Henning Breuer, John Bessant, Sune Gudiksen

Gamification for Innovators and Entrepreneurs

Henning Breuer, John Bessant, Sune Gudiksen

Gamification for Innovators and Entrepreneurs

Using Games to Drive Innovation and Facilitate Learning

DE GRUYTER

Co-funded by the European Union projects GAMIFY and IMPACT:
GAMIFY Project Number: 600947-EPP-1-2018-1-DE-EPPKA2-KA, Project Duration:
January 2019 – December 2021
IMPACT Project Number: 621672-EPP-1-2020-1-DE-EPPKA2-KA, Project Duration:
January 2021 – December 2023

Open Access funded by EU IMPACT Project

ISBN 978-3-11-072554-4
e-ISBN (PDF) 978-3-11-072558-2
e-ISBN (EPUB) 978-3-11-072566-7
DOI https://doi.org/10.1515/9783110725582

Library of Congress Control Number: 2022935572

Bibliographic information published by the Deutsche Nationalbibliothek
The Deutsche Nationalbibliothek lists this publication in the Deutsche Nationalbibliografie; detailed bibliographic data are available on the Internet at http://dnb.dnb.de.

Illustrations: Isabelle Kling
Cover image: Hiroshi Watanabe/Stone/Getty Images
Typesetting: Integra Software Services Pvt. Ltd.
Printing and binding: CPI books GmbH, Leck

www.degruyter.com

Dedicated to our kids: Inho & Jun, Lara, Matias & Leon

Agile Retrospective

Awareness Raising

Business Modelling

Business Simulation

Dilemma Solving

Crowdsourcing

Experiential Learning

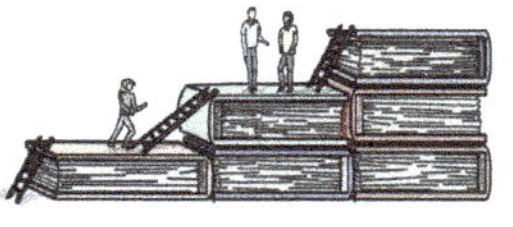

Ideation

Innovation Markets

Warm-ups

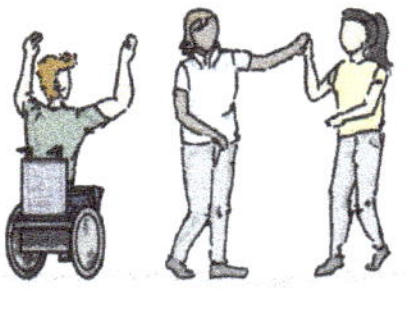

Workshop Facilitation

Branching Choices

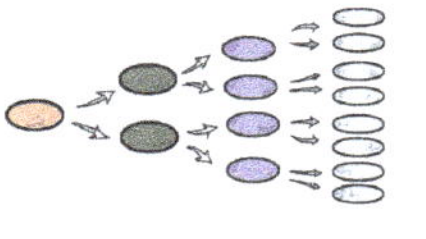

Cards

Challenges

Collective Decisions

Competition

Cooperation

Day in the Life

Dedicated Facilitators

Epic Meaning

Humour

Mapping

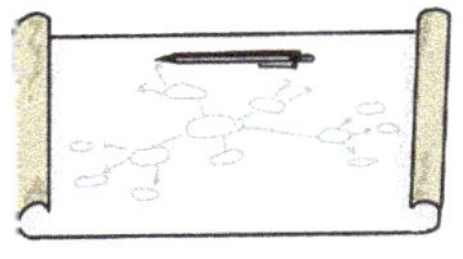

Metaphors

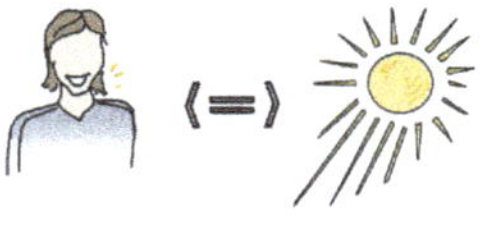

Modelling Materials

Mutual Goals

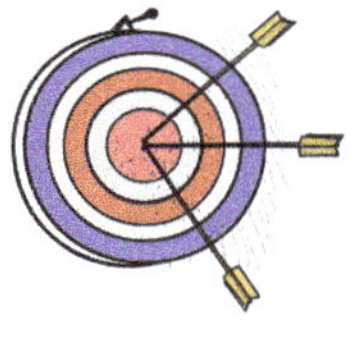

Negotiations

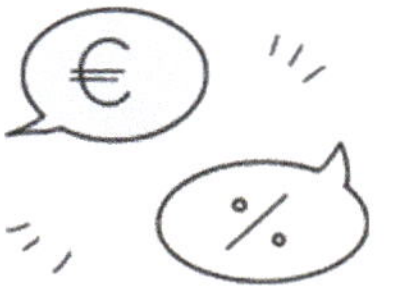

Pitch

Prioritization

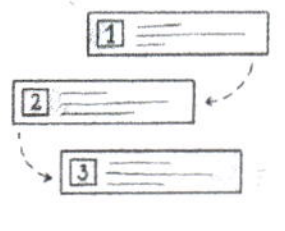

Quizzes

Resources

Rewards

Roles

Storytelling

Surprise

Trade-offs

Voting

About the authors

Henning Breuer

Henning Breuer consults, researches, and teaches in the fields of innovation management and business psychology using gamification and games in his consulting work and university teaching. He is a Professor for Business and Media Psychology at HMKW Berlin and founder of UXBerlin – Innovation Consulting. Since 2001, Henning has worked with multinational corporations, SMEs, public organisations, and start-ups, providing consulting on sustainable innovation culture and business models, future scenarios, and ethnographic stakeholder research. Henning has co-authored numerous journal and conference publications and textbooks on *Values-Based Innovation Management* and *Sustainable Business Model Design*. As a visiting researcher and professor, he has worked at the University of Chile (Santiago) and Waseda University (Tokyo). He studied psychology, philosophy, and law in Berlin and Tubingen, and received his PhD in psychology from the University of Magdeburg.

John Bessant

Originally a chemical engineer, John Bessant has been active in the field of research and consultancy in technology and innovation management for over 40 years. In addition to his role as Emeritus Professor of Innovation and Entrepreneurship at the University of Exeter he has visiting appointments at the universities of Stavanger, Norway and Erlangen-Nuremburg, Germany. He is the author of over 45 books and monographs and many articles on the topic and has lectured and consulted widely around the world. His most recent books include *Managing Innovation* (now in its 7th edition), *Entrepreneurship* and *Riding the Innovation Wave*. You can find more and follow his blog at https://johnbessant.org

Sune Gudiksen

Sune has worked extensively with design, innovation management, future scenario design and strategic foresight. One medium of choice for him is play and game-based techniques to support stakeholder participation, high engagement, novelty in directions and quality learning outcome. He holds a PhD in co-design of services and business models through design thinking games and is currently associate professor in strategic design and innovation management at Design School Kolding, Denmark. He has been a project leader of several projects at various national innovation networks. As well, he is project leader on international EU projects focusing on strategic design, innovation management and play and game techniques to support stronger development and learning. He has authored several international books over the years directed towards industries and practitioners, and published a number of conference papers and journal articles in design and innovation management.

https://doi.org/10.1515/9783110725582-001

Preface

This book

This book introduces the potential of gamification and games to solve the great societal and organisational challenges that corporations and public institutions are dealing with today. It is written for innovation professionals, entrepreneurs, game designers, and students who seek to understand and apply the potential of gamification and games in different organisations.

Part I introduces the power of games to drive innovation and tackle grand challenges. It also provides the conceptual foundations on games and gamification, learning and innovation management. Part II introduces a pattern approach to configuring, creating games and using games to drive innovation. Part III demonstrates the approach and presents different games that have been developed to solve innovation challenges in leading European firms – each of these formats is available online and can be adapted for different organisations. The final part IV presents educational approaches to training innovation professionals and teaching students how to create their own games. It ends with an outlook into the future of games and gamification, and provides some starting points for your own future with games. Appendices include a short version of the 36 gamification design patterns and a collection of 76 games already used for innovation and entrepreneurship. The whole book builds on insights we gathered in the gamification of innovation at leading European firms, and leverages knowledge from over 150 experts in the fields of gamification and innovation management.

GAMIFY

The essential insights from this book build on results from the European GAMIFY project: It leverages the knowledge of more than 150 experts we interviewed and the lessons learned from developing games responding to innovation challenges in leading European firms. It draws from the insights and outcomes of our research, and from our experiences with conducting and evaluating numerous gamified trainings and educational sessions.[1]

GAMIFY stands for 'Games as Methods to enhance Innovation and Entrepreneurship'. The project was motivated by the observation that games and gamification have been successfully used to increase productivity within organisations, and in isolated initiatives, also to facilitate the innovation and entrepreneurship (I&E) capabilities of organisations. However, the documentation of existing formats was scarce and inconsistent,

https://doi.org/10.1515/9783110725582-002

design guidelines and criteria for applicability and quality based on comparative evaluation were missing. Researchers, professional innovation managers and consultants from different organisations and industries discussed these observations at several conferences of the International Society for Professional Innovation Management (ISPIM) and an international workshop in Berlin. In some initial workshops on gamification in innovation at the 2017 ISPIM conference and 2016 at the University of Applied Sciences for Media, Communication and Management (HMKW) in Berlin we began to explore the potential of gamified formats in innovation management, education and training in a more systematic way. Through these events, we sharpened our understanding of the needs of managers and scholars that act as change agents in their organisations.

The *partner organisations* are leading institutions with strategic objectives that include the adoption of games and gamification for innovation in products and services, on the strategic level of business modelling and for entrepreneurship. They build on first-hand experience in the research, design, development and implementation of gaming approaches. Four universities from Germany, Denmark and Spain (HMKW Berlin, Design School Kolding, Complutense University of Madrid, HHL Leipzig School of Management) and six corporate partners from different industries (telecommunication, conglomerate, banking, metering, airline subsidiary for IT services and insurance: Deutsche Telekom AG, 3M España, Danske Bank, Kamstrup, Lufthansa Systems, Generali Group) set up a knowledge alliance together with ASIIN Consult and ISPIM (International Society for Professional Innovation Management). Later, several associated partners joined: UXBerlin – Innovation Consulting, and Play Serious Academy as consultants, ACTEE as a gamification software platform provider, and University College from Denmark. They were also supported by a wide network of innovation professionals from the ISPIM Special Interest Groups for 'Values-Based and Sustainable Innovation' and 'Teaching and Coaching Innovation'.

From the outset, all partners were convinced that gamification and gaming provide relatively new, attractive, and experiential learning approaches to promote corporate and academic innovation and entrepreneurship capabilities. They (respectively we) also understood that these approaches still needed to be further explored and developed. Together we designed, evaluated and refined many of the materials presented in this book. We conducted a comprehensive literature review and a needs analysis with our industry partners. Collaboratively, we created and evaluated most of the games presented in part III and tried several interactive formats to train trainers and teach students and professionals in the new approaches we developed. In sum, we found that gamification and games provide a unifying and fresh perspective across innovation domains and industries, allowing for transfer of best practices in compliance with established quality criteria. We also discovered the potential of a design pattern approach to document, teach and advance existing knowledge for future designers of gamification and games to tackle grand challenges.

IMPACT

The Gamification Design Patterns themselves (see chapter 4), the overview of games to facilitate values-based and sustainable innovation (chapter 5.3) and the collection of games were then created and validated by Henning Breuer and Kiril Ivanov as part of the IMPACT project. IMPACT stands for 'Creating values-based innovation cultures for sustainable business impact'. The project was based on the observation that many companies in Europe adopted sustainability goals as part of their mission and strategies, but few have established practices in their organizational culture and manage innovation based on values of corporate sustainability. The purpose of IMPACT is therefore to identify good practises as well as barriers for values-based and sustainable innovation, and to create appropriate methods to overcome the barriers and establish sustainability-oriented innovation cultures.[2] Gamification and games provide a golden path to facilitate these developments and were therefore systematically explored and included (see chapter 5.3).

Acknowledgements

Numerous voices and hands have contributed to this book and the ideas it presents. First and foremost, we thank the main academic partners who conducted most of the research, design and facilitation throughout the GAMIFY project: Sandra Dijk, Claudia Lehmann and Sina Plietzsch from HHL Leipzig coordinated the project, participated in research and game development and were quite actively engaged throughout the project. Kiril Ivanov of HMKW Berlin worked closely with Henning Breuer, assisting him for a major part of the GAMIFY project, and also in the IMPACT project. Together they created the design patterns and most of the educational materials including the collections of games in the appendices. Together they are now teaching in a new master's program module on 'gamification for organisations' at HMKW. Samana Subedi supported Henning and Kiril as a student assistant towards the end of the project. Carmen Abril and Mar Camacho, Elena Gimenez of Complutensé University Madrid worked very closely with us throughout the project as part of the academic core team, and focussed on the literature review and expert interviews. Keila Z. Péréz Quinones from Design School Kolding joined in and took part in the planning of game development, testing and train-the-trainer. A thanks also goes to Pia Schytz and Mathias Poulsen from Design School Kolding who were part of the teaching crew in the first two years of the course at Design School Kolding: Play-based intrapreneurship. We thank our industrial partners who shared their expertise in innovation and organisation challenges and their insights on the current use and future potentials of gamification, especially Stefan Kohn and Miriam Beljaars of Deutsche Telekom, Teresa Gallo and Jose Maria Benito of 3M in Spain, Jeppe Møller Thastum and Simon Ormholt Schrøder from Danske Bank, Lisa Weber of Generali, and Carina Leue-Bensch from Lufthansa Systems. Anna Bessant, Steffen Conn, Lucija Barisic and the whole growing community of the International Society for Professional Innovation Management (ISPIM) helped us to get further experts on board, to discuss intermediary results and to spread the word about our efforts – a great thank you to you all for your valuable support!

Paul Lauer did outstanding job in editing each chapter and part of the manuscript and the patterns. He substantially helped us to clarify our wording and to ensure a consistent flow across the chapters from different authors.

Special thanks go to Marie Isabelle Kling who contributed her artistic skills and created the illustrations based on visual ideas and discussions with Henning. We thank the contributors of the GAMIFY project who created the games we discussed in part III of the book:

- The *Corporate Sustainability Innovation (CSI)* game was developed by Henning Breuer and Kiril Ivanov from the University of Applied Sciences for Media Communication and Management (HMKW), Berlin and in collaboration with industry partners from Deutsche Telekom. We thank Barbara Costanzo (Vice President Group Social Engagement) & Melanie Kubin-Hardewig (Vice President Group Sustainability Management, Miriam Beljaars (Telekom Design Gallery) and Stefan Kohn (Innovation Manager at Deutsche Telekom Service GmbH) for their indispensable contributions to framing the challenge, creating the dilemmas and improving the game through their feedback, ideas and suggestions. Thanks to Marcel Oelschläger for redesigning the prototype of the game into a visually appealing format.
- The *Customer First Change* game was developed by Sune Gudiksen in collaboration with Lisa Weber of the German insurance company Generali and with use of Actee game software and guidance from CEO Leif Sørensen, as well as Gamify consortium feedback.
- The *Business Model Branching* game was created by Sune Gudiksen in collaboration with a number of SME companies and Danish design and innovation leaders from these companies.
- The *Shift* game developed in collaboration with Industry partners Lufthansa, Danske Bank, Kamstrup & Arla Foods. The Shift game was created by Emilie Bech Jespersen, Klara Birgisdottir, Lea Chenot and Sune Gudiksen in collaboration with Lufthansa, especially Carina Leue-Bensch and Jörg Liebe.

- The *Proximity Seeker* game was developed by Keila Z. Péréz Quinones and Sune Gudiksen from Design School Kolding and Carmen Abril and Elena Gimenez from Complutensé University Madrid in collaboration with industry partners from 3M with Teresa Gallo and Danske Bank with Jeppe Møller Thastum and feedback from the GAMIFY consortium.
- The *Ecosystem Canvas* game was created by Jacob Thomsen & Sune Gudiksen and tested with UCL teachers and ecosystem stakeholders in Odense, Denmark.
- *Lego Serious Play* is a method developed by LEGO, which is frequently and enthusiastically used in workshops by HHL Leipzig. Special thanks go to Sandra Dijk, Claudia Lehmann and Sina Plietzsch, who put their knowledge and experience with this method in the framework of this book.

The projects GAMIFY and IMPACT have been funded with support from the European Commission. This publication reflects the views only of the authors, and the Commission cannot be held responsible for any use which may be made of the information contained herein.

Co-funded by the European Union

GAMIFY Project Number: 600947-EPP-1-2018-1-DE-EPPKA2-KA
Project Duration: January 2019 – December 2021
IMPACT Project Number: 621672-EPP-1-2020-1-DE-EPPKA2-KA
Project Duration: January 2021 – December 2023

Contents

Part II
Using, adapting and creating games

Part III
Games tackling grand challenges in innovation and entrepreneurship

Part IV
Our future with games for innovation and entrepreneurship

Part I
Gamification, games and play as drivers of innovation and entrepreneurship

https://doi.org/10.1515/9783110725582-004

This book introduces an exciting, still nascent *superpower*: One that enables a person to use, repurpose and create games that will help solve the great societal and organisational challenges companies, startups and public institutions are dealing with – games that actually drive innovation, engage stakeholders and facilitate experimentation. We empower innovators and entrepreneurs by building on insights gathered in the gamification of innovation at leading European firms and leveraging knowledge from over 150 experts in the fields of gamification and innovation management. A design approach enables everyone concerned with innovation to create their own games based on state of the art academic and practitioner knowledge. We hope this approach will convey a new understanding of games and gamification and provide the means to put it into practise.

Several easily customizable games and gamified interaction formats, collections of patterns, and educational materials for training and coaching should help you to do so. (76 selected games used in innovation and entrepreneurship are described in the appendix.) For readers new to the fields of gamification, innovation and entrepreneurship (I&E), part I provides the conceptual foundations for the more practice-oriented chapters and cases in parts II and III.

Chapter 1
Challenges: Gamification and games to tackle grand challenges

Gamification and games can provide a safe space for experimentation and unconventional forms of interaction. They can be tailormade and iteratively improved to drive innovation and facilitate learning.

The *term gamification* originated in an emerging interface culture in which game design principles and patterns were transferred to many different kinds of interactive applications and even social configurations. Nick Pelling,[1] who coined the term gamification in 2002, initially understood gamification as making digital user interfaces more easily accessible, fun and in this respect game-like. He considers digital platforms such as Kickstarter and Alibaba as his 'gamification heroes' since they activate and bring people together, and change social activities around funding projects, and around buying and selling. By tracing the origins of the term, we can therefore understand gamification within the larger cultural trend towards digitization and the ubiquitous making of interactive interfaces available and accessible – a means to facilitate a layperson's flow in handling entertaining gadgets that may serve serious purposes.

Today gamification is usually seen as an 'application of game design elements in non-game contexts'.[2] In a context of learning, a game is defined as a 'system in which players engage in an abstract challenge, defined by rules, interactivity and feedback, and which results in a quantifiable outcome often eliciting an emotional reaction'.[3]

Many companies, innovation consultants and entrepreneurs, as well as higher education institutions, have embraced play, games and gamification to boost performance. Especially in the world of business, gamification has become established in a rather narrow sense: as new ways to increase the efficiency or productivity of the workforce, foster engagement and competition, and improve business performance in well-defined task domains. Think of a restaurant chain whose employees are rewarded points for selling the new kitchen specials, the top-notch servers not just being shown at the top of a leader board, but also receiving messages from management acknowledging their contribution to the company's success.

However, several of these initiatives were assumed to follow a behaviourist ideology that tries to manipulate people with extrinsic rewards, to trick people into game-like behaviour in a non-game environment[4] and to override or downplay rationality and agency.[5] Others have been criticized for incorporating insufficiently reflected values or

https://doi.org/10.1515/9783110725582-005

dominant societal mindsets (e.g. an overly narrow view on future energy transitions). Still, several authors including ourselves, see great business potential for 'game thinking' beyond narrow ideological underpinnings or reductionist approaches of mere 'pointification'.[6] Several pioneers have already used games to drive exploration and innovation and to master the great transformations ahead of us. A few are using gamified interaction formats and games to drive qualitative change and engage participants in collaborative, co-creative, action-oriented and experience-based learning activities. However, documentation and analysis of these formats is scarce and inconsistent, and design guidelines and patterns, as well as educational materials for professional trainers and teachers are lacking.

To tackle this gap, we talked to game developers, innovation managers and experts in the field to learn from their experiences. We reviewed all the cases we could find in the scientific literature as well as online and in white papers. We developed a design pattern approach to collect, consolidate and advance existing knowledge and organisational capabilities in games and gamification that drive innovation and entrepreneurship (I&E). And this approach allows you to create new training programmes, educational materials and curricula in which innovation professionals and students use and customize games for new purposes, or create new forms of gamification from scratch. These games introduce a safe space for experiential learning, experimentation in small groups, and trying out new, inclusive forms of collaboration. As we will see, they even provide a still widely unexplored means to address the great business and societal challenges we are facing today.

1.1 The power of games to tackle grand challenges

New grand challenges facing us now, and in the future, will require new methods if we are to successfully deal with them and find yet unforeseen solutions. In the context of this book, gamification does not mean motivating people to do things they wouldn't otherwise want to do, but creating formats of social interaction that boost our capacities to drive innovation or be entrepreneurial in approaching challenges. Gamification is about this search for and iterative development of tailored, yet unconventional methods to drive innovation. It is about exploring and paving entrepreneurial paths in an action-oriented and engaging manner. The 'superpowers' they equip us with should not suggest an easy solutionism, but a call to confidence in daring new and unconventional, highly interactive and action-oriented formats of tackling the great challenges we are facing today.

Games introduce a safe space for experimentation in small groups and for trying and establishing unconventional forms of (inclusive) collaboration. They are a powerful approach to address the great business and societal challenges we are facing today, because they can be purposefully designed and iteratively improved to do so. We briefly discuss the potential of each of these three aspects and then go into the innovation and entrepreneurship challenges that games are best suited to dealing with.

Experimentation in a safe space

Innovators and entrepreneurs are told to fail early, and fail often. The idea is to maximise learning which minimizes the costs of failure – whole process frameworks like the stage-gate process[7] and the lean start-up approach[8] ensure such iterations of prototyping, gathering feedback and learning to improve or step back. Gamification and games facilitate a different approach to entrepreneurial learning. They create a safe space for immersing yourself in a topic, feeling free to dream up solutions and acting out to celebrate a glorious success or to fail with a laugh just to stand up again with 'urgent optimism'[9] for the next round of the game. What comes at effectively no costs outside the game still benefits its players who carry over the ideas, concepts and knowledge they generated, the encouraging or disappointing feedback they gathered, the new perspectives or scenarios they experienced into the 'real' world. When these games work well, innovator and entrepreneurs leave the safe game space better prepared for the opportunities, risks and challenges ahead.

Still, 'I don't have time to play around' is a typical reaction of some busy managers and serial entrepreneurs when they come across a gamified workshop format or a game. Games are often not taken seriously and many designers and innovation professionals have avoided the term so as not to endanger their reputation and the funding of their efforts in this field. Proponents of using games in business often highlight the immersive experiences, challenging assumptions, looking for surprising viewpoints and perspectives to avoid tunnel vision rather than fun to convey the purpose of their activities. Indeed, when applying games in these settings the goal is not fun, but the interactive experiences in groups of peers. Some of this scepticism is due to the fact that – although most games do lead to new viewpoints, directions or decisions – they usually do not result in the immediately visible or tangible or measurable output that conventional work practices reliably produce. Besides, their often indirect and medium-term outcomes and business impact – much like innovation efforts themselves – cannot be easily measured. Still, the challenges that games provide resemble some of the challenges we face as innovators and entrepreneurs, and – as we will see in chapters 2 and 3 – they provide some indispensable capabilities for discovering and experimenting with novel framings, directions and possible solutions to challenges.

Gamification and games create an artificially constructed environment based on rules, goals, artefacts and boundaries and thereby provide a safe space for experimentation and play. Play may be fun – but it has a serious purpose. Our imagination and our adaptive behaviour in a variety of situations owe much to our ability to experiment and explore but also to the ability we developed as children to play in imaginary worlds as complements to the real one. Play represents a space within which things become possible, experiments can be safely made because consequences of failure are limited to the boundaries of the game. Just like life itself, games must be played forward, but can often just be understood backwards,[10] and a good facilitator can help us learn what we might do differently next time.

Innovating social collaboration with new interaction architectures

Under the viewpoint of social interaction, we can think of each game as an *unconventional form of collaboration* or as an interaction architecture. In large or small organisations, even as individuals and entrepreneurs, we have conventional ways of dealing with things. Processes are sets of activities to perform standard tasks and produce well-defined results, and projects are temporary courses of actions to deal with new and often unique, one-time challenges. We also have the formal structures and unwritten rules that guide an individual's action, e.g. rules of communication and progression across different hierarchical levels. As individuals we have our routines and habits that keep us on the beaten track. Gamification and games now put us on their own track. They replace the unwritten or written rules of social convention with new rules, ones that hold for the time of the game and provide a safe space for its players.

Game rules introduce a new architecture for interaction that differs from the conventional ways we see the world and relate to others. They turn individuals with their unique history and identity into players with different roles and submit them to the game's rules governing actions and turn-taking. These rules can cut across the formal hierarchies and structures and unwritten customs of an organisation. Historically and often hierarchically defined rules about turn-taking and speaking up can be replaced and lead to unforeseen forms of interaction among participants, who now find themselves on a level playing field.

An obvious example is role-playing games that ask us to step out of the conventional roles we grew into and learned to perfection over the years and to assume a new role that other players or the game assigns to us. The new role comes along with a new perspective on the task at hand, and new relations to the other roles convey a new experience and facilitate new insights – as organisational or family sculpting sessions in systemic consulting and therapy impressively demonstrate.[11] Not just empathy, also *collaboration* and cooperation can be enhanced when collaborative gameplay helps to establish mutual trust and social bonds and thereby improve cooperation. As well, game rules and procedures can activate and develop a multitude of perspectives on a challenge at hand before moving further into the innovation process. Role-play is especially good at enabling this, because it tends to break established thought patterns and allows our imagination to envisage new directions.[12]

In the field of education, learning architectures are supported by gamification and games that deviate from the standards of frontal teaching and group project work. For example, in a flipped classroom, students acquire textbook knowledge outside the classroom in order to prepare for more meaningful collaborative activities – like the ones that gamification and games can provide – that advance their understanding in the classroom.

Paved by its unconventional (or semi-conventional) game-specific rules, gamification opens a third path in the middle ground between process and project, with design patterns that can be used as components to facilitate standard tasks (like generating ideas or managing trade-offs) and repurposing them within a temporary setting to unique, organisation-specific challenges.

Tackling grand challenges

According to a Greek saying from the ancient Sophist Antiphon, 'Life is not a game that we can begin anew'.[13] Today, we are still learning the hard way that we do not have a planet B and that it may be impossible to fix some things. Luckily enough, however, we do have games that can be played in almost endless variations, and we do have future scenarios that allow us to anticipate alternative future developments and their consequences before we enter an irreversible path.[14] Sometimes complex knowledge, numerous stakeholder contributions and several iterations are needed to identify and consolidate the more desirable pathways and to translate these into appropriate decisions.

Games and gamified formats of interaction are powerful means to facilitate this process because they can be purposefully designed to tackle grand challenges. Such games couple the game challenges (stretching the players' capabilities) to innovation challenges and enable participants to generate new ideas, knowledge or solutions to a problem. Or they facilitate a transformative experience that enhances their awareness or capabilities and thereby create the precondition to overcome a barrier.

What makes gamification a 'superpower' is its capacity to adopt, repurpose and combine already powerful methods and techniques from different disciplines and traditions (like futures studies, user experience, agile management, design thinking or business design) into a new, action-oriented and engaging framework. We call this framework the ludic space, or an alternative world, purposefully designed to deal with innovation challenges. Therefore, one key to success is to frame the overarching story – that is, the game world – with suitable metaphors that turn the recombination of and interplay between these different techniques (e.g. card-sorting from user experience design, feedback methods from design thinking and agile management, and scenario writing and backcasting from futures studies) into one coherent flow of activities.

This recombination and design of action flows draws from and incorporates experience-based knowledge from professional workshop designers and facilitators (the pattern approach in chapter 4 serves to capture this knowledge). Moreover, once created, these games can be iteratively revised and refined – based on empirical evidence – to better fulfil their mission of solving a particular innovation challenge. They do not only provide a safe space for experimentation and unconventional means to involve diverse stakeholders, but structure the environments players play in. As part of the ongoing interaction (merging knowledge acquisition with problem solving actions), games can convey the information required – either on their own account or from knowledgeable participants. A simple example here is a set of playing *cards* that provide the information needed to complete a task (for instance, the *Business Innovation Kit* provides background knowledge on business model components and implementation challenges during an ongoing business modelling session). More complex formats call for participation in open innovation challenges[15] or in generating knowledge to solve societal challenges or even so-called 'wicked problems'.[16]

Typically, these challenges cannot be solved by isolated initiatives, individual actors or a within a single session, but require continuous engagement, learning and collaboration. Typically, they also involve several sub-challenges that are likewise unique (for instance, how to address a company-specific group of customers) and recurring (for instance, how to foster customer engagement). For this reason, many games in business and innovation are not designed to provide a single solution, but yield competing directions to discuss and reflect on.[17] Games and gamified interaction formats can be specifically designed to work on this middle ground, to leverage proven gamified formats (called gamification design patterns in chapter 4), and apply them to a company-specific innovation challenges that can still be customized for use by others. The games presented in part III exemplify this approach.

Sometime grand challenges – like improving corporate sustainability or renewing a customer-centric strategy – can be broken down into sub-challenges like raising awareness or facilitating knowledge acquisition. Games have been designed for a variety of serious challenges – for example as 'safe' ways to explore and resolve organizational conflicts, break down silos, build trust, enable more effective collaboration within and between teams, and more.[18] Challenges include the great societal challenges of our time (such as in the *CSI* game in chapter 7 or the UN *Global*

Compact Dilemma game[19]), organisational challenges (for instance after mergers and acquisitions, or introducing a new customer centric strategy, in the *Customer First* game in chapter 8), or the challenge to identify and overcome innovation challenges within the firm (in the *Shift* game in chapter 10). Likewise, the other games presented in part III of this book were all designed to address a specific recurring challenge. In the political arena, games for democracy and gamified applications help user to manoeuvre the complexities of political opinions, candidates and parties, and to facilitate their voting decisions.[20]

Innovation and entrepreneurial challenges and exemplary games addressing them

Games and their design elements can be mapped onto different normative, strategic, or operational management dimensions, or onto the major domains of innovation management described in the scientific literature and textbooks (as we will see in chapter 4). Scientific discourse also provides a rich repository of innovation and entrepreneurial challenges as well as the barriers that individual methods or complex games address. Empirically, we can identify current innovation challenges facing companies, start-ups and public organisations. More or less sophisticated research methods ranging from simple conversions and semi-structured interviews to standardized surveys and ethnographic field research can reveal hidden challenges and barriers in cultural practices. Identifying the right challenge to tackle is the first great challenge for innovators and entrepreneurs and the consultants and game designers supporting them.

Once the challenge is understood and agreed upon among the relevant stakeholders, a variety of existing games and gamification design patterns can be used to create new ones. Two appendices to this book provide you with an overview of both – a comprehensive collection of games and gamified formats that have been successfully used to drive innovation and facilitate entrepreneurship, and the short version of gamification design patterns to create new ones.

Before we turn to those games and gamification designs, and the theories behind them, a historical antecedent and two examples should illustrate how games can provide a safe environment for experimentation, how they allow players to take on unusual roles and create a framework for mixing methods to tackle strategic innovation challenges.

A historical antecedent stems from the history of war simulations, where game scenarios have been used to inform military strategies. In the Prussian army in the 19th century, big maps, cards, role-play, strategies, and 'hidden' enemy moves functioned as a way to simulate possible war events. The purpose was to explore a range of possible strategies and tactics, and later also became a way to train officers' ability to make decisions at the battlefield. The game was called 'Kriegsspiel'.[21] In these kinds of play in organizations a map creates overview – it is a landscape and world with actors who make specific moves and have specific skills, behave in specific ways. It is a landscape to comprehend and maybe to mould things differently – a landscape consisting of not one way to go but several, maybe competing alternatives.

The first recent example deals with strategy development in a business context. Strategizing is difficult because while a company can make their own moves it is hard to anticipate how other companies in the market will react. Games can be used to simulate this environment and market, giving key decision-makers the chance to test potential strategic moves and alternatives in a safe space before taking real action. *Strategic Derby* exemplifies this approach of providing a safe environment for experimentation and playing unusual roles – in this case as competitors.[22]

Unfolding strategic options and role-playing competitor moves in a telecommunication company

The telecommunication industry has been overheated for many years, forcing market players to reinvent and rethink their strategies many times in a year. In this case, an incumbent in Denmark was threatened by upcoming competitors offering cheaper solutions.

In order to respond to this challenge, a strategy game was staged. A big, table-based game was created with a number of categories illustrating potential competitive advantages both backstage, center stage and frontstage (i.e. backstage: best production line, best partnerships; center stage: first market offer, best quality and usage, best pricing; frontstage: best brand, best customer relationships, best distribution). In the game, participants would team-up in 5–6 pairs (a group of 10–12 participants playing in the same game). One or two of the pairs would play the company, while the other teams would play its competitors. Each pair was giving a mini-board in which they could confidentially discuss their moves. Each pair was given a specific number of resources (points) to invest in strategic moves and asked to note the idea behind the moves directly on the boards to make sure to focus on the content and be able to track moves.

A game rule – sometimes called 'fog of war' or 'hidden information' – was used. Pairs would create ideas and moves on their own mini-boards and then everybody would simultaneously move their markers to the bigger board. Thereby avoiding a team from getting an advantage by being for instance last in the turn-taking and seeing the others' moves. Depending on the positions on the board (e.g. if they were leading in best brand) teams would receive new resources to use in the next round, simulating some companies having more resources in real markets. Those behind with fewer points and therefore investment capital have to move around the main competition or fill up market spaces by making more radical moves to the board and situation.

In approximately 90 minutes, groups of up to 12 people would take a number of strategic moves, ideate on alternatives and always get instant feedback and potential competitor reactions through the moves made by the other teams in the game. For the department managers, innovation managers and project managers this activity led to more quality in the strategic options they might take afterwards, a better sense of potential alternatives and an overview of likely competitor action or reaction. Several sessions were conducted.

In reusable gamification design patterns, you can spot classic game components such as role-playing and branching choices, and interaction flows of awareness-raising and simulation at work. Thinking about the immediate output and mediate outcomes of the game, it also becomes evident that not just the resulting range of strategic options help to inform innovation-related decision making, but that training entrepreneurial thinking in alternatives is as valuable to many of the participants as the development of an innovation culture. The same is true for the second case, which also shows how different innovation concepts and methods are integrated into a gamified framework to facilitate entrepreneurship and foster cultural change.

Good practice case: an insurance company

Following a merger with a European partner, a large insurance company tries to reinvent insurance for private customers. Following a new strategy, it strives to have its customers experience it as a 'lifetime partner' (e.g. supporting prevention and promoting health) rather than as a company rarely contacted and then on unpleasant occasions. In order to foster cultural adoption of the new strategy, key behaviours are defined and addressed with a gamified workshop format that allows mixed groups of employees to experience and reflect upon them. For instance, simplification as one key behaviour is conveyed in an escape room setting with different puzzles (such as sequencing customer journeys) that need to be solved cooperatively under time pressure in a less complex way. Reflection upon the activity and its results reveals potential for future process simplification. Another activity focusses explicitly on strategic innovation. Participants apply the four actions framework of blue ocean strategy (asking what aspects of an offering can be eliminated, reduced, improved and created anew) to reinvent an ice cream shop and innovate its business model competing against a large competitor.

This standardized, gamified format lowered the access barriers to issues of strategic change using different conceptual frameworks (such as customer journey and blue ocean strategy). It enabled almost 80 percent of the employees to participate in these workshops, many reported eye-opening 'aha' experiences and most valued the activities. Facilitating comparable action-oriented, but still different experiences, reflection upon these experiences within and across the groups and aggregation of overarching insights allowed the new strategy to be conveyed in tangible and memorable ways. The playful approach also helped to reduce the distance between board members and their subordinates and helped to facilitate entrepreneurial thinking.

Equally rich is the variety of innovation challenges addressed by the many other games mentioned and described throughout the book: to get to know remote teammates and build trust across departments, to foster ideation and evaluation of new product, service or process ideas, to generate new, values-based business models, to foster cultural change and corporate sustainability, to empower underprivileged entrepreneurs – just to name a few. The full list of 76 innovation games, the challenges they address and the approaches they take in doing so you will find in the appendix.

1.2 Previous findings on gamification and games for innovation and entrepreneurship

Several studies and a few books have already addressed gamification's potential for innovation and entrepreneurship, at least on the periphery. Most of these works focus on related topics like gamification for learning and instruction,[23] gamification for business in general,[24] 'gamestorming'[25] to spur creativity or crowdsourcing ideas, to facilitate values-based innovation and cultural change, or even save the world. Still, they provide valuable insights for innovators and entrepreneurs. Some thinking and early publications have had a focus on using ludic elements or game parts in design, innovation and in general development processes. Here we point to a few of those.

Learning and instruction

Learning and innovation are two sides of the same coin. Karl Kapp gave the first comprehensive overview of the gamification of learning and instruction, showing a good part of the way beyond a stereotypical understanding of gamification as points, badges and leaderboards. Instead he calls for enhancing the learning experience: 'Let us situate learners in authentic environments in which they can practice skills and gain immediate feedback on progress and accomplishments, earn recognition for doing well, and feel good for overcoming a challenge.' He draws from Malone's theory of intrinsically motivating instruction[26] to show how it is the continuous learning challenge of the game, as defined by its rules, meaningful goals and uncertain outcomes which keeps players engaged.

In the context of this book however, a game's challenge needs to contribute to solving a real innovation challenge, in other words, to generate new knowledge not just for oneself, but also for others. Conveying this greater purpose of the game to the players, and clarifying how the game and its outcomes contribute to solving the innovation challenge, becomes an essential framing of the activity which contributes to the players' engagement. Of course, the game and the greater innovation challenge should be well aligned. Think of a dice game with rigid turn-taking rules and an outcome left purely to chance and without any opportunity to make an individual contribution – can you imagine how this could contribute to innovation?

Gamification for business and innovation

Some early examples of simulation games in management can be found in normally simple process descriptions with three to four steps and a few game rules. Chris

Elgood's handbook of management games from 1981 is an example.[27] Luke Hohmann was one of the first to directly use the term 'innovation games' in the title of a book focusing on product innovation.[28] He describes games and gives reasons and formulas for playing these games, and with tools and templates to further assist the process. They are good examples of how to use games in product development and are also connected to, for instance, agile development. More recently, Sune Gudiksen and Jake Inlove have shown several examples of how games can promote innovation. They explore games addressing general business challenges (such as breaking down silos, suspending power relations and establishing trustworthy relations), and examine innovation-focused challenges (such as mitigating conflicts between operations and innovation). Sune has contributed several games he co-created to part III below.

Gamification to spur creativity and crowdsource ideas

With respect to innovation, most authors focus on the potential of games in early stages of the innovation process.[29] as a means to spur collaboration, creativity and engagement as well as challenge assumptions and elicit surprising viewpoints.[30] Gamification is already established to facilitate ideation[31] or crowdsourcing.[32] Dave Gray and colleagues in their 2010 book *Gamestorming: A Playbook for Innovators, Rulebreakers, and Changemakers* provide the reader with an overview and short introductions of simple creativity games divided into design thinking-related principles like divergent, emergent and convergent modes of thinking and development. In the Scandinavian tradition of participatory design and innovation – and also in the connected design methodology found in *Lego Serious Play* (chapter 13) – the games and activities are highly tangible and visual. Many of these examples deal with challenges related to service design, business model development and strategic thinking. These materials are getting more attention as their tangibility provides a better way of thinking and a chance for tacit knowledge to surface in the activities.

Games of agile management

While many publications focus on the power of gamification to help in the early innovation stages of searching for and selecting ideas, there is a set of gamified techniques in agile management and software development. One of the best known is the widely played game *Planning Poker*[33] to estimate implementation efforts using Fibonacci numbers in agile teams. In team retrospectives, games are used to facilitate the forming and storming phases of small group development.[34] However, more general games for innovation tend to focus on the initial stages of innovation and neglect later stages of implementation and capture. Here, in driving the adoption of innovation and in capturing value from new products, services and business models, is where we see the greatest potential for games to serve innovators and entrepreneurs.

Games to facilitate values-based innovation and cultural change

With respect to social dynamics in interdisciplinary and cross-functional teams, games can leverage engagement and improve interaction.[35] In a broader perspective on organisational culture, first studies indicate that gamification has a great role to play in addressing cultural challenges and in facilitating values-based innovation. For instance, gamification aids manufacturing firms in their transformation to product-service systems and in overcoming barriers such as information-sharing with suppliers and customers in this transition.[36] In a previous study,[37] we explored recurring innovation challenges in European companies and gave an overview of the literature on gamification for innovation and its potentials and pitfalls for fostering innovation-supportive cultures and values-based innovation. We identified boundary conditions (such as fit to company strategy), requirements (such as providing clarity about purpose and real-world impact) and design implications (such as the need to carefully tailor task complexity and carefully work with competition and rewards).

World saving online games

Several location-based, alternate reality and multiplayer online computer games have been designed with the humanitarian mission of changing the world for the better. Some of them can be used or adapted to drive innovation in organisations and to empower entrepreneurs. Jane McGonigal[38] has popularized the idea of saving the world through playing games and created several games herself at the Palo Alto Institute for the Future; and she is a contributor to the non-profit platform *Games for Change.*[39] Several of these games facilitate innovation and social entrepreneurship – especially ideation on how to deal with societal challenges (e.g. *World Without Oil* and *Superstruct*)[40] and entrepreneurial skill development (e.g. *Evoke* and *Superbetter; for these and other games also see chapter 5.3).*

What we are still missing and want to provide here is a comprehensive overview of the potential of games and gamification for innovators and entrepreneurs, as a well-structured reusable resource for designers and practitioners that leverages state-of-the-art knowledge to create, repurpose and use games to drive innovation.

1.3 Preview of the book

If you find these conceptual discussions on games, play, learning and innovation enlightening, we suggest you continue reading the following chapters. If you are more interested in the pattern approach and how to customize or create games to work on your own challenges, you can skip to part II of the book and return to the conceptual foundations later. If you are looking for games to use or adapt for your own purposes, check which one of the games presented in part III would best fit your needs and continue there. The final part IV is primarily addressed to teachers, trainers and everyone with an interest in the future of gamification and games for innovation and entrepreneurial endeavours. Here we provide a short summary of each part and each chapter.

Part I introduces what we call – drawing on the language of games – a still nascent superpower: to use, repurpose and create games to solve the great societal and organisational challenges that corporations and public institutions are dealing with. These are games that actually drive innovation, engage different stakeholders and facilitate experimentation.

Chapter 1: Challenges
The power of games to tackle grand challenges relies on their capabilities to enable experimentation in a safe environment, engage stakeholders in unconventional forms of interaction and drive innovation by design. The chapter reflects on challenges to be addressed, reviews previous publications and provides a preview of the book.

Chapter 2: Play
We play games to develop ourselves. The chapter introduces the basic concepts of play, games and gamification and shows how they are fundamentally intertwined with our notions of learning and innovation.

Chapter 3: Innovation and Entrepreneurship
This chapter introduces innovation and entrepreneurship and provides a basis for mapping games and gamification to address I&E challenges.

Part II introduces a pattern approach to configuring, creating and using games to drive innovation. Gamification design patterns document proven solutions to recurring challenges and enable innovators and entrepreneurs to create their own games.

Chapter 4: Patterns
A pattern approach serves as a framework for thinking about and creating games for I&E. The chapter introduces gamification design patterns as an approach to document and provide knowledge on reusable solutions to recurring challenges. It distinguishes between flow and component patterns and develops a basic structure for collecting patterns.

Chapter 5: Games
This chapter explores ways in which innovators and entrepreneurs and learners can use, modify and adapt existing games. Existing games and proven gamification formats are mapped onto our framework of innovation challenges.

Chapter 6: Gamification
This chapter provides a simple process and a canvas to collect information and generate alternative approaches to creating new games for an organisational innovation challenge. We discuss different contexts for defining suitable game methods and design patterns.

Part III features different games addressing challenges in innovation and entrepreneurship – from the daily need to empathize with colleagues to redesigning the business model and overcoming innovation barriers and solving the great societal sustainability challenges. Each was developed in response to major innovation challenges that our industry partners were facing. These games and guidance for their customization to different contexts and challenges are also available on the companion sites. These cases demonstrate the potential of games by not just providing a safe space for experimentation and trying out new forms of collaboration, but also by tackling recurring challenges in organizations.

Chapter 7: Corporate Sustainability
The *Corporate Sustainability Innovation* game empowers participants to identify sustainability challenges at the workplace and generate ideas and future scenarios on how to address them.

Chapter 8: Customer-Orientation
The *Customer First Change* game deals with challenges related to creating more human-centric organizations that can respond to changing customer needs, regulations etc.

Chapter 9: Business Modelling
Business Model Branching (BMB) deals with difficult and complex challenges of balancing ongoing operations and new innovation-oriented activities.

Chapter 10: Innovation Barriers
The *Shift* game explores practical ways and strategies to overcome innovation barriers in established organizations. It assesses why companies have gates.

Chapter 11: Teambuilding
The *Proximity Seeker* game was developed to address the challenges of social dynamics, especially in remote teams.

Chapter 12: Entrepreneurship
The *Ecosystem Canvas* game allows future entrepreneurs to become aware of and explore the potential for joint value creation in networks.

Chapter 13: Enhancing Collaboration
This chapter discusses the potential of *Lego Serious Play* to facilitate communication about strategy and to address innovation and entrepreneurial challenges in face-to-face and remote settings.

Part IV derives lessons learned from the development of these games and the pattern collection to teach students and train innovation professionals to create their own games and address specific challenges. It ends with an outlook into the future of games and gamification.

Chapter 14: Teaching
The chapter shows how games are used to facilitate professional development and learning. Games facilitate new forms of encounter between students, teachers and companies. Gamification design patterns can be used for professional training and education.

Chapter 15: What's next?
This chapter focuses on persistent hurdles in tracking and sustaining the impact of games. Technological and material developments create new opportunities for gamification. Basic challenges in organisations and newly emerging grand challenges point to future applications of games.

Chapter 16: Your future
What's your future with games? This is an invitation to use and contribute to our online library of games and to join a wider community of practice.

On the final pages you will find the Gamification Design Pattern Collection featuring a short version of all patterns and an overview of all the games for innovation and entrepreneurship mentioned in this book. You will also find the full list of references and an index. Enjoy!

Chapter 2
Play: Playing games to develop ourselves

> A ludic space, its boundaries and rules, its artefacts and goals compose a purposefully designed structure for play and experiential learning.

Apart from their contributions to innovation projects and their objective results, playing games for innovation facilitates learning experiences that empower entrepreneurs and may be required to drive innovation.

Play is a serious thing. Watch any group of kids and you can remind yourself that this is something which comes naturally. Evolutionary psychologists point out that the ability to play, and therefore imagine and simulate a variety of situations, developed as an important adaptive mechanism.[1] Kids play because they are destined to do so, and the pleasurable experience ensures that they will want to keep playing, which also means learning from interacting with the surroundings and the people around them.

It's not just kids; all mammals display similar behaviour and this raises an important question. Why do these creatures play? Play is costly in terms of energy so why has evolution selected for this capacity? The argument is that play is not accidental but instead serves several important purposes. As Peter Gray[2] argues, play enables them to:

- practice skills that are essential to their survival and reproduction,
- learn to cope physically and emotionally with unexpected, potentially harmful events,
- reduce hostility and enable cooperation,
- generate new, sometimes useful creations.

This last point has particular relevance; play can be seen as a key factor in the innovation which has enabled our species to survive. Our ability to imagine and create lies at the heart of our emergence as human beings, whose main gift is not our size or strength but our ability to learn and adapt to often hostile and uncertain environments or to recreate the places we inhabit. We innovate, find solutions and, if our first options are blocked off, find alternatives. Arguably a key function of play is to generate – in an 'offline' mode – novel behaviours and creations which later on become useful in promoting survival.

https://doi.org/10.1515/9783110725582-006

Johan Huizingha writes extensively on this theme in his book *Homo Ludens*. He sees play as imaginative, and argued that it provides the engine for 'cultural innovations': 'It is an activity connected with no material interest, and no profit can be gained by it. It proceeds within its own proper boundaries of time and space according to fixed rules and in an orderly manner.'[3]

Caillois[4] follows up on Huizingha's work and distinguishes 'ludus', structured activities with explicit game rules, from 'paidia', rather unstructured and spontaneous playfulness. He associates the human tendency to transform 'paidia' into 'ludus', and the re-forming of rules to our cultural development. When watching kids play we see that 'paidia' is the essence of play. We don't lose this as we get older, though our instinctive desire to jump into playing may often be checked by a sense of decorum or etiquette or any one of a number of barriers. Adults continue to enjoy play in a variety of settings and for a number of reasons – not least as a way of structuring time. The English word 'pastime' captures this essence well – something to help pass time in pleasurable fashion.

2.1 Learning to play

Not surprisingly some of our creativity has been ploughed back into the design of play experiences which can be reproduced and shared – the idea of games. Games have a basic structure – the 'rules' of the game – which govern how the players can reach some kind of goal, producing a winner or a winning state. Whether on a sports field or with a deck of cards, games have long been a central feature of our lives. They date back thousands of years: archaeologists found a 3000-year-old set of dice during an excavation in Iran, Chinese tile games of similar vintage have been found and the Egyptians were playing board games close to 5000 years ago. But still games continue to evolve. The advent of the computer opened up space for digital games, as the internet and connectivity enabled massive online games and the smart phone mobile gaming, with virtual reality now shifting the frontiers still further. The scale is huge. Estimates for the market for computer games alone is over $150bn with an expected growth rate of 13%.[5] Individual games like Minecraft have a subscriber base estimated at 126 million.[6]

The range of games being played is still growing – also in the area we are concerned with, namely, the innovation process itself. A key component of play lies in the creation of something new through activities involving experimentation, interaction and exploration. It is not surprising that putting some structure around this urge – in the form of games – opens up new possibilities for accelerating and enhancing innovation, for creating new products, services and processes.

In a famous study in 1971 trying to understand what went on in the minds of creative artists, psychologists Mihali Csikszentmihalyi and Jacob Getzels[7] gave a group of art students a table of thirty items from which they were asked to construct a still life composition. The results were evaluated by a jury of experienced professors who rated their work on three dimensions – originality, craftsmanship and 'overall value'. What they found was that the artists spent time crawling around the problem and exploring its dimensions and opportunities. They were shaping the emerging problem. Csikszentmihalyi and Getzels called this behaviour 'discovery orientation' – and found that not only was this discovery-based approach a good predictor of artistic creativity, it also predicted future success.

This idea of playing around with elements of a problem before beginning to solve it isn't just relevant to the world of fine art. Exploring, reshaping and redefining the problem – playing with it – makes a difference in many spheres of innovative activity. For example, James Dyson wasn't the first person to be frustrated at the inability of his vacuum cleaner to pick up all the dust and at the need to keep changing the bag.[8] But eventually something clicked in his engineer's mind and he took the recalcitrant machine to his workshop to see if he could improve it. 'Crawling around' the apparent problem of an inefficient filtering mechanism – the particles of dust blocked the pores of the bag and so quickly reduced its suction power – he began to see a new approach. The actual problem wasn't one of creating a better bag, but whether or not you needed a bag at all. What if you could make a cleaner with no bag, using a different way of separating out the dust from the air being sucked through the machine?

In other words, he had reframed the problem – and in doing so opened up some new lines of enquiry. This moment of insight wasn't of course the end of the story but rather the beginning of a long, laborious process, involving five years and over 5000 prototypes before he got the idea 'right'. This story highlights the importance of problem exploration, an approach which Dyson continues to use in systematically reinventing a wide range of domestic appliances. He summarises it well: 'I spend a lot of time taking things apart and putting them back together, considering how they work and how they might work better.'

Sometimes the challenge is to look beyond the apparent pattern. We've evolved to be really good at making sense out of multiple bits of information fast – because our survival depended on it. That's often an asset – but it can be a barrier as well since we risk pigeonholing problems too early. Seeing a problem and thinking that we recognise it – 'it's one of those' – starts us off on a pathway applying old solutions which worked in the past. The trouble is that this particular version of the problem might not be 'one of those' but something different which needs a new approach. Once again, we need a capacity for problem exploration, examination, checking.

So how do we go about problem-exploring? How do we move from vague notions, hunches, half-formed ideas towards something more workable? Not by a single leap but by a series of stepping-stones, bridges, scaffolding – essentially playing with ideas about the problem, and building on the ideas of others in a fertile environment.[9] The artists in Csikszentmihalyi and Getzels' study picked up objects, weighed them, turned them around in their hands, looked at them from different angles. Dyson's method is the similar – create a prototype to help focus the exploration, since, as he explains, 'prototypes allow you to quickly get a feel for things and uncover subtle design flaws.'[10]

The clue is in the name – *proto*-type. It's not about the finished object but a stepping-stone, a test-bed for learning, some way of exploring in a laboratory, in an experimental mode. Kids do this naturally (which is a major reason why they outperform most adults in the Marshmallow challenge described in chapter 5.1). From the moment they can start to hold an object they begin to explore it, trying out all its possibilities. And when they play together they multiply the possible options in an inspiring fashion – a humble cardboard box can become a spaceship, a shop, a stage, an article of clothing. And it changes its identity with impressive speed!

Not surprisingly play has become a central theme in the research and practice around innovation and entrepreneurship (I&E). Books with titles like Serious Play, The Playful Entrepreneur or Experimentation Matters[11] underpin a host of workshop and training programmes designed to cultivate skills and practices associated with effective play. This approach – incorporated in bootcamps, hackathons and other activities – has at its heart a deep research base in the psychology of problem exploration and open-ended solution development.

What we are doing with these approaches is bringing play into the innovation process in a planned and systematic fashion, creating structures and contexts within which play can happen.

2.2 Creating structures for play and games as structured play

Innovation – converting ideas and knowledge into economic, social and environmental value – benefits not only from play processes like exploration and prototyping, but also from the structured environment within which play takes place. It is a space featuring elements that promote play. Think of how a kindergarten works. These are not minimalist and functional classrooms but rather stimulating physical environments which are equipped with resources of many kinds which can be used in play. These resources and 'play structures' provide scaffolding which encourages children to experiment and explore. What works in the world of children can also work for adults. Increasingly we are seeing attention being paid to environments to enable innovation – for example the Googleplex, Apple's new headquarters or the Pixar studios.[12] The need for dedicated spaces where experimentation can happen has led to 'innovation labs' becoming a 'must-have' for any organization concerned with innovation. They provide ludic or 'boundary spaces' – in which play can happen as a path towards innovation and everyday routines and on-going operations can be suspended while thinking of the new.[13]

And within these play structures we can find a growing use of *games* – as structured, goal directed patterns of play. In their playbook for Innovators, Rulebreakers, and Changemakers, Dave Gray and colleagues focus on games for creativity and ideation. They suggest that games represent a particular kind of play with five key characteristics:[14]

- *Game space:* an environment in which the rules of ordinary life are temporarily suspended and replaced with the rules of the game. In effect it involves a temporary alternative world.
- *Boundaries:* games have a definite point at which they start and end and other boundaries, for example in physical space. A football game has a certain duration and the pitch a particular size.
- *Rules for interaction:* these define the way the game is played together with the game space boundaries.
- *Artefacts:* these are elements which enable the game to be played or carry information about the rules. The counters on a board game, the ball, bat and other equipment in a sports game, etc.
- *Goal:* games have a purpose and an end point, a winning state when the objective is achieved.

The authors focus on creativity and ideation, but even beyond idea generation games are used to accelerate innovation, often involving surprising new insights, creative combinations and promising pathways to scale. Especially for more complex tasks, the participants and content have to be considered as equally important key characteristics of gameplay and its design. On the one hand, the *participants'* identity, professional background and their role and relations in the organisation may heavily affect their attention, their in-game behaviour and the results they generate. On the other hand, already grasping the *content* and the methods to process it can be demanding for those without specialized expertise in the domain. Therefore, content is king in innovation games – a tangible trace of the process and content need to be clearly visible.

Increasingly game elements inform professional interaction formats for creating new products, services and processes. The hackathon, for example, is a popular approach, which can be targeted at a major societal challenge around which teams compete over a specified time and with the promise of winning a prize. Companies and other organizations regularly organize these as a way of generating novel ideas and business models; for example, the German company Merck uses *hackathons* in its 'innovation playground' at its headquarters in Darmstadt. Such games and events do not just structure interaction, but contribute to what innovations and entrepreneurs are beginning to understand as essential enablers for enduring success in innovation: culture.[15] An innovation manager of a leading recycling and environmental services company in Germany explained the underlying trend: 'In the last years we went from exploring future scenarios, to building dedicated innovation labs to focussing on changing values and culture.'

2.3 Playing to learn

Learning to play is a key theme in innovation and entrepreneurship and an increasingly important set of skills. But there is a second important theme: the idea of playing to learn. The *constructivist* view of development sees learning as children-centred, involving not simply the passive receiving of inputs but active experimentation with them. For example, John Dewey argues for the key role of such experiential learning.[16] The power of play is that it allows simulation, rehearsal, experiment and – crucially – failure in a safe space. So using play as an educational device offers some powerful learning opportunities, not least because it works with our innate behaviour. Play runs through the work of many educational theorists. Jean Piaget sees it as integral to the development of intelligence in children.[17] Lev Vygotsky places a similarly strong emphasis on play as a learning device or enabler. His 'zone of proximal development'[18] suggests that play has an important role in enabling children (via social engagement and collaboration) to both reinforce their existing knowledge and reach towards new frontiers.

'Play structures' provide the context in which safe experimentation can happen, changing the role of teachers to helping guides who extract learning from play, translating between the worlds. Jerome Bruner talks about 'scaffolding', and the metaphor can be applied to teachers actively supporting learners but also to the play structures themselves: Providing a temporary support and framework for acquiring or constructing new skills and knowledge until it can stand and develop on its own foundations.[19]

In its purest form play is open-ended, simply a pleasurable activity from which learning may or may not emerge. Games create artificial worlds. Their boundaries, rules, artefacts and goals can be designed to fulfil purposes that reach beyond the goals of the game itself, for instance, to facilitate learning or address an innovation challenge by coupling the games challenge to an innovation challenge.

The experiential learning cycle

David Kolb's learning cycle is widely used to represent how learning takes place (Figure 2.1). According to this model, learning creates knowledge 'through the transformation of experience'[20] and integrates four stages. Learners make a new concrete experience, accompanied by observation and reflection. Abstract conceptualizations modify their existing concepts or generate new ones. Through active experimentation they apply the revised concepts and gather new experiences again. The model suggests that learning is about more than grasping abstract concepts. It is rooted in experience and different stages need to be visited before the loop is closed. Crucially it recognises the need to experiment as part of that process, creating experiences which can then be reflected upon.

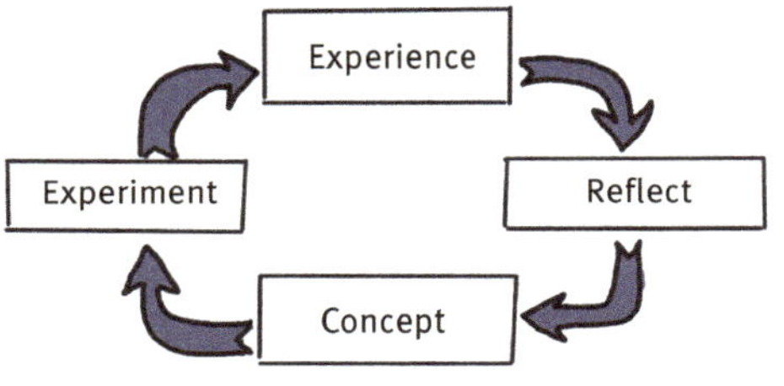

Figure 2.1: Kolb's four stage learning cycle.

It doesn't matter where we enter the cycle. It only matters that we complete the whole cycle for learning to take place, enriching, broadening and deepening the experience. In order to enable effective learning – for example, about how to manage innovation better – we need to:

- capture and reflect on our experiences, trying to distil insights from them about what works and what doesn't work;
- create models of how the world works – concepts – and link these to those we already have;
- use our revised models to engage again in innovation – and try new things out.

But learning is not automatic. There are a number of points at which learning can fail to happen unless a blockage is dealt with. Table 2.1 gives some examples. Importantly, play can help deal with these problems and resulting challenges. For example, component patterns like *EPIC MEANING*, *HUMOUR* and provoking *SURPRISE* can spur motivation for the innovation challenge at hand. *AWARENESS RAISING* workshops are one approach to sensitize for abstract guidelines and values. *EXPERIENTIAL LEARNING* can be a gamified interaction flow (pattern) in itself to convey innovation-related knowledge in a group experiential manner. For learners who lack concrete experience, the possibility of entering an artificial game world can bring experience to them. The risks attendant with many experiments in the real world can be offset by the use of games as simulations, again in a temporary artificial and safe world.

Table 2.1: Some key blocks to learning.

Learning blocker	Underlying problem
Lack of entry to the learning cycle	The motivation problem
Incomplete learning cycle	The completion problem
Not knowing how to learn	The skills problem
Tacit, hidden, informal learning	The elicitation problem
Local search for new solutions	The parochial/ not invented here problem
Uncritical reflection	The challenge problem
Infrequent, sporadic learning	The reinforcement /reward problem
Localised, unshared learning	The sharing problem
Unsustained learning	The motivation problem

Let's look at a game designed to help understand some of the challenges in new product development (NPD) as one important innovation theme. The *Self-Propelled Car* game involves teams competing against each other. There are boundary conditions, namely, teams have limited time and a limited set of resources which they can use. The overall goal of the game is to create the best self-propelled car – where best means performance (the ability to travel furthest under its own power) and provides a clear criterion to determine the winner. The underlying purpose is to create experiences with the NPD process, to enable guided reflection and the emergence and presentation of core concepts.[21]

This game allows for extensive experimentation and creativity. Observers are attached to each team to help the subsequent reflection. At the end of the time period, the resulting cars – finished or not – are presented and lined up. Each is allowed a demonstration run and then the winner is found.

Let's link this to the key aspects of the learning cycle. The game provides:

- motivation, the fun element draws people into the game;
- structured and controlled experimentation, with a clear beginning, middle and end as well as defined rules;
- simulated and safe experience – even if the content is challenging in the game and conflicts arise, the stakes are low and so there is little likelihood of real animosity;
- reflection guided by a facilitator, teacher or coach; and

- concepts are created, added or reinforced by matching reflective observation with relevant theory about project implementation.

Playing the *Self-Propelled Car* game helps deal with the challenges posed in Table 2.1 The motivation to learn is enhanced by the fun element of the game. While it draws into an immersive experience, it is the reflection phase afterwards which completes the learning cycle and allows concepts to be embedded and reinforced. Learning comes as a consequence of play and so engages existing skills around game-playing. The group discussion and reflection phases offer an opportunity to articulate and share tacit knowledge and to explore experiences. Having an experienced and *Dedicated Facilitator* running the game allows for probing and guided reflection, challenging participants to think about what they have just experienced. Above all learning is shared – and the enjoyment of this game sets up expectations for future game-based opportunities which nevertheless have a serious learning agenda embedded in them.

The ludic space and its organisational boundaries

The 'playing to learn' approach uses games and play structures to create a safe experimental space, an alternative world, in which experience can be generated. Reflection is then guided by teaching/coaching inputs (e.g. questions, probes, illumination) and concepts built or reinforced. Kolb and Kolb[22] suggest that setting up such a 'ludic space' is one of the highest forms of learning, since it introduces new perspectives to enhance familiar experiences, gives equal weight to process and outcome, and encourages learners to take responsibility for their own learning experience based on their own success criteria.[23] Setting up such a ludic space involves working with elements such as freedom to play, uncertainty and the use of artificial, alternative worlds within which a different reality can be experienced.

Figure 2.2 illustrates Kolb and Kolb's ludic learning model. The *ludic space boundary* is defined by the rules of the game. For example, the rules of turn-taking set a basic framework for interaction. The *ludic learning space* is made up of play elements: feeling free to play, tolerating uncertainty, welcoming foolishness, stepping out of real life, balancing competition (agon) and structured interaction (ludus) with free play (paidia),[24] community and communication, and the replicating the ludic space through recursive practice. *Deep learning* then takes place in the centre, involving tensions between competitiveness and fair play, self-absorption and empathy, experiencing an authentic self and one that is imagined.

While Kolb and Kolb describe these principles of a ludic space, their examples are taking from more broad play activities. What ultimately also confines and sets boundaries for a ludic space when dealing with innovation processes and management is the fact

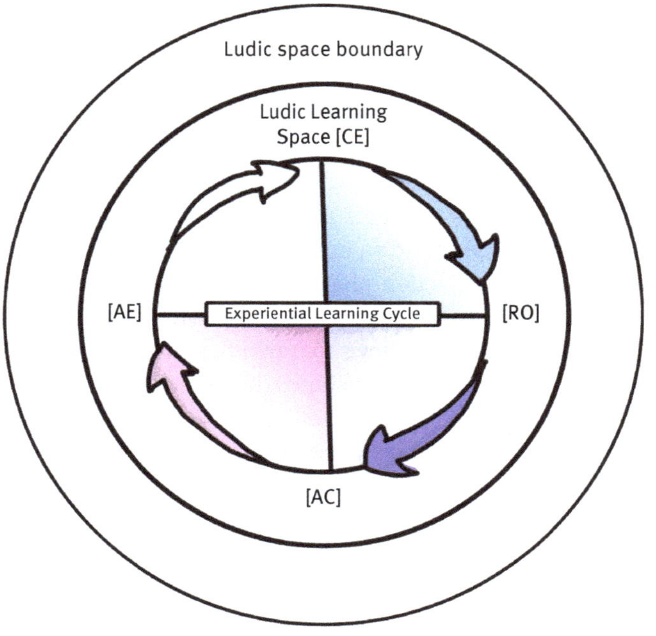

Figure 2.2: The ludic space and experiential learning cycle.[25] CE (concrete experience), RO (reflective observation), AC (active conceptualisation), AE (active experimentation).

these are also boundaries to an 'organization'. While games and the play within games can create a distance to on-going operations or everyday routines, various organizational elements still come into play – these cannot and should not be fully separated. We call these elements 'organizational constraints'. They are not necessarily negative or positive, but something one has to consider when creating a ludic space in an innovation context. Organizational constraints consist, for instance, in the times that can be assigned to different tasks, in historical and power relations, and organizational structures and culture, and governmental regulation (e.g. with respect to safety, data security or employee rights).

Likewise, language barriers play a role – and here we don't mean the language spoken in a country – but even more impactful the highly professionalized and specialized language that people use in innovation settings, where we often have to consider that people have a variety of disciplinary and work backgrounds. Games can be designed to feed in required background knowledge and mitigate similar barriers, but once in a while, organizational constraints can still pop up and influence – for better or worse – the play activity.

For example, in the *Self-Propelled Car* game mentioned above, it is essential when creating a ludic space to bear in mind the organizational constraints, allow players the freedom to move, acknowledge and accept uncertainty and create alternative directions, scenarios and stream of thoughts. Combining these with the highly experimental elements found in innovation processes over the course of a few hours results in dynamic, immersive activities that can lead to novel perspectives, uncovering hidden assumptions and other surprising insights that can lead to new pathways to pursue.

In the next chapter we will connect these concepts of learning and the ludic space to the core concepts of innovation and entrepreneurship. Based on these conceptual foundations we can then move on to looking at specific games and how they can be adapted and created to empower innovators and entrepreneurs.

Chapter 3
Innovation and entrepreneurship: Gamification and games in the innovation and entrepreneurship space

Different innovation management dimensions, process stages, and historically grown concepts span the background to situate and design gamified approaches to innovation and entrepreneurship.

These days we're familiar with the sophisticated devices embedded in our smart phones which give us access to a rich variety of geographical and travel guidance. Supported by a network of satellites and a huge library of programs interpreting information, we have literally at our fingertips the kind of navigation resources a 16th century sailor would have given riches for. The new and thriving markets in world trade which drove economic growth 500 years ago relied on accurate navigation to far-flung places which involved voyages lasting years. Accurate maps provided a considerable competitive advantage; they were tools to be kept secret and guarded, fought over and defended whatever the cost. Now at the flick of a fingertip we can map our route to anywhere and get directions to guide us on each step of the way.

The voyage and the map are useful metaphors for thinking about the challenges of managing innovation, corporate venturing and entrepreneurship. It involves an uncertain journey fraught with risk. Fortunately, we've been doing a lot of map-making over the past century. Both theoretical and practical research have enabled us to build a reasonably accurate guide to the known world and helped us develop techniques for mapping at the frontier.

There's now over one hundred years of such research on innovation management and the good news is that it is convergent. There are core themes which come up again and again. Of course, there is plenty of undiscovered territory – for example, the frontier world of managing innovation in virtual digital space. But quite a lot of territory has already been mapped, which converts to handy traveller's guides. Just as powerful map applications are available on any smartphone, there are thousands of books, courses, and even apps to help us navigate the journey of I&E. The International Standards Organization (ISO) is now actively promoting a 'standard' for a systematic approach for organizing and managing the innovation process.[1]

https://doi.org/10.1515/9783110725582-007

Games form part of this rich resource to help navigate the necessarily still uncertain world of innovation and entrepreneurship (I&E). But before we look in more detail at how they do so it will be worth briefly flying over the I&E landscape to remind us of the territory. Then we can move on to look at how games can help us learn to travel well, and take new journeys into less developed or explored lands.

3.1 What is the innovation and entrepreneurship landscape?

When did you last use your Spangler? This seems like an odd question and one which is likely to trigger a somewhat mystified response. Who or what is a Spangler? The answer is simple – Mr Murray Spangler is the man who invented and patented the electric vacuum suction sweeper. It might be an everyday object in our lives (going under various brand names), but the name of the innovator who struggled so hard to bring it into being is lost to us. But we often associate another name with vacuum cleaners – that of Mr William Hoover, who bought Spangler's patent, took over his struggling operation and built a global business out of the innovation.

This mini-saga[2] gives us a powerful reminder of a key point about innovation. It doesn't work like the cartoons in which a 'light bulb' suddenly appears when someone has a new idea. Innovation is a journey, not an event, and it's a journey across difficult and unfriendly terrain. It's full of risks and uncertainty, and those who've made the journey before us report the multiple false starts, dead ends, unexpected roadblocks and hidden potholes which might trip us up. It takes time and we may run out of the scarce resources we've scratched together to make the journey before we reach the end – the fate which befell poor Mr Spangler. But there is an end, a 'promised land' where we can rest for a few moments and enjoy the fruits of our hard work. Innovation is about creating value – whether economic, social or environmental – from our ideas and the end point is one where we have managed to achieve that goal at scale, where we've persuaded many to adopt our innovation, or we have changed the world to be a better place in some way.

The trouble is that the wanderlust gets in our blood. Once we've completed one journey we can't sit for long before our feet are itching to make the next journey, perilous though it might be. Once again, we gather ourselves, make new preparations and begin our next expedition – this time hopefully having learned the lessons from the first to help us become slightly better prepared for what awaits us. Whether we're talking about a start-up venture, making the journey for the first time, or a large corporation sending out yet another team to explore and colonise the new world, the underlying metaphor is the same. One of journeying and exploration.

The good news, of course, is that the landscape is not totally unfamiliar. We've learned a lot about its basic geography, the different climate zones we're likely to travel through and the general challenges such terrain holds. There'll still be surprising events to deal with but, thanks to a growing knowledge base, we're not simply venturing into the complete unknown. The maps that we rely on have been made by a mixture of people – fellow travellers willing to write down and share their experiences as well as researchers who have tried to systematically capture the contours of the landscape and make it available to others.

3.2 The core body of knowledge

In order to understand how games can drive innovation and facilitate entrepreneurship let us review the conceptual foundations and basic building blocks of the domain: its definition, word form, relevance and relation to entrepreneurship, its sources, dimensions, radicalism and process.

a) Definition: Innovation is about converting ideas or knowledge into economic, social and environmental value. The word is derived from the Latin *in* plus *novare,* meaning to make something new or to change. Innovation alters our capabilities to act,[3] and has been described quite simply as 'significant positive change'.[4]

b) Word form: The word 'innovation' has two meanings: it is used both as a noun (the outcome of a process) and a verb (the actions involved in making such changes). Research on innovation has not only looked at the what and its impact but also at the *how* – the ways in which the process is organised and managed.[5]

c) Relevance: Innovation is important for a number of reasons. It matters for employment, for economic growth, for social welfare and for the individual motivation and values of different stakeholders involved in the process.[6] William Baumol's work explores the insight that innovation is a key factor in economic development: extensive studies highlight the importance of 'the residual' due to innovation – the part of productivity growth statistics which is not accounted for by changes in labour or capital inputs.[7] Other studies look at the way innovation shapes competitiveness and enables the emergence of new industries and change in economic structures and firm level performance. Also, its role in social change has been well documented. Arguably the development of civilization is a history of social innovation in new forms of human interaction. Periods like the Renaissance and the Industrial Revolution are characterised by waves of social and cultural change enabled by innovation. In the last decade the pivotal role of innovation for urgent transitions towards a sustainable development has been widely acknowledged.

d) Entrepreneurship: Innovation is what entrepreneurs do.[8] Entrepreneurs are agents of innovation and they do it in many different contexts. Start-ups are the most familiar to us but innovation agents act in many other contexts: in growing enterprises, in large established organizations (LEOs) and in multi-organization networks and systems. This distinction is important because there is growing recognition of the various forms of innovation action – for example amongst employees, in corporate entrepreneurship, as well as with the individuals and teams who create new ventures.

e) Sources: Extensive research highlights the wide range of sources of innovation. These include formal research and development (R&D), less formal process improvement experimentation, sensing and analysing of market signals, competitor behaviour and emulation, user-led innovation, as well as changing values in society or governmental regulation. The underlying message is that effective innovation management requires a rich understanding of both the wide range of sources and the ability to search systematically across them to identify threats and tap into potential opportunities for innovation.

f) Dimensions: Multiple studies going right back to Schumpeter's early theories[9] point to innovation taking place in a number of different ways. These include product, process, marketing and organisational innovation.[10] Unique methods address different types of innovation in three management dimensions, namely the operational dimension with product, process and service innovation, the strategic dimension with business model innovation and strategic concerns (including market positioning and supply chain) and the normative dimension with innovations in organisational identity and networks.[11] Once again effective innovation management requires understanding of these different types and building a portfolio which reflects the range of opportunities and values to strive for.

g) Radicalism: Innovation involves a spectrum of novelty and risk along these dimensions of change, running from incremental improvement (doing what we do but better) through to more radical steps and at the limit doing something completely new. Sustaining innovation involves incremental and larger step changes within an existing technology or market framework while disruptive innovation involves more radical shifts such as the emergence of new markets, jumps to new technological fields or shifts in business model paradigms.

h) Process: Innovation involves a process – it is not a single 'light bulb' moment. While this process is not neat or simple there is an underlying structure to it over time and it requires innovation managers to pay attention to different activities within each phase. Typical models have a front end concerned with search, a phase associated with strategic selection of opportunities out of the many available at the front end and then a systematic elaboration of those projects. This process involves reducing uncertainty by investing in knowledge acquisition through development activities; it requires careful review and balancing of risk and reward and the ability to stop or pivot activities as learning takes place in cycles of experimentation. Once developed to the stage where a new product or service can be launched on the market (or a new process launched in an internal market) the emphasis shifts towards scale, diffusion and capturing of value. Finally, innovation as a process allows for review and learning to establish and innovation culture and build capabilities for the future – how to repeat the innovation trick more effectively. This process doesn't take place in a vacuum – it is shaped and influenced by a variety of factors. In particular innovation needs:

- Clear normative direction and strategic leadership, plus the commitment of resources to make it happen. Innovation is about taking risks, about going into new and sometimes completely unexplored spaces. It requires visionary leadership, the willingness to commit resources and effective communication in order to secure buy-in and the alignment of innovation efforts from all employees.
- An innovative organisation in which the structure and climate enable people to deploy their creativity and share their knowledge to bring about change. Research emphasises that 'one size doesn't fit all'. There is a need to determine the appropriate organizational structure given the operating contingencies. Too little order and structure may be as bad as too much.
- Pro-active links across boundaries inside the organisation and to external stakeholders who can play a part in the innovation process – for instance suppliers, customers, sources of finance, resources of skill and knowledge, even society at large. Twenty-first century innovation is most certainly not a solo act but a multiplayer game across boundaries inside the organisation and beyond those to the many external agencies who can play a part in the innovation process. Emphasis in the era of 'open innovation' is increasingly on building and managing in innovation ecosystems in which networks and relationships are critical.

The essential steps of a process model and the key innovation management questions are summarised in Figure 3.1. In chapter 5 we will see how different game flows can support each of these steps.

Of course, there are limits to such process models. Many commentators point out the complexities and uncertainties involved. But even they agree that there is a generic landscape through which we need to travel if value is to emerge from ideas. Anyone might get lucky once but successful organizations try to *manage* the innovation process and they do so at multiple levels – operational, strategic, normative – within an integrated management framework.[12]

To stay a little longer with the journey metaphor we need to recognise that innovation does not simply involve the same journey every time. There is enormous *variety* in terms of the travellers, destinations, level of risk and such. Organizations and

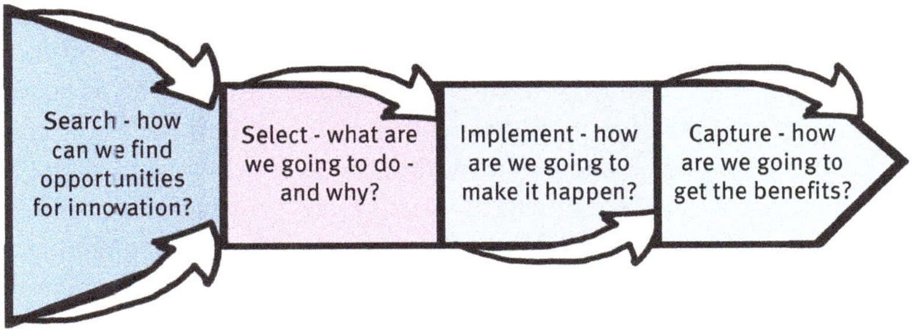

Figure 3.1: A four step process model to drive innovation.

serial entrepreneurs try to embed behaviour patterns which work – for how they search, select, implement, etc. – into behavioural 'routines' which become 'the way we do things around here', the culture of their organizations. But the reality is also that there is always a need to discover new ways of travelling and adding new skills and capabilities which we learn through travelling at the innovation frontier.

Organisational ambidexterity or the tension between 'exploit' – doing what we do better – and 'explore' – doing something completely different – is at the heart of organizational strategy concerning innovation.[13] The former benefits from familiarity, so maps can be used to good effect here. But the latter requires a capacity to make our own maps. When companies grow, many lose the capability to explore and make new maps over the years – in other words; innovation is at odds with ongoing operations. Companies become good at optimizing the current portfolios already at the heart of the organization. This has been referred to as the innovator's dilemma, organizational ambidexterity and sometimes also as corporate immune systems. Approaches are needed that can catapult selected company representatives out of the exploit mode and into exploring new directions, and eventually also launching and ramping these up.

It's also worth reminding ourselves that the *context* in which all of this takes place varies. Much of what we learned in the early days of our map-making about managing innovation began in large commercial organizations. The emphasis then shifted to smaller organizations in a start-up phase, looking more closely at the 'front end' of innovation and especially the role of the entrepreneur as an agent of change. Early work focussed heavily on manufacturing. More recent emphasis has been on services. Product and process dominated early thinking, now there is a strong focus on business models and value platforms. And the unit of analysis has moved from focusing on the enterprise to chains and relationships involving customers and suppliers, to today's view of innovation as an open multi-player game with an emphasis on networks and ecosystems.

In particular we've recognised that it's not simply a matter of plug-and-play. These lessons need configuring to contexts like social innovation or the public sector where different constraints apply and which require different or adapted models. For example, healthcare innovation involves a tension between risk and reward as would be familiar in any commercial venture. But it also involves reliability – the need to ensure safe healthcare provision – something which introduces a bias towards playing safe. In similar fashion, social innovation in a sector like humanitarian aid faces ethical challenges – slogans like 'fail fast' and experimenting with minimum viable products and rapid prototyping have no place in a context where the 'market' consists of vulnerable people traumatised by the after-effects of a disaster.

Eventually, acknowledging an increasing variety of social and sustainability-oriented innovations has contributed to our current understanding that any kind of innovation is to some extent based on values, i.e. driven by systems of priorities and notions of what is considered desirable, that innovations articulate a response to what is conceived of as a relevant challenge. Accordingly, innovation is increasingly recognised as a key resource to deal with 'grand challenges' confronting society today.

Games and gamification have played a relatively small role so far in the development of innovation approaches. However, their potential to promote safe experimentation, to facilitate collaboration amongst a wide group of stakeholders and to combine different techniques and methods suggests considerable potentials to expand this approach.

3.3 Games for map-making at the innovation frontier

As we have seen, there is a body of knowledge of I&E. The challenge becomes one of *how* to share this knowledge so others can make the journey. It's a learning challenge and, as we saw in the previous chapter, one in which games can play a big part. First let's remind ourselves of the key attributes games have to support the learning cycle.

- They create a temporary alternative world with boundaries in time and space, within which safe exploration can take place.
- They involve rules and other play structures and elements.
- They allow for interactivity between players and game objects, allowing them to experience of the 'drama' in the situation being modelled.
- They allow for multiple simulations in which players can experiment with different strategies.
- They provide motivation, the fun element of a game which draws people in.
- They permit experimentation within the game context.

As we saw in chapter 2 a widely used game in the field of innovation involves participants in teams competing to design and build a new product – a *self-propelled toy car* for example.[14] In this new product development game the players have limited resources so they need to be creative in their design, and they are working against the clock so they need to balance exploration with implementation. They are judged on a number of performance criteria – for example how far can the car travel under its own propulsion. In its simplest form this provides rich content for reflection on key themes like innovation search and experimentation and disciplines like project management and teamworking. Variations in the game can bring in a market element – success is judged partially on how satisfied the customer is so teams have to do market research to try and elicit and meet needs, or not!

If we map this game onto our model of ludic space we can see the role the game plays in allowing experimentation and exploration. Despite the element of competition, participants enjoy the interaction. The risks they take in design are calculated but the consequences are not career threatening. Importantly, the reflection phase after the game is completed allows participants to straddle both the game world and the real world; experience suggests there is considerable transfer of learning from the game to equivalent situations in the world of practice.

This discussion highlights the point that there is a rich set of resources involving games as a way of communicating and explaining the core concepts in innovation and entrepreneurship. They enable the exploration and elaboration of key themes and offer the opportunity for individuals to experience and make sense of the challenges I&E can pose. For now, it's worth reminding ourselves of this dual challenge – exploring the use of games to illustrate what we already know about I&E and developing new games to help extend or enrich that repertoire. We'll explore this theme and give some examples drawn from our current research in part II where we look at:

- using existing games for relatively simple, pre-defined challenges,
- adapting and customizing games for more complex or challenging individual organizations and innovation projects, and
- creating new games for new or 'hidden' and unexplored challenges.

Part II
Using, adapting and creating games

https://doi.org/10.1515/9783110725582-008

In this part we set out a pattern approach to configuring, creating and using games to drive innovation and describe how to work with them. Gamification design patterns document proven solutions to recurring challenges and enable innovation professionals, game designers and facilitators to create their own games.

Chapter 4 explains the pattern approach as a framework to thinking about and creating games for I&E. The chapter introduces gamification design *patterns* as an approach to document and provide knowledge on reusable solutions to recurring challenges. It distinguishes between flow and component patterns and develops a basic structure for collecting patterns.

Chapter 5 explores ways in which innovators and entrepreneurs and learners can use, modify and adapt existing *games*. Existing games and proven gamification formats are mapped onto our framework of innovation challenges.

Chapter 6 focusses on *gamification*. It provides a simple process and a canvas to collect information and generate alternative designs for addressing unique innovation and entrepreneurship challenges. We discuss different contexts for defining suitable game methods and design patterns.

Chapter 4
Patterns: A pattern approach to gamification for innovation and entrepreneurship

Gamification design patterns describe reusable interaction flows and components to address recurring challenges. They can be combined to empower entrepreneurs and to drive innovation.

Games have become an increasingly popular tool in a variety of organizations. In many cases, the purpose of these games is to enhance motivation of employees and to improve their productivity and the overall organizational performance. Beyond such an optimization of operations there is considerable scope for using this approach in innovation and acquiring entrepreneurial skills. Games have moved to a central stage in both classroom contexts and the world of practice. Institutions and actors now recognize and utilize gamification and games to engage stakeholders in collaborative, co-creative, action-oriented activities. Methodological frameworks like design thinking and agile management include gamified approaches in their portfolio.

However, in spite of this proliferation of interest we are missing an overview and structure that allow us to move beyond anecdotal reports to a more comprehensive understanding of games and towards an advanced, evidence-based knowledge about different options for their design. We need a framework within which to locate the rich experience we now have with games and to extract design and configuration principles to help their further application to both existing and emerging challenges.

In this chapter we move beyond anecdotal views on games and gamification and introduce such a structured approach associating game flows and components to innovation challenges. The purpose is not just to provide a classification, but also a resource for design, education and professional development. The collection of design patterns should motivate students and professionals to think about the relation between different components, flows and contexts of game design, and to develop their own alternative formats to address innovation challenges.

4.1 Design patterns to develop gamified facilitation formats for innovation

In this chapter we unfold a systematic framework and a design approach to analyse and design games that drive innovation. We reviewed the academic literature and interviewed numerous innovation experts. First, a systematic and integrative literature

https://doi.org/10.1515/9783110725582-009

review on gamification for innovation gave us an overview of the scientific discourse. Interviews with 59 experts in large European corporations or small consulting firms provided insights into corporate innovation challenges and the potential of games to address them. We continued with a collection and classification of all the innovation games we found, much like a biologist would collect, identify, group and name different species to create a taxonomy. We collected the different game formats and analysed their design elements as well as the purposes they were serving. Finally, we aggregated and structured the results of this analysis in a collection of gamification design patterns suitable to address recurring innovation challenges.

Design patterns were initially introduced in architecture through the works of the US-American architect Christopher Alexander. With the term design pattern, he refers to 'a combination of a problem and a corresponding solution that is described in a systematic and generic way, so that it can be used over and over again in different situations.'[1] Just like we did with the innovation landscape in the previous chapter, he introduces the approach using a spatial metaphor when he says that patterns create 'a coherent picture of an entire region with the power to generate such regions in a million forms, with infinite variety in all details.'[2] Design patterns have been successfully applied to other design fields such as software engineering,[3] interaction design,[4] pedagogy and educational technologies,[5] business model design[6] and sustainable business design.[7] These patterns not only document and structure design knowledge in a reusable way. They also offer a means to make design knowledge more accessible to a wider public, to encourage participation in shaping human environments and, in the end, to democratise the design process.[8] We want to follow up on this approach and provide an initial set of gamification patterns for innovation that is equally useful for innovation game designers as for teachers and professional trainers.

4.2 The structure of the gamification pattern collection

The pattern collection was derived from examining recurring innovation management challenges discussed in the literature[9] and from the results of a needs analysis with innovation experts from leading European firms.[10] Starting from these sources, we collected existing games and gamified responses to innovation challenges, identified their components and interaction flows and matched them to the following structure. It consists of four levels, two describing innovation challenges that can be addressed through gamification, and two describing design patterns responding to these challenges. Figure 4.1 shows the basic structure of the patterns overview.

These are the four levels of challenges and patterns to address them.

I. *Overarching domains of innovation challenges* from the literature: 10 domains associated to the operational, strategic and normative dimensions of innovation management.
II. *Recurring Challenges*: A typical innovation or entrepreneurship challenge to be addressed through gamification and selected flow patterns.
III. *Flow patterns*: Reusable flows of interactions between participants and artefacts to address an innovation or entrepreneurial challenge. Flow patterns combine several component patterns through a defined flow of interactions to address a specific innovation challenge.
IV. *Component patterns*: Reusable, stand-alone game elements that can be aggregated as building blocks in the design of innovation-specific game flows and game-like activities. They provide 'a set of building blocks or features shared by games.'[11]

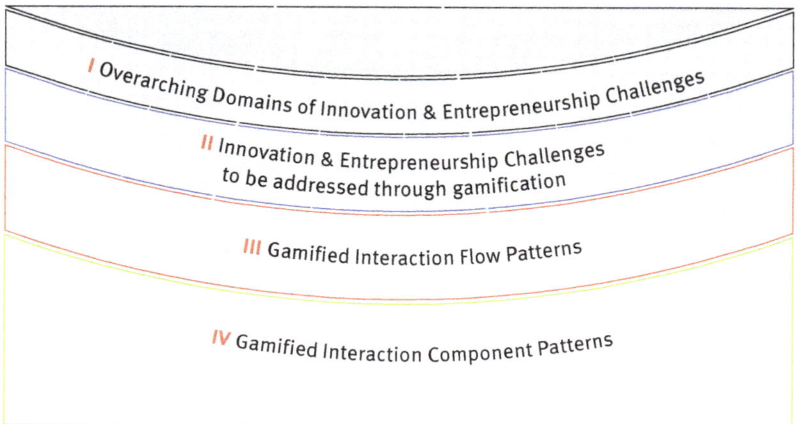

Figure 4.1: Four levels of the innovation challenges and gamification design patterns.

Overarching domains of innovation management and entrepreneurship challenges

An integrated management framework[12] distinguishes between normative, strategic and operative management dimensions. In this framework, normative management defines the overarching normative guidelines (such as vision, mission and purpose) of the organisation. They make up and preserve its identity and reach beyond its strategic goals. For example, serving humanity, ensuring safe mobility or combatting a severe disease would be examples of such normative directives, whereas increasing market share or becoming a leading healthcare provider would be strategic goals.

Strategic management secures the competitive edge of an organisation, and differentiates it from other market players. It translates visions, missions and purposes from the normative dimension into strategic programmes and business models, and provides orientation for value-creating activities in the operational dimension. Operational management translates normative and strategic dimensions into operational processes and daily practices; in the context of innovation management this includes the typical activities in a stage-gate process[13] of product or service innovation. The development of processes, products, services and further business model components is realised by operational management.

Based on this framework, and the recurring challenges described in innovation management textbooks,[14] we work with the following 10 overarching domains of innovation challenges (see Figure 4.2).

1. *Normative guidelines* and espoused values found in vision, mission and purpose statements and/or documented values of an organisation establish an enduring normative framework for all business activities including innovation management. Associated challenges include the sourcing, framing and communicating normative statements for innovation and ensuring alignment among the different stakeholders. For example, a company could ask: How can we best convey our values and improve our employee's commitment to them?
2. *Top management involvement* was identified early on by innovation research as playing a critical role for innovation to succeed, i.e. a power promoter for new ideas is required next to the domain experts that actually implement them.[15] Against resistance from top management, innovation projects are destined to fail, but we should also ask more broadly: How can we engage colleagues in promoting the innovation process by means of either hierarchical power, specific technical knowledge or as active mediators?
3. *Cross-functional engagement* and successful collaboration to succeed in innovation or create a new venture requires individuals and teams with different competencies and functions to join forces to reach a shared goal. Defining the goal, conveying a common understanding and enabling such collaboration creates multiple challenges. For instance: How can we align goals and priorities across the different departments needed to contribute to making an innovation happen?

On the strategic level management, (4) market and brand positioning, (5) business modelling, and (6) incentivisation of employees can and have been addressed though games and gamification.

4. *Human resource management* and employee incentivisation are designated toß attract, appoint, mobilize and retain employees as capable resources to turn innovation projects into success. Incentives range from tangible benefits to trust-building

and self-determination measures, for instance having employees themselves decide which projects they work on.[16] A question could be: How can we manage our human resources and design our incentive system to align corporate sustainability with our strategic goals?

5. Market and brand *positioning* secure competitive advantages and differentiate products, services and business models from potential and existing competitors on the market. Associated challenges include those of brand management and development, managing product and service portfolios and understanding (future) markets, e.g. identifying 'blue oceans'.[17] A decisive question could be: How should we reposition our product or brand?
6. *Business modelling* and business model innovation develop new and viable forms of value creation, delivery and capture. Recurring challenges for innovators and entrepreneurs include exploring the scope and depth of business design options, evaluating the strengths and weaknesses of different business model components, and creating a shared understanding and conviction among participants that the new model is worth doing.[18]

On the operational level we followed a widespread sequence of process stages[19] (chapter 3) including futures search and framing, idea generation and selection, prototyping and implementation, capturing benefits of going-to-market, commercialization and diffusion.

7. *Search* includes the exploration of future scenarios or unmet customer needs and preferences, values-based framing of the search field and generation of ideas to find opportunities for innovation. A typical challenge would be: How can we increase the number of promising ideas for our new service offerings?
8. *Select* reduces the number of candidates to a small number of ideas to be pursued. Selection can involve different roles within and outside the organisation and is based on criteria such as fit with the normative frameworks and strategies, expected market potential and technical feasibility. One question could be: How can we select ideas collaboratively without sorting out radical or disruptive ideas for the wrong reasons?
9. *Implement* can include several iterations of prototyping and development to assess technological feasibility, desirability for potential customer and/or viability of different business model components. A critical question could be: Which aspects of an envisioned product or service should be prototyped first and how should its potential be assessed in order for it to become a breakthrough innovation?
10. *Capture* is concerned with ensuring expected (economic, social and environmental) benefits in the real world – a test market for a new product, service or business model, or an organisational setting for a new process. A critical challenge in this stage is how to push adoption or how to sustain expected benefits.

Figure 4.2: Three management dimensions and ten overarching domains of general innovation challenges from the literature.

Innovation and entrepreneurship challenges to be addressed through gamification

These three management dimensions and ten domains were also used to structure a series of expert interviews that helped us to better understand the current needs in organisations to address innovation challenges through games and gamification.[20] Analysis of these expert interviews, an extensive literature review, and a collection of innovation games (with a special attention to games that facilitate values-based and sustainable innovation) allowed us to compile a list of ten recurrent innovation challenges that gamified interaction formats are already addressing. We are listing these empirically found formats with an exemplary question for each.

1. *Values Adoption*: Cultural issues related to an ongoing organizational transformation hamper innovation. How can we facilitate communication, understanding and adoption of organizational values (such as giving a higher priority to corporate sustainability) among employees?
2. *Empathetic Learning*: Lack of a shared understanding of other stakeholders' perspectives creates the need for stimulating learning. For example: How can employees better understand their customers' needs and spur customer centricity throughout daily practices?
3. *Professional Facilitation*: Sometimes substantial knowledge and resolving process ambiguities are needed for innovation. How can we facilitate participation in workshops that require substantial background knowledge?
4. *Team Energizing*: Most successful workshops depend on energizing participants and promoting team spirit in a limited timeframe. How can we engage workshop participants to rapidly co-create outstanding results and to collaboratively exceed their individual potential?
5. *Behavioural Uncertainty*: Risk and uncertainty are constant companions in business processes and ecosystems. How can we manage limits to controlling process-oriented and behavioural challenges on an organizational level?
6. *Collaborative Modelling*: When exploring new and viable business models, entrepreneurs, corporate venture managers and different stakeholders need to explore the design space, compare different options, come up with a shared understanding

and compare different options so that we can commit to the ones we want to proceed with. How can we facilitate such collaborative modelling?
7. *Effective Ideation*: Conventional ideation methods often fail to stimulate confidence, allow balancing between freedom and constrains, and deliver the right ideas. How can we facilitate the generation of a broad range of ideas involving diverse stakeholders?
8. *Motivated Engagement*: Insufficient stakeholder engagement and motivation hamper innovation projects. How can we involve and motivate diverse stakeholders to generate ideas and drive innovation and entrepreneurship?
9. *Situated Adaptation*: When implementing new business ideas, entrepreneurs and corporate venture managers need to manoeuvre between the dedicated pursuit of strong values and a vision and the readiness to pivot in the development of new offerings. How can we adapt flexibly to new information, feedback and insights while staying true to our values and vision?
10. *Collaborative Assessment*: At different stages of the innovation process or development of start-ups and new ventures, intermediary products need to be assessed. How can we facilitate such collaborative screening, evaluation and prioritization of ideas and prototypes?

Figure 4.3 maps these challenges to be addressed through gamification onto the framework of management dimensions and major domains in innovation management and entrepreneurship.

Innovation management challenges and gamification patterns

The pattern collection can be used by innovation professionals, game developers, teachers and students to sketch alternative gamified solutions to innovation and entrepreneurship challenges, and to think about the relations among different challenges, design flows and components. Since several responses in our expert interviews indicated the need to sensitize employees to organisational values and to introduce sustainability-oriented practises, we particularly looked into games and gamified formats to address these challenges. As a result, there might be room for expanding the current collection of 36 patterns into other domains. Its conceptual distinction between innovation projects and gamified activities addressing innovation challenges through flow patterns and subordinate component patterns can be further developed with reference to the theoretical distinction between activities, actions and operations.[21]

The current compilation was created from various sources, including the literature review on games and gamification to address cultural challenges and to facilitate values-based innovation,[22] a dedicated search for gamified formats facilitating sustainability-

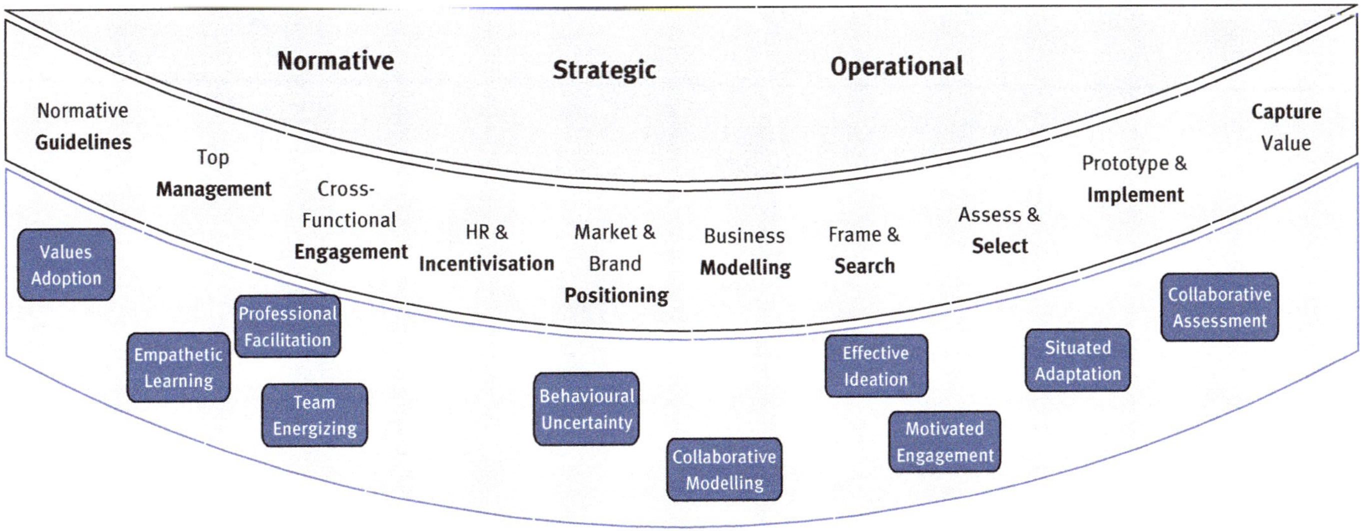

Figure 4.3: Ten innovation and entrepreneurship challenges to be addressed through gamification mapped onto management dimensions and overarching domains of innovation.

oriented innovation activities (as part of the development of the *Corporate Sustainability Innovation* game described in chapter 7), and selected games from design books not exclusively focused on innovation.[23] We reviewed each source and analysed each game and gamified format to understand the particular innovation and entrepreneurship challenges being addressed. We then documented the patterns as either a flow or component pattern.

Flow patterns describe reusable flows of interactions between participants and artefacts to address an innovation or entrepreneurial challenge. Each flow can involve several component patterns (see Figure 4.4).

Component patterns represent reusable, stand-alone game elements that can be aggregated as building blocks in the design of innovation-specific game flows and game-like activities (see Figure 4.5).

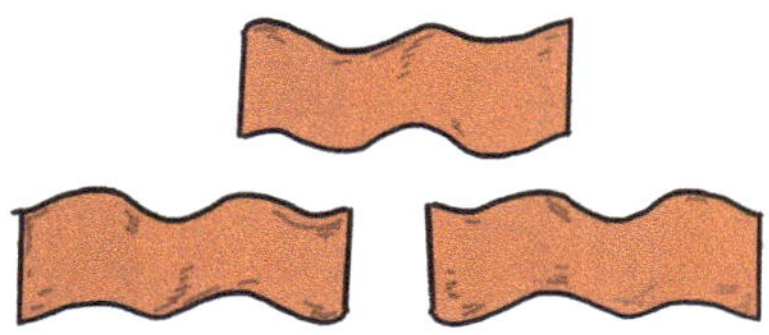

Figure 4.4: Flow patterns illustrated as wavy shapes.

Figure 4.5: Component patterns illustrated as blocks.

In designing gamified answers to innovation challenges, game designers or facilitators can work from top (i.e. challenges) to bottom to find suitable gamification flow and component patterns (see Figure 4.6). If recurring innovation challenges are not sufficiently addressed by the current collection, then new patterns can be added at the bottom.

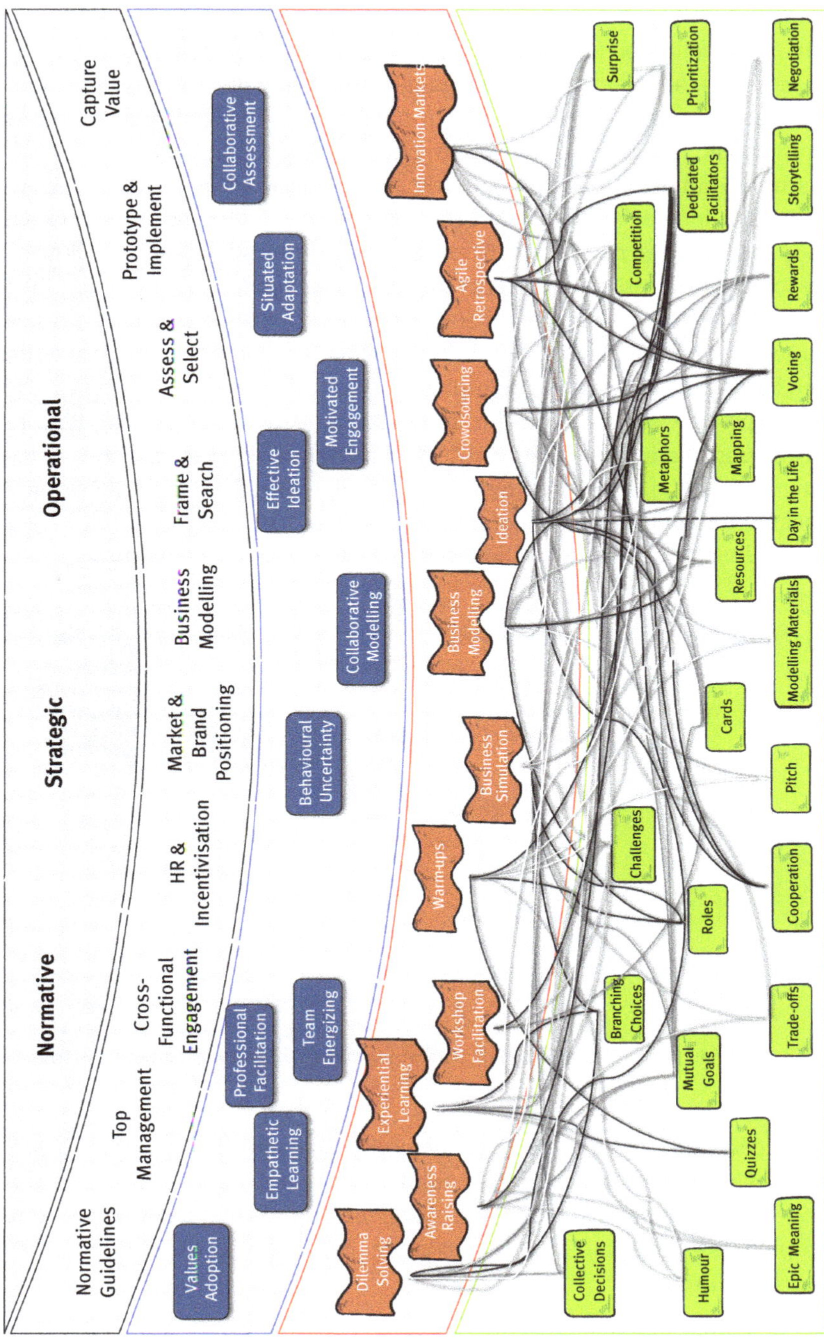

Figure 4.6: Overview of 36 flow and component patterns with associated challenges sorted by management dimensions and domains of innovation challenges.

4.3 Individual flow and component patterns

Each pattern of the collection is described with a name, a visualization, a challenge, a solution, some notes, an example and related patterns. The name captures in one or two words what the pattern is about (pattern names are set in italic capital letters throughout the book). An iconic illustration depicts some of its key aspects. The challenge sums up the innovation challenge that an organisation or an entrepreneur needs to address to succeed in innovation. These challenges can be addressed through gamification, and their description always ends with a key question that the following solution responds to. The solution presents the main idea about the pattern and then spells out why it works and which key characteristics are involved. The notes provide lessons learned for implementation and further insights. An example then features an actual game in which the design pattern plays a central role – these examples and related sources provide starting points for further research about the pattern, its conceptual background and implementations. Related patterns refer to other flow or component patterns that are often used together with the pattern – for designers and students looking for additional flows or components to enrich their game ideas (see Figure 4.7 – the first overview cards of flow patterns and component patterns).

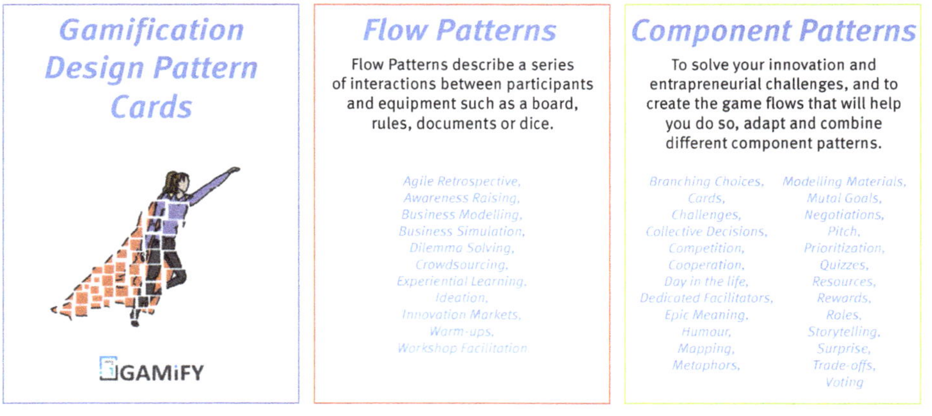

Figure 4.7: Gamification Design Pattern Cards[24] with an overview of flow and component pattern names.

The complete collection of patterns with comprehensive descriptions of each pattern and further references are accessible online, and in a shortened form as a *Gamification Design Pattern* card deck. Here we show one exemplary flow and one component pattern to illustrate what they contain and how to work with them (see Figure 4.8 and Figure 4.9).

One of the challenges organisations are facing is how to facilitate the adoption of abstract organizational values among employees. In one case an insurance company

Flow Pattern Example: *DILEMMA SOLVING*

Figure 4.8: Iconic illustration of the *DILEMMA SOLVING* pattern.

Innovation challenge: When decision-makers 'choose between multiple courses of action that each seem right from a certain perspective', values can be used to make choices that are 'maximally beneficial to all stakeholders'.[25] But individual values and the systems of priorities they represent[26] have to be interpreted and weighted against each other in order to guide decision making and devise courses of action. This makes it challenging to translate organizational values into strategic decision making and operations. *How can we turn abstract organisational values into actionable heuristics?*

Solution: *DILEMMA SOLVING* games help people interpret values (and associated purpose, mission and vision statements) and their implications through examples involving specific behaviors. They are based on typical dilemmas encountered by organizational members and prompt employees to apply organizational values through direct and concrete interaction. By clarifying networks of beliefs, attitudes and intentions, they help align individual and organizational values and establish them as principles by which organizational actors live and perform. Furthermore, they sensitize employees for potentially conflicting values and clarify associated networks of beliefs, attitudes and intentions.[27]

Notes: The resulting alignment of values promotes vertical as well as horizontal communication across boundaries.[28] Dilemmas need to be crowdsourced from organizational members and regularly updated in order to ensure that they represent organizational challenges accurately and realistically.

Example: The Danish company NETS used the *DILEMMA SOLVING* pattern to develop ACT, a game that promotes the company's organizational values of being 'accountable', 'customer driven' and 'together'.[28] Players assess specific dilemmas and give scores on how much they affect the three values. They then suggest different ways to solve or work with the given dilemmas. Next, players evaluate their approaches to solve the dilemmas by referring to the organizational values. Finally, a debriefing session allows participants to discuss the values and reflect on lessons learned from the game.

Related patterns: *AWARENESS RAISING, BRANCHING CHOICES, CHALLENGES, COLLECTIVE DECISIONS, COOPERATION, MUTUAL GOALS, ROLES, TRADE-OFFS.*

was implementing a new set of core values after an international merger. In another case a telecommunication provider wanted to sensitize its employees to the implications of its new sustainability orientation. Alternative flow patterns have been successfully used to develop gamified approaches to face dilemmas and difficult trade-off decisions, and to engage employees to deal with conflicting values and norms.[29] The *Global Compact Dilemma* game (all games are described in the appendix) is one prominent example of the *DILEMMA SOLVING* pattern. Alternatively, the *AWARENESS RAISING* pattern can be used to integrate a series of game-like activities in an experiential workshop format. Both flows integrate several components used in other flows as well. For instance, playing *ROLES* of different stakeholders is a typical component of dilemma games.

When an organization is facing similar challenges, the *DILEMMA SOLVING* pattern describes one potential flow of activities through which these challenges can be addressed. As is the case with any pattern, it can be interpreted and applied in quite different ways – 'a million times over without doing the same thing twice', as Alexander put it. For instance, players can be given predefined dilemmas they then respond to, or they can choose the ones they best relate to from a set of dilemmas. The dilemmas can be more generic (like those in the *Global Compact Dilemma* game), or more specific with respect to the individual organization. They can even be based on real situations. Also, players can address the dilemmas (or assess how other players respond to the dilemmas) from their own perspective or from the point of view of the *ROLES* they are playing in the game.

Just like the *DILEMMA SOLVING* pattern, the *ROLES* pattern can and needs to be interpreted and specified for the contextual flow, here the dilemma game. *ROLES* can be assigned or be chosen by the players. *ROLES* can range from a simple good cop versus bad cop, heaven's versus devil's advocate. A conceptual role definition can follow brainstorming methods (like the dreamer, realist and spoiler in the Walt Disney method) or the six thinking hats[35]. Of course, these can also be real roles as in a design sprint team, or the roles of stakeholders in an innovation ecosystem.

Playing with different combinations of flow and component patterns, and different interpretations of each pattern, game designers and innovation professionals, teachers and students can explore the design space at hand and probe alternative gamification formats to address their innovation challenges. They can sketch alternative gamified solutions to innovation challenges, and think about the relations among different challenges, design flows and components. Design patterns facilitate communication and comparative evaluation, stimulating the uptake of gamification in the context of teaching, training and consulting. They allow participants to acquire knowledge, hands-on experience and skills for developing new games and gamified formats for innovation.

Component Pattern Example: *ROLES*

Figure 4.9: Iconic illustration of the *ROLES* pattern.

Innovation challenge: A major challenge and opportunity in the process of developing successful innovations is the adequate and empathic recognition of customers and other relevant stakeholders. Although research-based input is helpful in this regard, such insights provide only a limited and static perspective about the stakeholders' needs, wants and values. Furthermore, sometimes employees may approach the innovation process with a habitual mindset and fail to think 'outside the box'. *How can we facilitate empathy and the taking on of different viewpoints?*

Solution: *ROLES* playing participants assume the goals and behaviors of fictional agents[30], enacting their goals and behaviors in a playful manner, and thereby acquiring a deeper understanding of their emotions and motivations. In addition, *ROLES* allow certain desired behaviors (e.g. leadership, cooperation) to be practiced in a risk-free environment. Such practice can be followed by a feedback or debriefing session in which participants reflect on how effective they were in their roles and where they need to improve.[31]

Notes: To support participants in better understanding and performing their roles, they can be provided with cards or other cues indicating typical aspects, such as common behaviors, values, needs or interests. The *ROLES* can represent members of relevant stakeholder groups or roles within a team, e.g. conceptualizers, coordinators, implementers (see[32,33]), stereotypes like a good and bad cop, or conceptual roles.

Example: The *Innovation Diamond Learning Game*[34] enables the development and internalization of four leadership behaviors associated with the early stages of the innovation process. The game draws on theoretical work by Darsø[33], who defines four distinct roles for supporting innovation processes: gardener, jester, conceptualizer and challenger. Throughout the game the players handle different tasks to gain hands-on experience with the four leadership roles and thus learn how they offer differing approaches for advancing innovation in its early stages.

Related patterns: *BUSINESS SIMULATION, CARDS, DAY IN THE LIFE, DILEMMA SOLVING, EPIC MEANING, IDEATION, NEGOTIATION, MODELLING MATERIALS, STORYTELLING, WARM-UPS*

Chapter 5
Games: Using and adapting games for innovation and entrepreneurship

Numerous games are already available to address recurring innovation challenges. Many of them can be easily repurposed or adapted to facilitate innovation-related tasks.

In the previous chapters we looked into some of the conceptual foundations of play, games and gamification, and gave a sense of the unique potential they have to address the typical challenges we are facing as innovation managers or entrepreneurs. We discussed several examples and introduced a collection of reusable design patterns with flows and components to create new or adapt existing games. Now, we will invite you to utilize these formats yourself – to enter your own gamification journey that can take you from using existing games (chapter 5.1), to adapting and customizing them for your specific purposes (chapter 5.2), and considering different games to utilize or adapt (chapter 5.3). Afterwards we show how to create new games and gamified facilitation formats yourself (chapter 6).

To explore new formats for interaction or even to handle many typical situations in innovation and entrepreneurship (like warm-up or retrospective sessions, or boosting creativity for ideation), it may suffice to just use some of the proven formats already out there. In many cases though, you will need to use games as templates to develop more tailored methods and content that fit to your organisation, its current challenges and the participants you intend to work with. Practising both approaches will give you the courage to apply not just the more established 'serious games' (designed for more 'serious' purposes than just entertainment such as learning, training or working), but also the more 'dangerous' ones (that might cause severe, but not fully predictable consequences outside the game world). It will also empower you to create your own formats that respond to grand challenges (like changing organisational culture) or even the wicked problems (like those associated with sustainable development). We start with a simple call to gamified interaction.

5.1 Using existing games for relatively simple, pre-defined challenges

We have seen that playing games comes naturally to us as humans, but introducing games and gamified formats for interaction into a business ecosystem may still be a

https://doi.org/10.1515/9783110725582-010

significant step. We might be tempted to 'just do it', but just doing it will fail if no one plays along. From the outset we should not just consider our own willingness and competence to introduce new gamified formats that break with established routines, but also the willingness of the would-be game participants to play along. We should also ensure that the organization possesses the absorptive capacity to experiment with different gamified formats and make them part of its routines. Once we acknowledge the need for support from these three parties – the initiator, the players and the organisation – it should be fairly easy to introduce games one step at a time.

There is always one simple game format you can start with. We're not thinking of betting on horses at lunch here – 'I bet you a six pack that this new management campaign will fail!' – but a rule-based system to help you engage in a challenge (chapter 2). Think of what this first game could be for yourself and your organisation.

Short and simple warmup exercises to group meetings are always an easy start to a journey. Instead of each player just mentioning their name, position and responsibilities in a certain project, you can try to set a more playful tone by using a *Name Alliteration* game or a warmup exercise related to the topic of the meeting. For instance, ask participants to *Bring an Object*, or a picture of an object that they associate with a new topic you are dealing with and use it as a stepping stone for storytelling and sharing their perspective on the topic.

Name Alliteration

Ask each participant in a meeting to tell the others their name by modifying it with an adjective beginning with the same letter (instead of just mentioning their name and position in the organisation). The first person starts with, for example, 'I am the sensational Sebastian.' Then the second continues, repeating the name of the first player, and making up their own adjective plus name, for example: 'This is the sensational Sebastian and I am the creative Carlos.' Each person adds to the list until everyone has had a turn, with others helping out when names, or adjectives, are forgotten. This exercise works in meetings with up to 12 participants. You can vary the exercise using animals, colors or hobbies instead of adjectives.

When introducing such simple and widely used game formats, consider how you can avoid resistance and ensure that the exercise fulfils its purpose. Many facilitators have found it is advisable to carefully use the *terms* game and gamification, so as to avoid discussions about whether, given time constraints and external pressures to succeed, these formats are appropriate to solving serious challenges. While you might be able to convince your colleagues that these formats are indeed well suited to the task at hand, it is much easier to justify the approach once it has already proven to be successful. But there is no need to name it in any particular way at all if you think this will help you to increase acceptance.

What is important to convey is the *purpose* of the activity, as it will not necessarily be immediately apparent to participants in the game. The purpose of the *Name Alliteration* game, for example, is not to collect funny combinations of names and adjectives, but to introduce the participants in an entertaining way that catches everyone's attention, and to encourage everyone to be creative in the upcoming meeting. It can also lighten the atmosphere, promote familiarity and provide some fun for smooth follow-up interaction among the participants who reveal a characteristic of themselves with a wink in the eye.

The purpose of *Bringing an Object* is not to end up with a collection of objects (although they actually make a nice photograph for a workshop documentation). Instead the exercise promotes collaboration in a number of different ways. Participants are often caught up in their daily work and usually haven't found time to choose an object until just before the meeting begins, and so they arrive already mentally warmed up for the topic. Second, it allows a participant to introduce their hobbyhorse, an issue or aspect they want to be considered in the new project while at the same time considering the objects of others in a relaxed atmosphere. Finally, it closes the loop at the end of a workshop, and provides an opportunity to reflect on the distance they have crossed as a group. The end of a session can also be a good moment to reveal the purpose of the exercise – not to spoil the fun, but to promote understanding and acceptance for more advanced forms of gamification.

In addition to providing an easy and unsuspicious entry point to the gamification journey, some standardized formats come with some benchmarks that further enhance the experience. A classic example from teaching and coaching innovation and entrepreneurship is the *Marshmallow Challenge*. With some basic materials and carefully described instructions, it provides an entertaining group experience to reflect on innovation and entrepreneurship issues like teamwork, collaboration and leadership, creativity, ideation and prototyping. And since the same format has been conducted thousands of times in a similar fashion, participants can compare their performance to other groups of players – and think about why preschool kids often outperform business school students and even CEOs (unless they come with their executive assistants).[1] In any case, collecting and reflecting on the results of different game sessions helps to improve one's own moderation skills. In some cases, it even feeds into eye-opening discussions when the results of one session are compared to those of a larger sample of sessions with different players or with variations on the same theme. Each new session equips the facilitator with new benchmarks for future use.

Marshmallow Challenge

In the classic *Marshmallow Challenge* small teams of players compete against one another in an attempt to build a tall freestanding structure. The structure must support the weight of the one marshmallow that goes on the top. Its height is measured from the surface it stands on (meaning it cannot be suspended from a higher structure). Each team has 18 minutes time and the same set of materials: 20 pieces of dry spaghetti, 1 marshmallow, 1 meter of scotch tape, and 1 meter of string. No other materials can be used, and after 18 minutes the structure must stand on its own. The team constructing the highest structure wins.

In a well-known 2010 TED talk, Tom Wujec compared results from about 70 workshops with different participant groups. On average they achieved a height of 20 inches. While students of business schools made it up to about half of this average, kindergarten kids outperformed the average, adults and even CEOs. Only CEOs accompanied by their executive admins and a second group of architects and engineers achieved higher results. Reflecting on your own experience with the exercise and comparing your results to those of other participant groups is a good opportunity to learn something about innovation topics like prototyping and about experience, collaboration and leadership, group dynamics and creativity.

There are several collections of easy-to-use games for use in the context of innovation and entrepreneurship. These include formats for 'gamestorming' and ideation, for customer integration and design thinking, and for agile retrospective games to improve a shared understanding of values and project-related objectives in small group development.[2] Most of the component patterns can also be adapted as stand-alone activities in a meeting or workshop setting. The key to using them successfully is to make sure they support the overall purpose of the meeting, workshop or innovation activity. Practising simple formats with few, clear instructions for all players allows you to explore the possibilities of each format. It also gives you the confidence to adapt more complex games and gamified formats to tackle innovation challenges.

5.2 Adapting and customizing games for individual organizations and innovation projects

While the general-purpose games and formats mentioned above provide some of the low-hanging fruits to enter the gamification journey, in some cases you will need to take the next step to make existing games fit better to your organisation or the challenges of a particular project. Not having to create a new game from scratch has two important advantages: you can keep time and effort for preparation within reasonable limits, and you can build on proven formats while learning about the experiences and insights others have already gathered. Moreover, customized or adapted formats can be used not only to support any innovation project (for instance team-building, energizing the spirit of collaboration or boosting creativity), they can also directly contribute to the particular innovation or entrepreneurial challenge you are dealing with. Sometimes variations can be designed to work with different cohorts of participants.[3]

One basic format is the design thinking exercise of *Draw a Vase*,[4] which asks participants to either draw an object or a context of experience (Figure 5.1). The following discussion then sensitizes them to the implications of framing problems, helps them deal with a design task from different perspectives – either focused on the product or its user.

Draw a Vase

This is a short playful exercise, rather than a game, to sensitize participants to the impact of framing challenges, for instance creating a user point of view. There are three steps. In the first round everyone gets a few minutes to draw a vase on a sheet of paper, and then pin their drawings onto a board.

Figure 5.1: Illustration of different results of *Draw a Vase*.

In the second round the same participants are asked to design a way for people to enjoy flowers in their home, and again pin their results onto the board.

Figure 5.1 (continued)

In the final step they compare the drawings and discuss how reframing the task has affected the results, and what that implies for their own project.

The vase can easily be replaced by the object you are designing. Thinking about new infotainment features in a car could be framed by having team members visualize the physical aspects of the feature (like a button in the cockpit allowing you to send audio notes to yourself), or the experiences it creates (using time spent driving to come up with and capture ideas, and being able to memorize them for yourself or to share them with others). Likewise, variations of *ROLES* and *PITCH* as in the television formats of *Dragon's Den* or *Shark Tank* are widely used in bootcamps and university courses and also in companies trying to encourage intrapreneurship. For example, different kickbox formats (like the *Values-Based Kickbox*)[5] or Liberty Global's Spark programme[6] culminate in a pitching session in which entrepreneurial teams formed in a company compete for funding and support.

Adapting or customizing existing games can take many forms, from just changing single words or replacing items to redesigning the structure of whole parts of a game. Like in the example above, you can transfer the content and structure to a new task, or replace pieces of content to fit your own organisation (e.g. the names of departments, or role descriptions of participants) – even for more complex games.

For instance, we developed a *Corporate Sustainability Innovation* game (chapter 7) together with a large telecommunication provider. The games' purpose is to translate sustainability challenges in the organisation and its business operations into seeds for innovation by applying the flow patterns *DILEMMA SOLVING, EXPERIENTIAL LEARNING* and *IDEATION* through a sequence of activities that involve component patterns such as *QUIZZES, ROLES* and *STORYTELLING*. The whole game was designed with potential customization in mind – free to download in an open, accessible format. Adapting the game requires changing some of the quiz questions, identifying and describing authentic dilemmas for the particular organisation and selecting the appropriate templates for a storytelling exercise to conclude the session.

Content adaptation can go one step further. The *Corporate Sustainability Innovation* (*CSI*) game format for instance can also be adapted to translate other values-based challenges (not necessarily sustainability-oriented) into seeds for innovation. For instance, a national bank asked for an adaptation of the *CSI* game that would support the alignment of shared values in an organisational change process. This requires a completely different set of quiz questions and dilemmas, even though the structure (including the digital templates) and the sequence of activities or flow patterns can be kept.

The final stage of adaptation also involves changing the structure of the gameplay. You can replace one component pattern by another (for instance, using a *PITCH* instead of *STORYTELLING* as a final exercise) while keeping the same flow; or you can substitute one flow for another (for instance, using *AWARENESS RAISING* instead of

DILEMMA SOLVING to facilitate the adoption of abstract organizational values among employees). In any case working with the gamification patterns involves adapting and specifying them for a particular innovation challenge, and embedding them in the context of some game.

Changing the structure[7] by exchanging or introducing new patterns makes a good exercise for teaching gamification to students or innovation managers. It also provides a powerful lever to evaluate the impact of different patterns by comparing the outcomes and output of games composed of different patterns with similar groups of players. Apart from the intellectual challenge of experimenting with these differences, changing the structure of a game provides the confidence needed to design completely new games. Use the patterns and a blueprint for gathering the information so that you can then select and adapt the patterns to address your innovation challenges.

5.3 Innovation and entrepreneurship games to use or adapt

Utilizing games and gamification, not to booster performance or education as such, but to drive innovation and solve grand challenges, is still a relatively young aspiration. However, there are already numerous formats out there that can be used or adapted to tackle innovation challenges or facilitate entrepreneurial endeavours. A handful of innovation practitioners, consultants, trainers and teachers have experimented with formats and shared their experiences on their websites, in white papers and other publications. As an innovator or entrepreneurs who seeks to utilize the power of gamification you will find numerous examples online. Still you might struggle to find the right ones that are practice-proven and suited to tackle your unique challenges.

Based on a decade of research, designing and teaching in this field, we have gathered all the games and gamified formats we could find, and can now provide a quite comprehensive overview. To ease access, they are categorized and clustered according to the three management dimensions and ten overarching domains of innovation challenges (Figure 4.2 above). In the appendix you will find a collection of 76 games with their titles, an innovation challenge they address, the solution they provide and a link. The following Figure 5.2 shows a selection of 40 games discussed throughout the book that are associated to the key fields of innovation. However, there is no rigid one-to-one assignment of games to the overarching management dimension and innovation domains. For instance, a simple exercise like to *Bring an Object* is quite useful as a conversation starter in cross-functional teams, but can also be used as a *WARM-UP* with *STORYTELLING* in any kind of meeting or workshop. Figure 5.2 therefore just captures one of the many different associations between games and innovation domains.

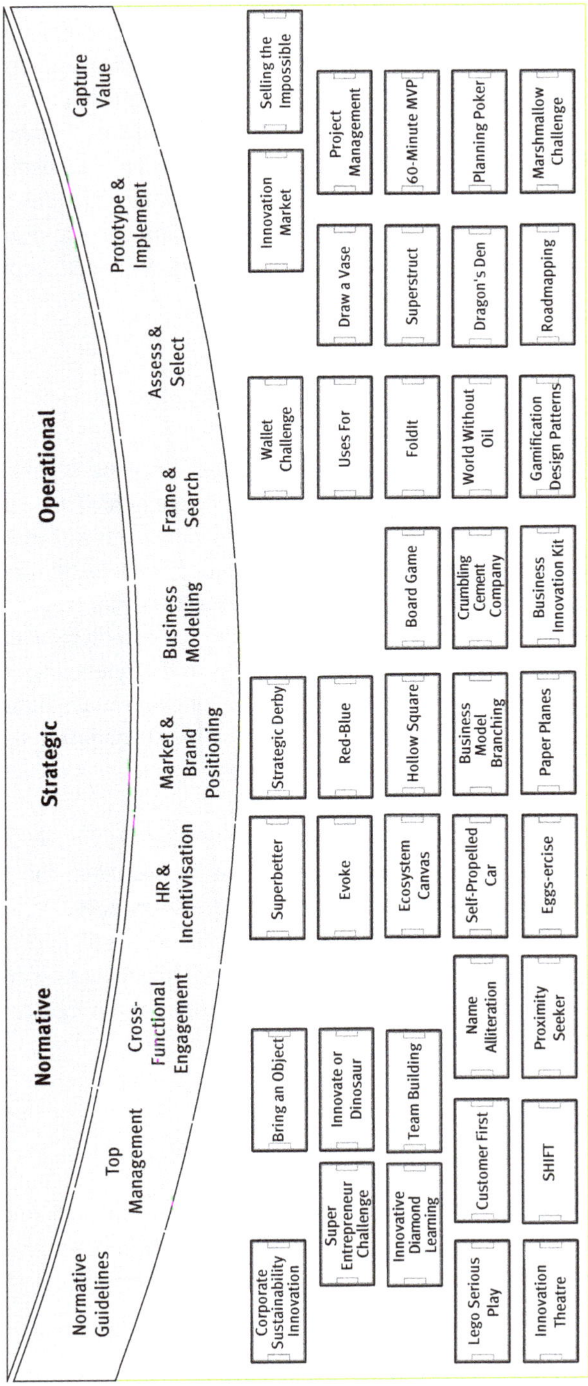

Figure 5.2: Overview of 40 games and gamified formats to drive innovation and entrepreneurship discussed in the book (more on each in the appendix).

Across all management dimensions, games can be used to facilitate values-based and sustainability-oriented innovation (a selection of 36 games with this focus is also included in the appendix). In particular they can contribute to innovation development in a normative management dimension along with gamified formats to facilitate organisational learning and the development of future capabilities. Games addressing the strategic dimension contribute to building an innovative organisation through human resource management and strategy development. Games facilitating the different stages of the innovation process on an operational management dimension support the search for opportunities, selection of ideas and concepts, implementation and value capture.

Driving values-based and sustainability-oriented innovation

The values that are constitutive for an organisational culture are often implicitly effective, difficult to access and to translate into appropriate behaviour and practises. Here, gamification offers one particularly well-suited approach to facilitate values-based innovation workshops. It provides a collaborative, experiential and practise-oriented mode of corporate learning. Gamification can be used, for instance, to specify global values and normative directives (such as introducing corporate sustainability as a new top management priority), sensitizing employees to their meanings and implications, and translating global values into field specific innovation activities. Therefore, we paid special attention to the emerging topics of values-based and sustainability-oriented innovation and found many inspiring formats.

A good example of values-based innovation games is the *ACT Dilemma* game. It helps to generate dialogue and improve awareness of the values in the organization as well as guide everyday innovative actions referring to the values. Participants proceed through gradually more complex dilemmas and *TRADE-OFFS* and suggest solutions referring to their organisational values. Apart from improving awareness it can facilitate a reinterpretation of the values and discussions on ambiguity and how to work with them.[8]

Learning and developing future capabilities

Some games focus on critical reflection and review, developing an understanding of core I&E concepts and using them to direct the exploration of structures and behaviours to prepare for desirable and alternative futures. Examples of games in this domain are:

- Games which enable critical reflection and review – for example taking an example of an innovation failure and (using the metaphorical world of the 'post-mortem' examination of the innovation corpse) carrying out a systematic analysis of what caused the 'patient' to die.
- Games which facilitate *EXPERIENTIAL LEARNING* and create a '3rd eye' perspective – for example a *ROLE* play based on 'half-time team talks' in which the 'coaches' review how things are going and make recommendations for how the next part of the match might be played. Once again players might be given examples of early stage innovations which have been launched but have not yet moved to scale. Their role is to stage a motivating team talk to inspire the innovators for their next project phase, but also to provide some hints about how to play the next stage of the game.
- Futures *STORYTELLING* and backcasting – for example, telling your grandchildren about the events which led to the demise of the great organization you worked with and how, with hindsight, they might have done things differently. Similar formats ask players to rewrite history or to imagine and depict parallel universes.
- *Evoke* is a multi-player educational online game that uses social networking, storytelling and other game design patterns to teach social innovation skills. It enables young people to acquire skills and gain confidence to address global challenges such as displacement, hunger, poverty and water scarcity.[9]
- *Superbetter* is another game designed to empower not just entrepreneurs, but anyone facing a major personal challenge. It consists of a number of life hacks or techniques (such as daily quests to tackle, power-ups to gain strengths and 'bad guy' obstacles to deal with) to improve mental health and resilience.[10]

Building an innovative organization through human resource management

Top-management and cross-functional engagement as well as innovation-related human resource management deal with questions of how innovation is handled by individuals, teams and organizations. There is a rich variety of games-based material which can be borrowed from general organization courses – for example in team-building games. Core themes include motivation, creativity, inter-group conflict, organizational climate, and culture and knowledge sharing across boundaries. Examples include:

- Games – often individual or paired reflection – around personas and ideal types such as the *Super-Entrepreneur Challenge* in which players are asked to paint a picture (or otherwise represent) the 'superhero' view of entrepreneurs who have all the skills and personal qualities needed to succeed. It is a simple warm-up which focuses attention on key attributes of entrepreneurs and stimulates a discussion on them.

- Competitive team games – for example the *Marshmallow Challenge* or *Eggs-Ercises* – followed by guided reflection[11] on the team dynamics leading to successful (or other) outcomes.
- Team *ROLES* games – as above but focused particularly on team roles and their interplay.
- Conflict-engineered games in which teams compete and are encouraged to find ways of exploiting their differences. These provide a valuable 'laboratory' for reflection on the inevitability of conflict in many kinds of innovation context (for example the need to share information and work across organizational boundaries) and the ways in which conflict can emerge and be resolved.
- *Hollow Squares*, *Jigsaw Puzzles* and other variants in which different players hold different key pieces of knowledge and they need to find each other, negotiate and share to create the whole.
- Brainstorming games, creativity tasks and guided reflection – games designed to demonstrate that more minds on the task can lead to more ideas and more different ideas, but that successful teams depend on the management of key underlying issues like psychological safety if brainstorming and shared creativity is to happen effectively.
- *ROLES* play and innovation theatre – psychodrama and forum theatre techniques in which real interpersonal situations in innovation can be brought to life and explored through role play.
- Visualisations – for example live sculpture, *Lego Serious Play*, rich pictures – in which exploration and simulation of roles and relationships in novel ways can be visualised and then modified
- Images of organization – using metaphors to explore and illuminate different situations.[12]

Strategy development

Here key learning is about the need for choices about resource allocation, business modelling and positioning, the need for a long-term and wide horizon perspective, the challenge of strategy deployment and communication and the underlying conflicts which strategy development reveals. Example games include:

- *Paper Planes* and variants in which teams compete to make something.[13] They need to choose which combination of market, design and difficulty they go for (strategy based on cost, on features, on modularity, etc.) and compete on access to scarce *RESOURCES* (technology, key skills, etc.) and the winners are those whose strategy best balances the costs (money, time, etc.) against benefits like revenue, customer satisfaction, etc.

- *Red/Blue* and similar 'prisoner's dilemma' games highlighting the risks and value in collaboration.[14] In *Red/Blue* players are split into two teams and have to choose between playing 'red' or 'blue' as their next move. The outcome is based on the prisoner's dilemma game; depending on whether both sides play the same colour or how points are allocated. The key feature of this version is that there are several points at which discussions are possible between teams, allowing for the possibility of collaboration (and of occasional 'double-crossing').
- *Hollow Squares*, jigsaw puzzles and other variants in which different players hold different key pieces of knowledge and they need to find each other, negotiate and share to create the whole.
- *ROLE* playing games which simulate strategic conflicts over selecting projects or allocating *RESOURCES*. For example, the *Crumbling Cement Company* stages four divisions in a large company arguing over the allocation and use of a limited R&D and innovation budget.[15] *Strategic Derby* (described in chapter 1) is another example.
- *BUSINESS SIMULATIONs* built on teams developing a consultant pitch to the board to promote different strategic options – for example presenting a SWOT or PEST analysis and recommendations, or arguing for the creation of corporate venturing capability. These can be linked to real case data which the teams assimilate and use in assembling their arguments.
- The *Business Innovation Kit*[16] is a gamified tool to collaboratively develop values-based business models. Its *BUSINESS MODELLING* flow involves *QUIZZES* to review and discuss good practice cases from different companies, facilitates *IDEATION* in a self-moderated process and uses *CHALLENGES* to convey basic knowledge and to guide self-moderated groups to develop alternative business models for a new business idea.

Search

In this phase we need to explore and learn about the sources of innovation. Many games help entrepreneurs and learners do just this. Some involve *BUSINESS SIMUMLATIONS* and *MODELLING MATERIALS* like using paper and cardboard, LEGO bricks and other simple materials to set up an imaginary factory or office. The game asks participants to play a role in the simulated factory/office and work according to a number of key performance indicators such as time, quality, output. These games are designed to cause problems and highlight in exaggerated fashion the significant scope for process innovation.[17] Another game with multiple variants is the *Wallet Challenge*, which explores user perspectives as an input to the innovation process.[18] Another set of games explores opportunities based on exploratory and normative future scenarios: an example is the *Roadmapping Game* developed by the Institute for Manufacturing at Cambridge University.[19]

In online games like *FoldIt* non-experts fold and pack proteins into 3D structures, allowing them to predict protein sequences. By experimenting with new ways of folding proteins, gameplay can actually contribute to the development of new vaccines.[20] Some multiplayer online games developed by Jane McGonigal and her colleagues prompt players to generate ideas about how to deal with upcoming *CHALLENGES*, and can be used or adapted to facilitate *IDEATION*. *World Without Oil* (created in 2007) projects an oil shortage and prompts players to react and share their ideas on how to deal with the consequences. McGonigal reports that many players actually keep up the new attitudes they learned from the game.[21] *Superstruct* depicts a rapidly approaching dystopian scenario of world collapse and engages participants in crowdsourcing ideas to secure the future of energy, food, health, security and the social safety net.[22]

Select

Here the question moves from 'What could we do?' to one of 'What are we going to do, and why?' Given scarce resources, how do we choose and build a balanced portfolio of innovation projects? What criteria should we use and how can we convince others to 'buy in' to our idea, either as external venture investors or internal resource allocators?

Games can illuminate this space – for example, *Innovation Markets* (or prediction markets) ask participants to bet on and trade different product and service design options to generate indicators for the future implementation and market success of concepts.[23] Alternatively, similar games or crowd-*VOTING* platforms can feed these indicators and involve different stakeholder representatives in stage-gate decisions. Visual templates and *MAPPING* tools are used in entrepreneur 'bootcamps' in which intense efforts culminate in a *Dragon's Den PITCH* to potential investors.[24]

Implement

At this point the journey begins in earnest as games become powerful ways of exposing players to the role uncertainty plays in innovation and the need for an agile approach which pivots and adapts to changing circumstances. Games supporting implementation introduce the typical stages from refining the outline concept, through prototyping and testing to the final launch. Examples include:

- Designing and building something – like a car, an app, a film – in competitive fashion. In each case the setting is usually a *COMPETITION* between teams with various performance criteria such as cost, customer satisfaction, non-financial criteria used to determine winners. As part of an entrepreneurship program the *60-Minute-MVP* is a powerful energising game built around building an app in one hour as a competitive exercise to create student engagement.[25]

- *Project management* games in which a complex activity – like making a film – has to be managed in a short period of time. This involves tasks like the search for limited *RESOURCES* and co-ordination, time management and team role allocation.
- Creating an innovation game (for instance a board game or card game) in which the snakes and ladders of uncertain events and *SURPRISE* are brought into play as participants try to negotiate the innovation journey. The *Shift* game (chapter 10) is an example of such a game.
- *BUSINESS SIMULATIONs* in which a number of rounds simulate different external conditions and force strategic review and pivoting.

Capture

A key problem in innovation is that launch does not necessarily mean success, even if early pilots are promising. The journey to scale involves key elements like assembling complementary assets and understanding what shapes adoption and diffusion. Games which can help here include:

- Variations on the above new product development games with *ROLES* of suppliers, customers or other stakeholders in the loop. This increases the uncertainty and requires participants to explore and build relationships with multiple stakeholders. By having a live customer, players have to work out how to really understand user needs rather than make assumptions. And in similar fashion bringing in the supply side shows the potential of complementary assets – what else can suppliers bring? These benefits will only become available, however, if the players work at developing relationships with suppliers which enable 'win-win' outcomes.
- *Selling the Impossible* games and variants in which key adoption factors are mobilized by the selling team and used by the resisting team in an adversarial debate format with the audience *VOTING*. This fun *PITCH* game allows exploration of the multiple factors likely to influence adoption and hence diffusion to scale.
- Rewriting history games in which innovations are reconstructed in ways which exaggerate adoption elements to ensure a different course of history – for example, the reason why fire never caught on or what was wrong with the wheel.

Experiences with these and other formats are more or less well documented, and their success depends not just on the innovation challenge, but on many organizational, situational and personal factors of those involved. In any case, existing formats can be modified and new formats can be tailormade and iteratively improved for unique innovation challenges and contexts. In the next chapter we describe how to proceed with this development.

Chapter 6
Gamification: Creating new gamified formats and games for unique challenges

A simple process model and a Game Design Canvas can be used to guide gamification and game design for different contexts.

Whether you are just using or customizing an existing game or developing a new one, the first steps are actually quite similar. In creating a whole new game, you should clarify some basic assumptions and then proceed step by step, before investing too much of your time and effort. We will describe those steps here in more detail, and introduce a canvas to gather the essential information in a structured way.

6.1 Five steps and a canvas to create new games from scratch using patterns

Proceed following a simple sequence of activities in five steps: understanding, briefing, concepting, sketching and prototyping (Figure 6.1).

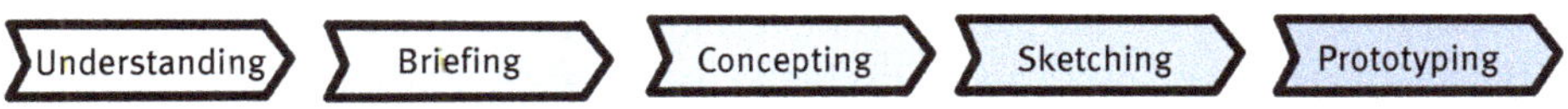

Figure 6.1: Gamification in five steps.

First, you need a profound *understanding* of the innovation challenge. This may seem an obvious step when meeting up with innovation professionals. You might begin by just getting to know each other and doing a warm-up exercise to exchange what you know about the topic. But for more complex challenges such as exploring the potential of new sustainable business models or renewing the innovation culture of the firm, this step can be much more demanding. Methodological approaches to gathering essential information include contextual inquiry and stakeholder interviews, ethnographic observation[1] or crowdsourcing challenges from employees. In the development of the *CSI* game we conducted six interviews with innovation experts in the company to define the basic challenge of 'promoting sustainability as a driver for innovation' and supporting the new framework of the corporate responsibility group and its normative directives. Understanding the basic challenge should also clarify who to involve in the next steps: namely, the key stakeholders and internal 'owners' of the gamification project.

https://doi.org/10.1515/9783110725582-011

In a second step, you need to bring the main stakeholders on board and agree on a basic framing of the challenge and a *briefing* for the design team. You will also need to decide on the purpose and methodological approach of the gamified format to be created. To document the cornerstones of the project in a structured manner you can use the canvas below (see Figure 6.2 on next page). It is important to consider the connections between the blocks, as together with the unique synthesis of the patterns they will constitute the game as a system (rather than a collection of elements) feeding innovation or entrepreneurial activities. The canvas indicates what should be considered when designing a new game. By making the basic assumptions behind your format explicit, it serves as a simple formal briefing.

First, the *challenge* captures the innovation problem or entrepreneurial challenge you want to address. The distinction between 10 domains of innovation challenges from the literature (introduced in chapter 4.2) can help you in situating the challenge on an operational, strategic or normative management level. The empirically found challenges (Figure 4.2.3 above) can provide additional clues for you to frame your unique challenge. Formulate the challenge as a 'how-might-we' (HMW) or 'how can we' question to frame it as an opportunity for collaborative design. In the development of the *CSI* game, we conducted a framing workshop with corporate project owners and formulated the challenge: 'How might we establish, think ahead and translateinto everyday corporate practices the topic of sustainability in its various facets?'

Second, *participants* are the players of the game. In order to identify them, consider different stakeholders inside and outside the organisation. Stakeholders include everyone who can contribute to the project or should be informed about the game and the intervention it targets: not just the project owners within the organisation, but – depending on the intended format – also the higher management, staff representatives and of course those people who will eventually play the game. Boundary conditions for the engagement of these different groups might include potential language barriers, privacy concerns, temporal and spatial conditions (if teams located around the world are supposed to play together). For the *CSI* game we identified small groups of employees of up to 12 players as participants and facilitators, who also served as multipliers for the format and communication of results.

Third, the *purpose* describes the intentions behind the game and its desired outcomes. Usually a single game format is not comprehensive enough to address great innovation challenges in their entirety. Instead focus on what can be achieved by means of gamification. For the *CSI* game, three purposes were defined: a) imparting knowledge and raising awareness in three focus areas of corporate sustainability(climate action, circular economy and human rights & digital inclusion), b) motivating reflection on participants' own impact, and c) generating ideas for improvement.

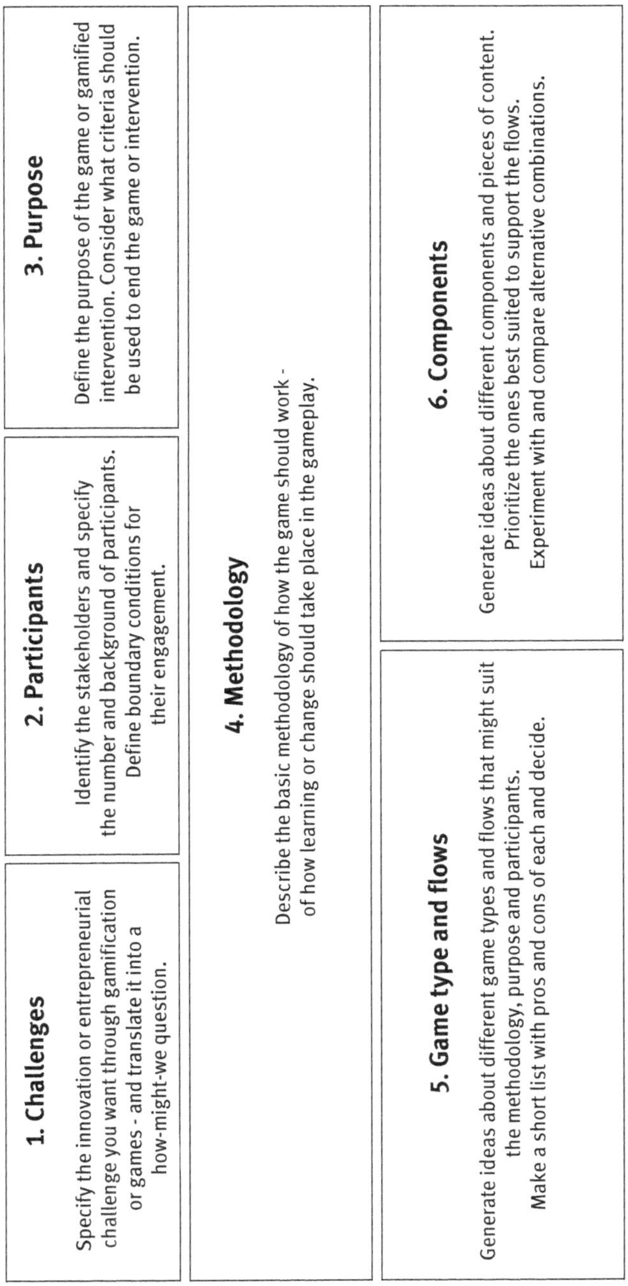

Figure 6.2: Game Design Canvas to collect information and sketch alternative designs for gamified formats[2].

Fourth, the *methodology* describes how the game should work and how learning or change should take place. Also, the contexts for gamification and basic decisions for gamification should be considered (e.g. online or offline, see chapter 6.2 below). While instructional methods are ways to facilitate learning processes, instructional media are surface phenomena that solely deliver the methods.[3] To ensure a user and learner-centred approach, describe the methodology from the participants' point of view. For the *CSI* game the methodology was described in four aspects: a) to enable learning (imparting knowledge & raising awareness) about corporate sustainability, b) to promote interpretation and reflection with respect to each player's work situation and practices, c) to use ideation to identify approaches for action, and d) to consider ways to transfer and implement results. In this case, the four aspects also yielded a basic sequence for the activities.

Here you should also decide between more exploratory and more instructional methods, that is, consider the range of options between a focus on playful encounters or structured games. Open-ended games that are loosely structured (similar to Caillois'[4] concept of 'paidia') can create an interaction architecture in which diverse interpretations and different actions can emerge and lead to previously unforeseen results. Alternatively, games can be structured more narrowly so that they lead players to predefined goals (similar to Caillois' concept of 'ludus'). The former facilitate a 'journey of discovery'[5] and exploring new frontiers; the latter are a powerful means of training and instruction that communicate what is already known, and is based on a predetermined sequence of activities that participants engage in, taking one step after another. While innovation and entrepreneurship – and the many games facilitating them – are open-ended by nature, they may still involve instructional parts to convey basic knowledge and contribute to a shared understanding among the participants. Some are even designed to produce specific outcomes, and we are just starting to understand and leverage their potential to tackle some of the great challenges we are facing in business and society.

Fifth and sixth, initial ideas about the game itself, the media types you want to consider, the interaction *flows* you might want to use as well as their sequence, and the *components* required to set up the flows can be mapped into the last two boxes of the canvas. Basic decisions – including, for instance, if the format should work online, offline, both or be hybrid – should be discussed and made early on with the key stakeholders. You can also probe your initial ideas regarding the interaction flows with them, using the collection of flow patterns as a valuable resource for considering the pros and cons of alternative flows. This discussion can also serve to align expectations. Likewise, for the component patterns. First collect all the patterns that might be applied and then prioritize the most suitable ones to support the flows, the participants and the purpose of the game. Experiment in small groups and compare alternative compositions. The *Gamification Design Pattern* card deck (available on the companion sites) can be used to facilitate a moderated card sorting session by the design team or even in a larger group including key stakeholders and representatives of the players. For the *CSI* games, flows included *DILEMMA SOLVING* and *IDEATION*, while the components included *QUIZZES*, *VOTING* and *DEDICATED FACILITATORS* as well as *ROLES* and *STORYTELLING*.

Different canvasses can be filled with alternative ways to frame the challenge and purpose, with different definitions of the participants and the methodology, with different collections of flow and component patterns and relations between them. This will allow you to directly compare alternative design sketches or gather feedback from stakeholders or external experts in an early stage of development. These comparisons are also well suited for educational sessions, as students can come up with their own designs and discuss the rationales behind them.

Once the briefing is fixed, the real work begins with *concepting*, sketching and (iterative) prototyping. Search for and define the basic storyline of the game to create the basic concept. In the case of the *CSI* game, this storyline was defined in a rather prosaic way as a progression from learning to interpretation and ideation. In other cases, richer *METAPHORS* are used to frame the interaction and to provide the players with a mental model for the whole gameplay.[6] For instance, a metaphor of growing trees provides the conceptual framing for a *Business Modelling Branching* (chapter 9) game. The *Customer First Game* (chapter 8) uses the metaphor of a boat. Participants have to move the boat, each of their choices can make it move forward, stay in its position, or move backward. Other people on the boat might push it forward or just jump off – while at the same time keeping people onboard. The tangible and visual metaphor of a boat connects well with typical change management challenges in which participants must stir things around and keep people onboard at the same time.

Once the storyline is set, the patterns can be selected, shuffled and turned into actual flows or components of the game – a creative process we call *sketching*. The examples provided with each pattern provide powerful stepping stones and inspiration in this phase. Patterns and elements will need to be added, taken out or modified to support the overall storyline and the flows of the format. For instance, when developing the *CSI* game it took numerous iterations to reformulate the quiz questions and dilemmas so they would better support the later stages of the game. To streamline the flow of interaction we also decided to take out an exercise for participants to learn from other companies' sustainability innovations.

Finally, *prototyping* parts of the game (for instance the quiz in the *CSI* game) or even the whole game enables you to collect some feedback in a structured way that will lead to further refinement. The time and effort needed for this iterative prototyping and testing and feedback-based refining should not be underestimated, as it often takes the most time in the project. Start testing parts and then the whole game with representatives of the participant group before taking it to the company or entrepreneurial setting (for instance in an incubator) and unrolling it across a whole organisation. (Different templates for feedback forms, observation guides and surveys for participants and observers can be found on the companion sites.) For instance, when designing the *CSI* game, it took us until the first real test to learn that the length of the gameplay exceeded the four-hour timeframe we considered tolerable in the framing workshop. Going through the feedback from the participants we also learned that the sequence of activities was fairly easy to follow, and that we could improve the novelty of results by designing the ideation progress less incrementally and asking for more radical ways of thinking before bringing some of the more utopian views of the participants down to earth.

6.2 Contexts for gamification and selecting the right methodology

There are different contexts for gamification and using games that preform the methodology, media types and design patterns we can apply. We can design games for a classroom or a workplace setting. We may have a few participants, or we may have a large class. We may be working online and remotely, or we may be able to engage in an intense in-person workshop mode. We may have a short time frame or be using games in the context of a multi-day training event. In other words, there is considerable variety in the context in which we might use games.

A simple metaphor for this challenge might be shopping for a meal we want to prepare. We can visit the supermarket and browse the shelves, choosing ingredients for anything from a simple snack to a five-course dinner, to be served informally on paper plates and eaten buffet style or as a formal meal with waiter service, detailed and expensive place settings and the best cutlery and china tableware. We may have planned an intimate supper for two, a small social get-together for close friends or a full-scale party to celebrate a big occasion. In other words, there is plenty of variety – and we will fill our supermarket trolley accordingly. We can take a similar approach to thinking about how games can be used, planning ahead as we wander the aisles of our games supermarket, deciding what and how to meet the needs of many different learning contexts. We need to keep in mind that the 'meal' we intend to cook represents the game as a system that feeds an innovation or professional development project. Its ingredients are the main practical dimensions to consider when setting up the methodology.

Individual versus group

While many games are designed as collaborative group activities, there is also scope for individual centred play. Reflective activities, personal quizzes, individual interaction with a computer-generated world and exploring challenges in building a robust business model are all examples of games played at an individual level. In a classroom setting this might be used to provide a gamified way of assessing individual performance; in a corporate setting it might help in creating professional development pathways.

Collaboration versus competition

Sometimes play activities benefit from a competitive element, others might work better with collaborative play. Novel ways to create collaborative play exist where the 'enemy' might be found in the rules or you compete against the 'board' instead of the other participants. Group dynamics in play activities, also in organizations, are vital for successful activities. Competition within an organization, if it needs to be integrated or moderated, is normally better between groups than between individuals.

Loose versus tight focus

Some games are designed with a clear focus to illustrate or explore a specific topic. Others are more generic in their applicability and provide a way of generating experience in playful fashion from which a number of reflective strands can be drawn. Good examples of such loose focus, broad spectrum games are the *Paper Planes* exercise (in which teams compete to design and build paper planes)[7] and the *Wallet Challenge*, a design-thinking game which can be used to draw out a number of key themes related to understanding customer needs, prototyping, etc.[8] By contrast an example of a tight-focus game might be versions of the prisoner's dilemma game (such as '*Red/Blue*'), which highlight the challenge of collaboration or competition in innovation decision-making.[9]

Micro-games versus full-size

There are many situations in which a simple game which can be easily set up and played quickly will have advantages – for example as a warm-up or 'icebreaker' exercise. Other games are designed for extensive exploration of a key theme and may involve detailed rules, supporting equipment and even a dedicated playing area. An example of a lightweight micro-game would be '*Uses For*', a simple activity designed to explore concepts in creativity.[10] At the other end of the spectrum the *Crumbling Cement Company* is an extended role play game around strategic resource allocation for innovation.[11] The games described in Part III of this book would also be examples of full-size games.

Length

Linked to this idea of scale is the time needed to set up, play and debrief games. Simple micro-games can be slotted to small time periods but others carrying more weight will have a longer duration. Another variant here are games played with sequenced rounds of activity – for example, many online business games are set up so that teams compete by making strategic decisions at various stages during the life of an enterprise.

Online versus offline

As the name suggests this dimension is linked to whether the game is played virtually or in-person face-to-face. The Covid-19 pandemic triggered development of a variety of online activities and games to support learning in this mode. It is important to recognise that both types of game have advantages and disadvantages. For example, face-to-face games allow for extensive group and intergroup dynamics, whereas online games can offer opportunities for large numbers of participants.

Other contextual conditions

There might be situations when we need to use games or when games might help in a particular context – for example in providing an alternative kind of experience in a training programme during the periods when energy levels are low (such as after lunch or during the so-called 'graveyard shift'). A more significant situation might be when it is important to explore a theme without the risk of failing – for example, simulating a factory process change rather than making it in real life. The alternative or artificial worlds in games, as we have seen, offer safe spaces in which experimentation can take place. In similar fashion, games offer ways of working through difficult issues – for example, using *ROLE* play to work with sensitive political or interpersonal issues in an innovation context. *Innovation Theatre* offers some good examples of this approach.[12]

Games can also provide a useful mechanism for changing the mind's learning state, signalling an alternative approach which might help open minds. For example, one of the authors was involved in a course developing creative skills in senior managers, with an audience drawn from the military and defence-linked civil service. The context in which this was to take place was at a military establishment in the 'war room', an operational facility with no windows (to allow for projection on all sides) and the seating layout was in rigid lines of chairs. It was also clear early on that different ranks and civil service grades were represented, causing a degree of inhibition amongst junior participants to speak their minds or volunteer ideas. A simple egg-manoeuvring game (*Eggs-Ercise*) was used to change the context and learn about creativity.[13] Eggs were hung at various places from the ceiling and the game challenge was to devise ways of catching them safely when, after a period of time, the strings holding them up were cut. This required participants to move around, and it changed the physical space. By temporarily changing the learning context and approach, the game stimulated considerable reflection and exploration in a fun fashion.

6.3 Guidelines and insights for design and implementation

Some general guidelines will help you to use gamification and games within innovation processes or entrepreneurial projects. They reflect some of the lessons we have learned from these highly iterative processes of creating and implementing games like the ones featured in part III. In a nutshell our insights are these: You should attend to when and where to use games and link the activities to the right innovation processes and supports. Appropriate framing of the conversation and using the right metaphors are vital for successful communication. Equally important for your intervention to succeed are simplicity as an essential design principle, considering changing requirements, and allowing for the time it takes to get the game right.

When and where to use games

Games are normally mostly a means and not the end goal – or at least both are important. In some cases they are meant to simply reach the next step in a longer process, moving past the first obstacles and finding novel directions through a two or three-hour activity. In other situations, they are full day workshops with a series of interconnected game-based activities. However, usually such innovation game activities are part of a larger innovation process in which it might only make sense to use games one or twice throughout the full process. Determining when to use them for the highest quality process and outcome and how it plays together with the rest of innovation-related activities becomes crucial.

Another critical requirement is not to tie the gamified intervention to a single person in the organization who might not have much decision-making power. Instead it helps to link game activities to innovation processes and methods that are already established and supported by decision makers. A stand-alone game that is not part of a larger innovation initiative can work in educational settings and shorter corporate training courses, but risks being less relevant.

Framing the conversation

Initiating or promoting an innovation or entrepreneurial process based entirely on games is not wise. As play, games and gamification have spread to various fields, participants immediately sense different connotations when they hear these terms. Innovators, entrepreneurs and developers of these games should keep the innovation challenge at the front and then integrate a few, but potentially crucial game activities at the right places – and then build on their experiential learning qualities.

Also, listening to the organization and what terms they normally use helps you align games to the specific context. Sometimes related terms like 'dynamic map making', 'tool', 'co-creation', 'simulation' etc. might provide a better entrance point to avoid misunderstandings. Geographical, sector or social based cultural differences also play a role in this.

Communication is key

It's not just about instructing players how to play, it's about telling them what the game is about. Finding conceptual metaphors[14] is often a major milestone guiding game design. One single metaphor that is immediately understood can help the participants make a quick dynamic start which will influence the rest of the session. Such a metaphor can be hinted at in the name of the game but, more importantly, it should be found in the visual maps of the game. Finding the best metaphor for a game isn't easy and will most likely take a number of iterative turns.

Simplicity prevails

Games in the entertainment industry are often highly complex and many-layered. However, innovation games need to be simple, instantly understandable and uncomplicated. Participants need to understand not only the game architecture but also the innovation topic and challenge at hand – a double mental effort. Peeling off layers and making the game as simple as possible is normally good advice. If that is impossible then at least introduce the layers of the game as the play progresses, and not all at the beginning.

Anticipate changing requirements

While games are not set in stone, they still rely on a well-defined format and set of rules. But as games typically involve more than one player, it's critical to build flexibility into the rules and adapt them to the situation. The number of participants, their background and organizational role sets the frame together with the game. Careful thinking needs to go into the participation set-up for each use situation.

The time it takes

Developing games takes time, time that a single organization cannot afford. You can reduce the effort needed to create innovation games by considering what generic principles in the flow and rules can be reused in your organizational setting and what new content is needed for your situation. This balance of generic patterns and content is crucial for creating games with minimum effort and expense. Like any other innovation method an innovation game can be refined over time.

Bear these suggestions in mind when browsing through the games described in part III. In an educational setting each of these games can be taken as a case study. Students (or you as an active reader) can reconstruct each game's development by using the Game Design Canvas, the contexts for gamification and by selecting the right methodology and applying these insights for design and implementation.

Part III
Games tackling grand challenges in innovation and entrepreneurship

https://doi.org/10.1515/9783110725582-012

The following chapters demonstrate the potential of games, not just to provide a safe space for experimentation and trying out new forms of collaboration, but also to tackle recurring challenges that innovators and entrepreneurs need to deal with. Each game was developed in an iterative manner with leading European firms, responding to core challenges they were facing in the context of innovation, challenges such as facilitating group collaboration, fostering sustainability and customer orientation, and overcoming innovation barriers. Part III presents the games resulting from this effort,[1] each chapter following the same structure starting with a short summary and key visual, then describing the challenge, purpose, methodology, participants, gameplay, experiences and results, exemplary walkthrough, customization and patterns used.

Chapter 7: The *Corporate Sustainability Innovation* game has a short and a full-length version. The short version, the *Corporate Sustainability Dilemma* game, raises awareness for issues of corporate sustainability and helps participants to be better informed. The *Corporate Sustainability Innovation* (*CSI*) game builds on the dilemma game exercises and their results. It empowers participants to identify sustainability challenges at the workplace, and generate ideas and future scenarios on how to address them.

Chapter 8: The *Customer First* game deals with challenges related to creating more human-centric organizations that can respond to changing customer needs. It leads participants through three steps with multiple choices that stimulate preliminary thoughts about how steps can be taken toward a more human-centric organization in which customer needs and challenges are acted upon systematically in order to keep them satisfied and onboard.

Chapter 9: The *Business Model Branching* game deals with the difficult and complex challenges of balancing ongoing operations with new innovation-oriented activities. It engages decision-makers and innovation managers in allocating resources and developing competencies for specific lines (branches) of their business, deciding when to reconfigure and close existing ones, and when to launch and ramp up new ones.

Chapter 10: The *Shift* game explores practical ways and strategies to overcome innovation barriers and organizational ambidexterity paradoxes in established organizations. Five categories of innovation barriers are used to spur strategic thinking about how to work around them and sometimes also how to remove them completely. This game helps participants assess the reasoning behind having specific gates in a company.

Chapter 11: The *Proximity Seeker* game was developed to address the challenges of social dynamics, especially in remote teams. It is used as a check-in or check-out exercise in meetings, and often when participants do not know each other well but have to develop a work relationship quickly and at a distance.

Chapter 12: The *Ecosystem Canvas* game allows future entrepreneurs to become aware of and explore potential for joint value creation in networks.

Chapter 13: *Lego Serious Play* is used to address innovation and entrepreneurial challenges in face-to-face and remote settings.

Chapter 7
Games: Corporate sustainability innovation

Henning Breuer & Kiril Ivanov

How can we turn sustainability challenges in the workplace into seeds for innovation? The *CSI* game conveys basic knowledge and raises awareness for corporate sustainability. It taps into the participants' experience to help them generate ideas for sustainability-oriented innovation.

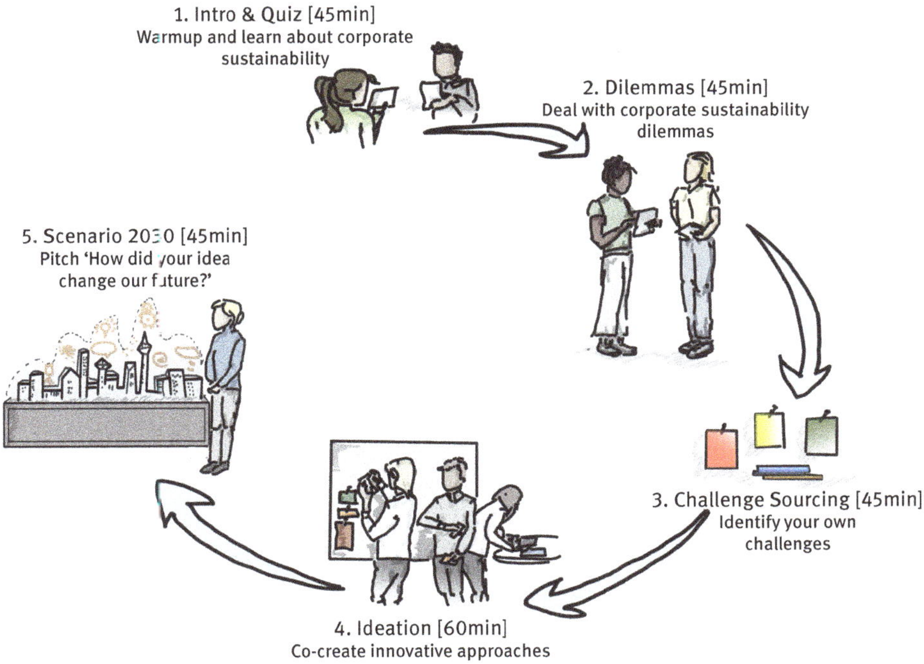

Figure 7.1: Gameflow in the *CSI* Game: Turn sustainability challenges at your workplace into seeds for innovation.

https://doi.org/10.1515/9783110725582-013

The *Corporate Sustainability Dilemma* game raises players' awareness for issues of corporate sustainability and helps them learn more. The *Corporate Sustainability Innovation (CSI)* game builds on the dilemma game exercises and results (Figure 7.1). It empowers participants to identify sustainability challenges at the workplace, and to generate ideas and future scenarios on how to address them. Both gamified workshop formats combine a sequence of competitive and collaborative exercises, and both can be adapted to different organisations and values-based policies.

Challenge

Corporate sustainability aims to create long-term environmental, social and economic value for different stakeholders of a business. The engagement of private companies is indispensable for any effort to achieve the sustainable development goals, and executives as well as employees are increasingly discovering that pursuing long-term values of corporate sustainability creates new opportunities for business and innovation. However, many firms and their employees are struggling to make the values associated with sustainability, and business's shifting priorities, explicit, and to turn sustainability-oriented strategies into daily practises. Gamification is one approach particularly well-suited to facilitating values-based and sustainability-oriented innovation.[1] Games can be used to clarify global values and sustainability-oriented policies, to sensitise employees to their implications and to translate values into field-specific innovation activities.

Two formats of corporate sustainability games have been designed to sensitise participants to related challenges and to explore the newly emerging opportunities. In collaboration with partners from a large telecommunication company we formulated the challenge as: How might we establish, think ahead and translate the topic of sustainability in its various facets into everyday corporate practices? We realized early on that we would need a facilitator to guide participants through the process, and a preliminary online format to allow distributed teams to engage, as well as to make the game accessible to a wider audience.[2]

Purpose

The *Corporate Sustainability Dilemma* game helps raise awareness for issues of corporate sustainability, while the Corporate Sustainability Innovation game builds on the dilemma game as a basis to identify sustainability challenges at the workplace and turn them into seeds for innovation. It provides a playful approach to addressing some of the great challenges we are facing today. The *CSI* game does not define potential solutions straight away – this must be left to follow-up workshops, activities or working groups. But it can help us to better understand where to start, how to deal with some of these issues at work and how we can create a positive impact on our company and the world we live in over the long run.

When to use it? The game is suitable when the top management and employees of an organisation are seeking to explore the potential of sustainability concerns to drive innovation. Such an exploration can be motivated through the introduction of a new sustainability-oriented innovation strategy, or when there is a desire to screen for further potential to improve the sustainability performance of an organisation, whether in terms of costs, risks, revenues and profit margins, corporate reputation and brand value, attractiveness as employer or innovative capacity.

Methodology

Three activities define the methodology of the *CSI* game: learning, interpretation and transfer. First, a quiz format game helps participants learn about essential concepts and different stakeholder perspectives on corporate sustainability. By being confronted with different dilemmas, trade-offs and stakeholder perspectives on critical issues, they are sensitized to conflicting values and interests. Second, participants reflect on the general dilemmas and trade-offs and make sense of related issues in their own organisation. Third, they collaborate to come up with new ideas on how to address the challenges, and then engage in future storytelling to think through the consequences of their intended interventions.

Participants

Groups of 3–12 participants, usually employees from any part of an organisation or a network of collaborating partners, play simultaneously online or in a face-to-face environment. Playing in cross-functional groups allows participants to sensitize themselves to and learn from sustainability challenges and solutions in different departments and subsidiaries, and thereby contribute to the development of an innovation culture based on shared sustainability values. With professional moderation and the use of breakout rooms, the online format can be scaled up to serve different groups at the same time. In the two-hour dilemma game format, participants finish with a reflection on the lessons learned and come up with a compelling 'call for action'. In the full-length 4-hour format (or more) of the *CSI* game, participants come to better understand basic concepts and dilemmas of corporate sustainability, identify and formulate their own situated sustainability challenges and co-create innovative approaches to address them.

Gameplay

A facilitator guide provides instructions on how to prepare the activity using a video conferencing system, an online collaboration environment (such as Miro or MURAL). The facilitator provides instructions and keeps track of participant scores and the stakeholder cards each one of them chooses. In the full *CSI* game, gameplay then proceeds in five steps:

1. In step 1 a *warm-up quiz* introduces the players to basic definitions and the general sustainability challenges companies are facing today. While answering the quiz questions and resolving the dilemmas participants gain Impact Investment Points. The player who gets the most points from the two first steps becomes the leader of their group and is able to use two extra votes in the voting sessions afterwards.
2. In step 2 the players choose to deal with either *closed or open dilemmas*. Closed dilemmas describe situations in which the players need to decide between imperfect alternatives, while open dilemmas allow them to come up with their own response to situations characterized by a dilemma. The other participants judge the response and assign points by taking different stakeholder perspectives.
3. Step 3 prompts the players to *share related experiences and challenges*that they have been facing at work. They translate these challenges into how-might-we questions and select the most relevant challenges that they want to address.
4. In step 4 the players can be divided into subgroups. They begin by generating radical approaches and utopian visions to overcome the challenge, and then they generate some ideas on how to bring those utopian visions back down to earth. These more realistic responses are used to *formulate their own ideas* on how to tackle their challenge.
5. In step 5 the players work with different templates again to *create scenarios*depicting how – thanks to the ideas and measures they are initiating today – the world and our business may look in the year 2030. They present their ideas to the other groups in a short pitch and vote to decide which solution to implement.

Experiences and exemplary walk-through

Players appreciate the creative exchange, the relevance of challenges, and the safe environment for experimentation. Following a testing session, they commented that the game allowed them to raise their awareness about sustainability challenges at their workplace, and to change and broaden their views on sustainability (e.g. sustainability is not only about dealing with resources). It also facilitated team building (e.g. through the warm-up activities). Observers noted that participants learned new facts and each other's point of view on sustainability issues. In the second part, participants were able to come up with, prioritize and further develop new ideas based on their own experiences.

For example, the discussion of a dilemma titled 'An employee's right to speak or remain silent', could lead to the sustainability-related challenge at the workplace that 'few colleagues are actively engaged with the corporate sustainability strategy'. A radical response would be to activate them by starting each day with a reminder. A more realistic approach could be to distribute prompts around the office or to encourage sharing insights and crowdsourcing ideas on internal social media channels.

In the *QUIZ* participants earn investment points by finding the correct answer to multiple choice questions. For instance, they need to find the right definition for 'greenwashing' or the key components of the 'circular economy'. Or they are given a quote and have to decide who is the author: 'Our world and what we have achieved cannot be taken for granted. We have to stand up for our values' (quote from Telekom CEO Timotheus Höttges, the alternative, and incorrect, answers were Donald Trump, Ursula von der Leyen and Greta Thunberg).

After the quiz, participants are asked to react to *DILEMMAS* or *TRADE-OFFS* like operations versus innovation: 'As one of Europe's largest providers of critical infrastructure, Deutsche Telekom is focused on running its processes to provide secure and reliable services to end users. You are in charge of one of Telekom's data centres and are striving to provide uninterrupted service. Innovation development would allow you to enhance your data centre's energy efficiency and environmental sustainability by introducing, for example, new processes for upgrading, refurbishing and recycling obsolete hardware components or by integrating state-of-the-art smart grid technologies and energy storage facilities. Such innovations lower costs and mitigate environmental impact in the long run, but they require substantial investments and compromise the reliability of service provision in the short-term.'

Closed dilemmas offer three different options to deal with the situation, whereas open dilemmas ask the participants to come up with their own response. Responses are then rated by the other participants, who take the role of important stakeholder personas (Martin the customer, Robert the shareholder, Sara the journalist, Jennifer the NGO representative or Tobias the colleague). They also justify their rating, which often triggers an intensive discussion.

Now that participants are better informed after the quiz and sensitized by discussions of the dilemmas, they identify sustainability-related *CHALLENGES* from their own work experience. In one of our past sessions a challenge was seen in transforming the corporate design gallery into a best practise case not just for innovation, but also for meeting corporate sustainability aspirations, inspiring customers and business partners.

Ideas addressing the challenge were formulated and visualized, for instance how to improve the server infrastructure, or how to implement new mandatory sustainability targets and criteria for all business decisions. Another challenge was seen in the need to collect and recycle even more plastic waste (from masks, lunch bags and such) due to the Corona crisis. This challenge was addressed with ideas for a gamified environmental heroes app and autonomous collectors turning recycling into a fun and rewarding experience.

In a last step, these ideas were spun out ten years into the *future* and participants visualized the positive impact they achieved by putting their ideas into practice.

Customization

The game was developed and is publicly available in an open PowerPoint format to allow professional facilitators, consultants or innovation professionals without advanced programming or design skills to adopt and customize the format for their own purposes.

Some of the quiz questions and dilemmas in the current version are suited for any organisation, while others (and these are marked as such) are more characteristic for the telecommunications industry, but can be adapted to another industry or organisation-specific context (e.g. including quotes from one's own CEO in the quiz, or dilemmas that are characteristic for your industry). The format can be extended to facilitate alignment of values in different phases of organisational change and to define project-specific objectives and initiatives based on new organisational values (a request we received from a large bank).

Once the first two essential steps (the quiz and the dilemma) of the Corporate Sustainability Dilemma game have been adapted, the following three steps in the Corporate Sustainability Innovation game can easily be reused to share experiences and identify challenges in your firm, to co-create ideas on how to address these sustainability challenges and illustrate them through future scenarios. The companion sites for the book allow you to download the games with additional instructions summed up in a facilitator's guide.

Patterns

The Corporate Sustainability Innovation game addresses the overarching challenge to facilitate the adoption of abstract organizational values, in particular sustainability-related values, among employees. It fosters corporate sustainability by identifying sustainability challenges and turning them into seeds for innovation. It utilizes the flow patterns of *AWARENESS RAISING*, *DILEMMA SOLVING*, and *IDEATION*. These are realized based on the component patterns such as *QUIZZES*, *SURPRISE*, *ROLES*, *TRADE-OFFS*, *DEDICATED FACILITATORS* and *COLLECTIVE DECISIONS* (see Figure 7.2 for visual depiction).

Figure 7.2: Breakdown of the *CSI* game into its flow and component patterns and its innovation challenge.

Chapter 8
Games: *Customer first change*

Sune Gudiksen, Lisa Weber & Leif Sørensen

How can we introduce and adapt change processes with a customer first orientation? Customer First demonstrates the effects of organisational changes on various stakeholders, including the customer.

Figure 8.1: Actee *Customer First Change* board, a multiple-choice system with algorithms that create the movements of fictional, but realistic stakeholders.

https://doi.org/10.1515/9783110725582-014

The *Customer First Change* game deals with challenges related to creating a more human-centric organization that can respond to changing customer needs, regulations and more, as well as training participants in overcoming organizational inertia (Figure 8.1). It is harder for companies to create customer retention, even in those industries where customers normally keep the same relationship for many years, for instance banking and insurance products or services. Loyalty to a company can no longer be taken for granted.[1]

Challenge

Picking up leads and responding to them are crucial. Developing strategies for staying connected and extending temporary loyalty are key to develop strong customer relationships.

Statistics show that loyal customers are worth up to 10 times as much as their first purchase, creating an urgency for companies to reconfigure their organization towards a customer first strategy, which historically has been difficult to implement. This pressure can be linked to at least five reasons: (1) Data protection regulations provides challenges in how to reach customers, placing a high demand on internal resources and units of internal 'regulators'. (2) New services help the customer to compare products and services and change to new providers or vendors, normally a difficult thing for customers to do. Customers are becoming aware of the number of similar products available on the market. (3) Customers can learn about services from a greater number of customers due to online reviews. A single negative review can lead to a storm of supporting comments. (4) Customers expect on-demand services, for instance smooth processes, instant replies and 24/7 availability. They react positively to unexpected services (which are not part of the visible package). (5) Covid-19 has intensified this process – customers are now even more focused on digital services and options.

Building together pioneering customer-first strategies using organizational change principles in a game format can help to advance understanding, potential and workarounds. Strategy and operations experts Nicolaj Siggelkow and Christian Terwiesch refer to connected customer strategies as a new source of competitive advantage.[2]

Purpose

The core objective of the game is to work with and develop strategies for customer journeys and lifecycle relationships in a rapidly changing customer behavior landscape, and train new forms of organizing around customer-first strategies as well as put systems in place that can create responsiveness with high speed.

The game provides a chance to prepare, through interactive sessions with colleagues and internal or external experts, upcoming focus points on customer-first strategies and awareness. Playing Customer-First Change gives participants the chance to discuss perspectives, approaches and organizational dynamics with colleagues and comment on the things they recognize in their own companies – or the things that they might implement.

The game builds on practice-based principles and dilemmas from various companies, and theories combined from both organizational change and change management,[3, 4] and relationship marketing and lead management.[5]

Methodology

The game is created with a cycle of recognize, request, respond and repeat (corresponding to theory and principles from Siggelkow and Terwiesch)[6] formatted as four phases the participants play through. The game moves through the cycle in a visual model in which a number of stakeholders are involved. The Actee game engine is basically a multiple-choice system with algorithms that create the movements of fictional, but realistic stakeholders in the game.

Participants

The game can be played alone, in groups or in large virtual group settings where movements, choices and scores can be compared. Participants can also play asynchronously during, for instance, a week and then meet up after completing the game – in so-called micro-learning sessions.

Gameplay

The fundamental learning element in the game is to observe and react to the stakeholders' movements and responses to a specific choice and strategy. Stakeholders begin at change resistance levels: I don't get it, I don't like it, and I don't trust you.[7] Will the stakeholders join you on the boat, fall back or jump off? Participants react to a prompt text that ends with a call to action in each of the four phases of the game, for instance: 'Diana launched the initiative because of a visible decline in getting new customers on board and holding on to existing ones. You also find it difficult to get in contact with customers and understand their 'pain points' and, internally, customer needs are not interpreted in the same ways. It is clear that digitalization, EU regulations and Covid-19 have had an effect on how one can approach customers.

What will be your first moves to pick up on customer needs and leads? And how will you communicate these internally?'

Participants now select a specific option and see how stakeholders move and react. Participants – if it is a group setting – then discuss the various choices they took and reflect on what to focus on and remember for the next phase of the cycle (and their next choices). By the end of the game participants can compare the overall strategies and choices they made throughout the game for a final reflection on their actions, a step that supports meta-level learning.

Exemplary case

The game was first used in a session with cross-unit representatives from a European insurance company that was struggling with access to customers and keeping them onboard due to new EU regulations and competition. The group went through the four phases and discussed the various choices and options, and the way these affected the stakeholders' attitudes and movements in the game. From this a good dialogue emerged, also on potential strategies.

Customization

In the back-end of the Actee software it is simple to change, for instance, the number of stakeholders and their movements, the number of phases and content in each phase – allowing the game to be easily customized for each session and group.

Patterns

The Customer First Change game addresses the overarching challenge of how to always keep customer needs at the centre of the attention, work processes and innovation. It utilizes the flow patterns of *AWARENESS RAISING, BUSINESS SIMULATION*, and *DILEMMA SOLVING*. These are realized based on the component patterns such as *ROLES, SURPRISE, BRANCHING, MAPPING* and *CHALLENGES* (see Figure 8.2 for visual depiction).

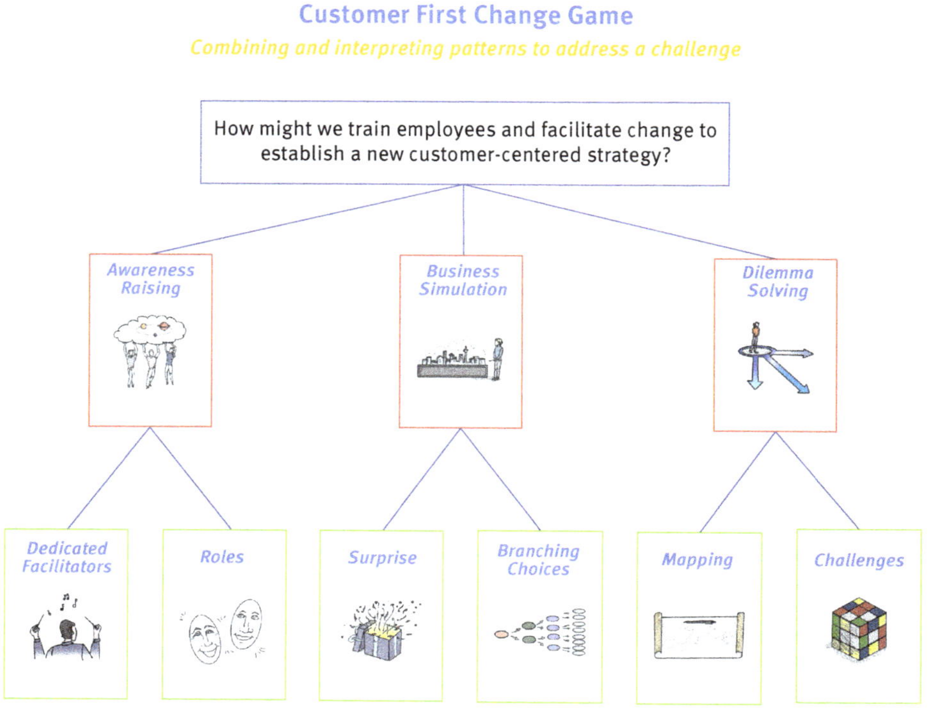

Figure 8.2: A selection of flow and component patterns contributing to the *Customer First Change* game and its innovation challenge.

Chapter 9
Games: Business model branching

Sune Gudiksen

How can we facilitate considerations whether it is the right time to reconfigure existing portfolios? *Business Model Branching* works with visual mapping models to create strategies for when to reconfigure existing business branches, and when to ramp up new ones.

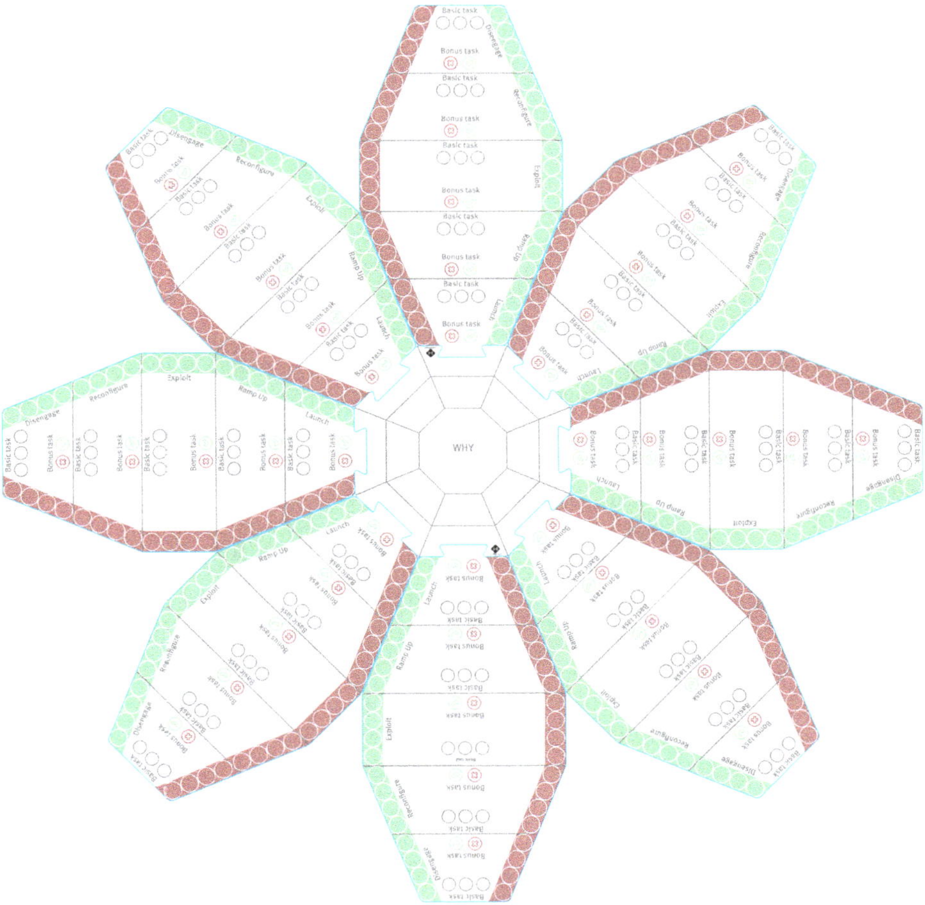

Figure 9.1: Business Model Branching game board with eight branches indicating the current lines of business and potential future ones.

https://doi.org/10.1515/9783110725582-015

The innovation game *Business Model Branching* (BMB) deals with the difficult and complex challenge of balancing exploitation and exploration, that is, of ongoing operations with new innovation-oriented activities (Figure 9.1). According to the influential business thinker and researcher Rita McGrath, companies can no longer expect sustainable competitive advantages and are forced to regularly seek out temporary advantages in order to be competitive. Here, Rita McGrath asks the question: 'How do you reconfigure the organization to simultaneously disengage from the original advantage while moving resources into the next one?'[1] It is vital for all companies to constantly find this balance through resource allocation, competence development, and generally understanding the need for both parts of the dilemma to be present in everyday business situations. Therefore, it is crucial for organizations – private and public – to build up a portfolio of business opportunities so they can avoid significant losses in profit when markets are disrupted by continually seeking out new business opportunities.[2]

Challenge

It has been investigated and widely discussed in business and the innovation research community that finding the balance between ongoing operations and new initiatives is key to successful operations on a leadership level.[3] For instance, Govindarajan and colleagues describe this as an inevitable paradox for businesses: Ongoing operations are characterized by short-term thinking, repeatability and predictability, whereas innovation is based on long-term thinking, chaos, serendipity and unpredictability. Govindarajan and Trimble argue that: 'Organizations are not designed for innovation. Quite the contrary, they are designed for ongoing operations.'[4]

On a further note, Rita McGrath unfolds principles in moving from one business model branch to another – from an existing advantage to a new one when the time is right. And timing is everything in this transition flow. McGrath's principles are framed in the two themes assets and competence allocation, especially when to use competencies. According to research from McGrath, a transition from 'access to assets, not ownership of assets' can be observed as key success parameter in 21st-century business markets.[5]

With temporary rather than sustainable advantages being the new norm, the existing value model in companies will always come under pressure, suggesting the need for reconfiguration and renewal of advantages at a more rapid pace. Here it is important to prepare new business advantages ahead of time, rather than wait till economic decline sets in. In a more recent book called *Seeing Around Corners* Rita McGrath argues for the importance of organizations being able to see around corners, detect inflection points, and work systematically with portfolios of possible new branches.[6]

Reconfiguration and exit decisions – that is, closing one business to launch a new one – are vital. Moving from one advantage to another is essential for continual profitability, which means that organizations need to master the transition of assets and competencies.

Purpose

Consequently, leaders and innovation managers need to know how to:

- align organizational structure and culture with ambidextrous developments, balancing resource allocation between ongoing operations and innovation.
- develop future business model scenarios and possible new branches and consider what types of declines in existing branches are visible and what reconfiguration could look like if these trends continued.

Methodology

The *Business Model Branching* game gives participants practice in allocating resources to launch and ramp-up concrete new business branches while also exploiting, reconfiguring and disengaging from old business model branches. It rests on different foundational business theories related to vital 21st-century challenges, and the game incorporates them into a combined business game world with systematic approaches: Rita McGrath's business value cycles, and Govindarajan and Trimble's strategy concept on balancing ongoing operations and innovation.

Based on Rita McGrath's extensive work on how to compete with temporary business advantages, *BMB* is about how to deploy the right resources in the five stages of a business branch, also called upstream flow in the game, which goes as follows: (1) Launch, (2) Ramp up, (3) Exploit, (4) Reconfigure and (5) Disengage. As one can imagine, each stage comes with its own challenges. Launching requires an entirely different set of competencies and resources than Ramping up or Exploiting. Here, the game offers several insights to the participants on how the current business branches are doing and how they can be managed. Many companies and leaders are competent in certain stages of the cycle but fall short when faced with challenges in other stages. Several companies have been exploiting for so long that when faced with the need to reconfigure, they do not know how to launch new initiatives. Conversely, several companies are good at launching but fall short in their ramping-up efforts. Through tasks related to each upstream movement, the participants create concrete initiatives to advance upstream movement and learn when to use which types of competencies.

Building on Govindarajan and Trimble's strategy concept on balancing ongoing operations and innovation, the game framework uses the insight that it is not enough to depict a single value cycle if the purpose is to visualize the complete picture and move resources to new business branches. To do this and develop the needed competencies, the participants need to move between reconfiguring and closing down existing advantages while launching and ramping up new ones to create a perfectly timed sidestep movement. The first step of the game is to map the complete set of the company's business branches and mark which stage participants believe each branch is in – is it currently launching, ramping up, exploiting, reconfiguring or disengaging? Participants also mark how the company's resources are currently allocated to the business branches.

Once participants have mapped their current business branches and resource allocation, they go straight to the base of the branches – the reason why the company exists, the big Why. Here, participants examine the 'tree trunk' that holds different business branches together. It begins with the question Simon Sinek is famous for asking: 'Why does your organization exist?'[7] Here, participants can explore potential business branches and examine their fit with the company's reason to exist, thereby either transforming the why or advancing new understandings and interpretations. Since business advantages are shorter-lived, the WHY of a company becomes more flexible. Even though fundamental elements are intact – for instance, values and core beliefs – new interpretations of the Why are often inevitable.

Participants

Groups of 4–5 participants play the game. The innovation game is analogue and meant to provide a visual overview, tactile experiences and dynamic conversations using the materials at hand. Typically, participants are innovation managers and leaders, but as the game deals with the paradox of ongoing operations and innovation, the best results and impact are achieved with both operational leaders of existing branches and those looking into new ones, so that they can develop the flow together. Scaled-up versions developed by product developers, project managers and others can be used in large room set-ups to compare outcomes and assess quality. By the end, participants can secure alignment and achieve a better common understanding of the need for being able to continuously move from ongoing operations to innovations, namely, develop an ambidextrous mindset. The game also functions well in groups of business professionals where participants do not come from the same organization but have the chance to communicate with their 'peers' in other companies and organizations.

Gameplay

The game consists of a centerboard and up to eight possible branches. The centerboard includes the Why in Simon Sinek's golden circle.[8] Variations on this Why can be based on how new branches provoke new aspects of the Why. Different interpretations of the Why of a company are always emerging, either proactively or as a reaction to market changes. The branches illustrate value proposition cycles on a scale: (1) Launch, (2) Ramp-up, (3) Exploit, (4) Reconfigure, and (5) Disengage. Participants are challenged to move both upstream and sideways. Challenges in moving upstream are related to each stage in the value cycle. A variety of competencies, examples and strategies are needed for each stage. Participants have basic tasks to fulfil and bonus tasks that provide extra resources and movements in subsequent rounds.

Sideways movement marks the transition from one branch to another. Here, the participants have to devise resources and place people either in the red zone (in need of competence development) or in the green zone (ready to fulfil tasks). As McGrath mentions, 'another factor in play in companies that can move from one set of advantages to another is that they consciously set out to educate and upskill their people.'[9]

The game lets groups of participants work with the basic tasks for minutes to hours based on the time available and then return to the board to discuss changes related to both the Why of the company and the specific balance between ongoing operations and innovation. Based on McGrath's theory, BMB has a scoring algorithm that pressures participants to launch new branches before old branches die out, or else face the same fate as companies in the real market – going bankrupt. This helps participants look further into their future than their current business branches while also letting them see that they should not be launching new initiatives all the time. It strikes a balance between being so enamoured with existing value propositions that they fail to launch something new and, conversely, launching too many new value propositions without having the necessary resources and the right competencies in place.

The value of the game lies in the concrete actions in upstream flows and sidestep moves, alongside learning about how to master this balance. The timing in the movement of resources and competence development is the key to the game and regularly creating temporary competitive advantages. Participants gain new insights into how to act by making moves right after completing an activity based on the concrete situation they are in, and thus learning how to manage this crucial balance. Since the game moves between concrete co-created actions and advancement in overall understanding and learning, the game has the following outcomes:

Co-creation outcomes

- Concrete ideas on moving upstream (advancing existing business advantages) and also when to leave them behind, including when to use which types of competencies and available resources.
- Concrete ideas on creating strong sidestep moves, including moving resources and building up competencies to support potential new advantages in a careful and optimal transition.
- Keeping the Why flexible and advancing new interpretations continuously in the struggle to stay afloat and update business relevance.

Training outcomes

- Learning how to survey a company's business branches and resource allocation so one can spot weaknesses and pitfalls and progressively handle them before an economic crisis arises.
- Learning how to plan well-timed resource allocation and competence development so one can diminish wasteful use of resources and resources held hostage and progressively build competitive advantages.

Exemplary cases

In a case clearly illustrating the dilemma between ongoing operations and innovation, we worked with a company with years of success with its existing value proposition based on promotion and marketing. They then experienced their first declines in business dynamism and signs that reconfiguration and disengagement were not that far away, but they also found that scaling up an existing business branch might lead to better times.

Based on this initial mapping of *Business Model Branching*, the team had identified existing value propositions and new potential business branches. Subsequently, the team was divided into two groups. One group focused on an existing business branch and scaling this up in fierce competition (upstream movement on an existing branch). The other group focused on a new value proposition of outdoor promotion events (sidestep movement to a new branch). The groups went through a series of idea generation activities to further unfold the potential of each branch and then returned to discuss what these potential moves would mean for status quo practices in the company.

Based on the game, the team concluded that they were currently using all their energy on a declining business branch without advancing new business branches. Resources were needed to experiment and test new business branches – and quickly, since they were currently falling behind competitors, such as in digital solution promotions. Additionally, employees quickly gained new competencies related to the new business branches while there were still resources available and time to gain them.

In many ways, this case illustrates the dilemma between ongoing operations (existing value propositions and practices) and innovation (identifying and launching new value propositions). It is not an either/or approach but rather a balancing activity for leaders and employees. For this reason, it is also of vital importance that this perspective is not geared only toward leaders but also employees so that everyone understands that moving from one competitive advantage to another is happening at a rapid pace.

Customization

Business Model Branching (BMB) can function as two game types. First, Business Branching can be a co-creation game with a focus on concretely mapping your company and figuring out how you can allocate resources in your company's current situation and move forward. Here, the game offers practical insights to launching, ramping up, exploiting, reconfiguring and disengaging from your company's business branches. You co-create possible strategies to allocate resources and optimize your company's economic situation.

Second, BMB can be a training game with a focus on helping managers learn how to handle the various problems related to balancing innovation with ongoing operations. Here, the game is played with fictional but relatable cases using a selection of built-in tasks to focus on the timing of resource allocation.

The game has been played in both small and large companies. Based on these experiences, dealing with the problem of allocating resources to both ongoing operations and innovation appears to be a dilemma companies face regardless of their size. It is relevant for the entrepreneur, who has launched, ramped up and exploited one business branch, but is hesitant to launch another. It is relevant for large companies, where middle management is too closely tied to a particular business branch and therefore hangs on to it for too long, even when critical indicators tell them to launch something new. As McGrath states: 'Preventing resources from being held hostage by the leaders of a particular advantage will become more standard as firms become aware of the dangers of a leader hanging on to an old advantage for too long.'[10]

The same also applies the other way around. Many leading managers and business developers with an extensive portfolio of strong ideas and potential new value propositions, however, do not have the nerve and an overview to launch and ramp-up the one with the most promise and then follow through.

Patterns

The Business Model Branching game addresses the overarching double challenge to allocate resources to launch and ramp-up concrete new business branches while also exploiting, reconfiguring and disengaging from the old business model branches. It utilizes the flow patterns of *DILEMMA SOLVING* and *BUSINESS MODELLING*. These are realized using component patterns such as *BRANCHING CHOICES*, *CHALLENGES*, *RESOURCES*, *MAPPING* and provoking *SURPRISE* (see Figure 9.2 for visual depiction).

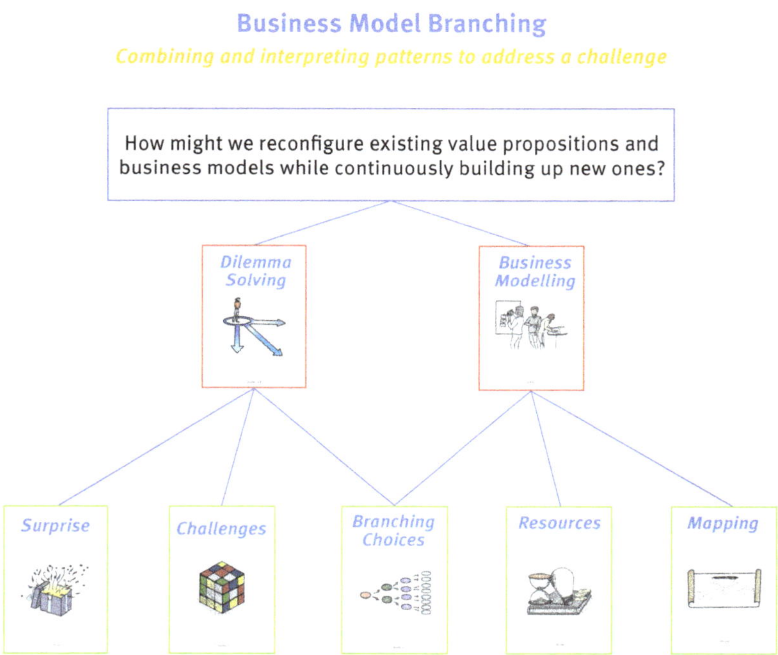

Figure 9.2: A selection of flow and component patterns contributing to the Business Model Branching game and its innovation challenge.

Chapter 10
Games: *Shift* innovation barriers

Sune Gudiksen & Carina Leue-Bensch

How can we overcome typical barriers in full scale innovation processes? *Shift* is a is floor-based game with stakeholder roleplay as participants work through a number of innovation barriers and develop strategies to overcome them.

Figure 10.1: *Shift* floorboards with one player responding to one of the innovation barriers written on tiles and others taking stakeholder roles to respond.

The *Shift Innovation Barriers* game deals with practical ways and strategies to overcome innovation barriers in established organizations. When working through development, design and innovation processes in both private and public organizations, stakeholders stumble over a number of gates and challenges which are difficult to overcome. A floor-based game with a three-stage progression with hidden barriers helps participants to develop strategies for overcoming the innovation barriers, before actually running into them (Figure 10.1).[1]

https://doi.org/10.1515/9783110725582-016

Challenge

It is a well-known phenomenon that organizations run into a series of dilemmas when specific company units propose radically different future directions – involving for instance new types of products, services and business models – that do not align with the company's current organizational infrastructure and operations. Innovation must pass a series of implicit or explicit 'gates' which are often created by operational managers who determine the value of new innovation proposals based on criteria based on current operations rather than on future ways of organizing the new services and business models. This has been called the 'the innovator's dilemma' in research by business professor and influential thinker Clayton Christensen in the 1990s.[2] This paradox was later framed as organizational ambidexterity, and led to ways to manage and overcome these innovation barriers being widely discussed.[3]

The innovators' dilemma has sometimes led to what has been called 'the fix that fails',[4] where private companies under the control of owners or shareholders only have the short-term bottom-line in sight. Or when public organizations under changing political winds or with political alliances and voter satisfaction in mind respond with quick fixes that help in the short term but cause damage in the long term.

This has led to several business and innovation researchers claiming that organizations, through the operations and routines associated with current practices, develop a kind of corporate immune system. A classic example would be the decline of the home video rental service Blockbuster – from a market leader to almost a closed business. Completely disrupted over a period of only a few years by technological developments, new customer demands and streaming services, Blockbuster Video, according to internal sources, did have opportunities to pursue the radically new ways of doing business in this market, but was stopped at the internal gates of the company.

With quick technology developments and societal movements comes rapid market shifts and times of high uncertainty. The need for organizations to move between current operations and radical innovations becomes increasingly urgent each day.

Shift works well as part of a cyclic format starting with a few preliminary processes. For instance, as participants need to first have a good understanding of possible future directions for their company, begin with an *IDEATION* session on future scenario development, then leap into a follow-up activity on how to branch out through the *Business Model Branching* game (chapter 9). The cycle would close with *Shift* to develop strategies for influencing, communicating and overcoming innovation barriers in the organizations regarding organizational structures, cultures, current business models and regulations. This might eventually push more radical developments through 'eye of a needle' gates in the organization and train employees – product and service developers, project managers and innovation managers – to build up an intrapreneurship mindset and needed general competencies.

Purpose

Consequently, employees and leaders need to train how to:

- develop strategies to overcome specific organizational innovation barriers based in business model operations, organizational structure and culture, and regulations.
- assess the logic and reasoning for having specific gates and determine whether they should remain unchanged, be altered to work differently or be completely removed.

Methodology

Shift is a floor-based game with a three-stage progression with hidden barriers that helps participants to develop strategies for overcoming the innovation barriers before actually running into them. Barriers are hidden to begin with and as participant progress through the tangible tile barriers their descriptions are revealed.

Participants

As many as three groups of 4–5 participants can move through the game if enough space is provided. This innovation game is analogue and floor-based to provide a visual overview, tactile experiences and dynamic conversations with the materials at hand. Typically, participants are innovation managers and leaders, but as the game deals with the paradox of ongoing operations and innovation, the best results and impact are achieved when both operational leaders of existing branches and those looking into new ones develop the flow together. Scaled-up versions with product developers, project managers, innovation managers and others can be used in large room set-ups to compare different strategies to overcoming the innovation barriers through the tangible traces playing the game leaves on the floor. The game also functions well in groups of leaders or employees, or in an MBA programme where participants do not come from the same organization but have the chance to communicate with 'peers' in other companies and organizations, thereby getting external input on their practices.

Gameplay

Shift is a floor-based game with a three-stage progression and hidden barriers written on tiles on the floor. The game has two content versions – either it can be played with a narrow focus on *IDEATION* stages or more broadly on the full run of innovation processes. Archetypical *ROLES* are incorporated to change perspectives and viewpoints. The barriers are divided into five categories:
1. Business model
2. Organizational structure
3. Organizational culture
4. Regulatory elements
5. User & front-end employees

Each barrier description on a tile on the floor contains a description of a specific situation that the participants have to face. First, the group (4–5 participants) needs a future direction, a new innovation proposal – this can be one developed in a previous session or one prepared for training purposes. After this, *ROLES* are assigned to the group, as described below:

- Project owner: Assign a project owner from among the participants. The project owner has the most knowledge about the case and gradually provides more context as the play unfolds.
- Team members: The project owner selects two members to join his or her team. They can also be chosen randomly.
- Role card players: The rest of the participants randomly select a role card from the table, which assigns them the *ROLES* of either marketing, design, finance, the user, the boss, or the devil's advocate. A minimum of 2 role cards and a maximum of 4 should be in play.

As the group progresses through the stages, the barriers gradually contain more complexity and difficulty. At the end of the game, the group and a *DEDICATED FACILITATOR* backtrack the movements and strategies through the tangible traces left on the floor, enabling a critical group reflection on the process and the insights gained in the game.

Exemplary case

In a case clearly illustrating the paradox between ongoing operations and innovation, we worked with German airline subsidiary for IT services. The company had years of success with their value proposition based on carefully planned flight services and a holistic development of complete customer journeys. *Shift* was applied to engage and train employees at Lufthansa to develop new idea projects and subsequently prepare them for potential barriers they would likely run into in their organization – making them more aware of these barriers and building strategies for overcoming them. The *Shift* innovation barrier game was employed at Lufthansa during the opening of Flying Lab (Lufthansa's innovation lab) with 3–4 groups of participants completing the game. The outcome yielded critical reflection on how to develop concrete strategies to overcome the barriers.

At this point, the Covid-19 pandemic and its heavy impact on the airline industry led to the closure of its markets and eventually forced Lufthansa to overcome or remove barriers at a faster pace than usual.

Customization

There is another version of this game we call *Shift* ideation. It can be played in the same way as *Shift* innovation barrier game but using the *Shift* ideation questions instead of the *Shift* barrier statements. Both questions and barriers, alongside templates to create tailor-made content and facilitator roles, are available on the EU Gamify website.

Likewise, the content of the barriers and the specific gameplay can be connected to a broader strategic level or for a specific project in its early stages to guide product, service and project developers through innovation processes. In this way, the game can be played on two levels.

Patterns

The *Shift* game addresses the overarching challenge of preparing participants deal with and work around typical innovation barriers in larger organizations. It utilizes the flow patterns of *EXPERIENTIAL LEARNING*, *IDEATION* and *WORKSHOP FACILITATION*. These are realized based on the component patterns such as *SURPRISE, ROLES, CHALLENGES, CO-OPERATION* and *MAPPING* (see Figure 10.2 for visual depiction).

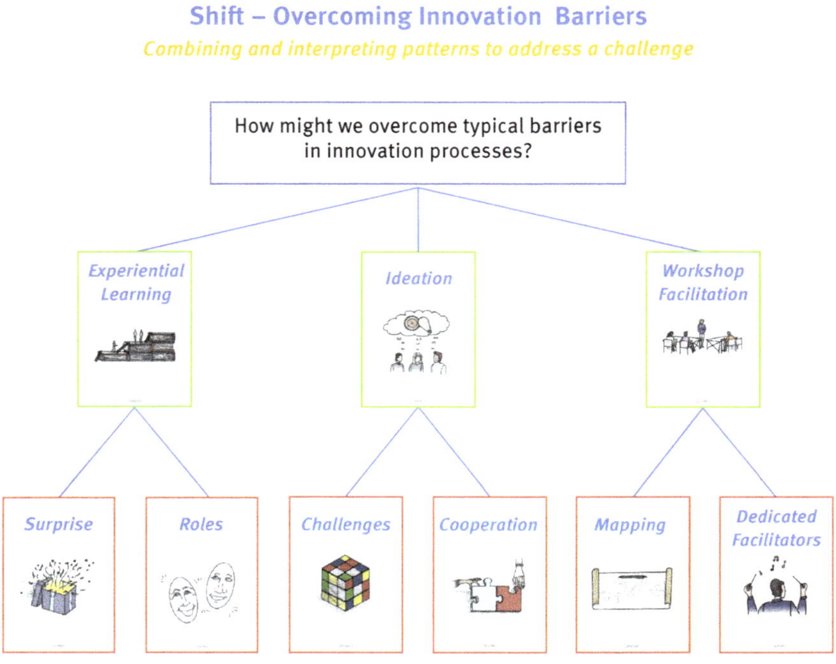

Figure 10.2: A selection of flow and component patterns contributing to the *Shift* game and its innovation challenge.

Chapter 11
Games: Proximity seeker

Keila Z. Pérez Quiñones & Sune Gudiksen

How can we promote trust and empathy among remote team members to cooperate effectively and efficiently? The Proximity Seeker game facilitates sharing experiences and knowledge through fun and engaging questions.

Figure 11.1: The *Proximity Seeker* Game, a little magic protocol for distant teams.

It is crucial that we become better prepared and proactive in dealing with the difficulties that remote teams face. Much effort is being placed into creating even more efficient meetings – shorter and task-focused. However, what is still needed is a way of dealing with the challenges of social dynamics that efficiency and productivity tools cannot address.[1] The Proximity Seeker game was developed to fill this gap (Figure 11.1).[2]

Challenge

Global organizations have been working with remote teams and distributed tasks for many years. The rest of the world has been forced to follow suit due to the global pandemic. Luckily, the technology for this shift has been available to us for many years, making the practical side of remote work a small challenge. Especially for

https://doi.org/10.1515/9783110725582-017

global companies and organizations, remote work is here to stay and is even standard practice. The main problem is the potential lack of trust and the social complexity of cross-cultural remote collaboration. The richness that collaborative work brings can lead to unexpected problem solving and diversity in ideas. This is even more crucial when we talk about teams with multi-cultural backgrounds, a common characteristic of remote teams in bigger organizations. When we miss the informal communication that normally occurs in the physical workplace, we lose many opportunities to build a sense of familiarity and connectedness to our colleagues and the company mission. Proximity Seeker is a social innovation game based on creating a space for informal exchanges that would occur naturally in a physical working environment.

Purpose

Innovation leaders and project managers need to develop ways – at a distance – to create social dynamics for better team development and cultural understanding. In this game, participants gain the following:

- Participants gradually learn more about each other, reveal aspects of their ways of thinking and culture, which tend not to be clear and explicit in 'classic' online meetings.
- A group dynamic of openness, communication and respect is fostered through the gameplay that translates back into the team's work dynamic.
- Participants' social barriers are challenged in a safe space created by playfulness, by taking the risk to speak up and by becoming somewhat vulnerable in front of others, strengthening the feeling of connectedness to other participants.

Methodology

The Proximity Seeker game is used as a check-in or check-out exercise in meetings, and often when participants do not know each other well but have to develop a work relationship over sometimes short periods and at a distance. The game was developed to fit existing presentation software such as PowerPoint, Keynote, or others, and a web-based edition is also available. Taking inspiration from an earlier game,[3] the reason for choosing PowerPoint is that it can be easily shared in online meetings. Facilitators and participants are both already familiar with the medium and save time they would otherwise need to dive into an unfamiliar application (which typically steals much time in meetings).

Participants

This game can be played by 4–8 people. More than this in an online meeting would slow down the flow of the game, and the participants' motivation. In seminar and conference settings, breakout rooms can be used to divide the participants into groups, with many participants playing the game in parallel rooms.

Gameplay

The game progresses through five steps:

1. Determine the turn-taking order (for instance, by starting with the person who most recently had a birthday).
2. Press the 'Play' button to view the card menu and select one of the three modes – social check-in, team synergies, or made-to-fit. The social check-in mode is about learning information we typically acquire through informal interactions in the workplace. They tend to get lost when we do not have the opportunity to share a physical environment. Exchanges by the coffee machine or in the hallway create a sense of familiarity with our teammates. The team synergies mode facilitates unexpected synergies among colleagues working on different projects. When working remotely, our chance to exchange knowledge and inspire each other is minimized, as our interactions are mostly scheduled and follow specific agendas. Knowing more about each other's professional background builds our sense of trust and familiarity with others. The made-to-fit mode allows you to customize your categories to best fit the needs of your team or session.
3. The participant stares into the color-changing eye and says 'Stop!' The facilitator presses stop, and the eye displays a colour. Depending on the color, the moderator then asks a predefined question to trigger a conversation. For instance, 'Forget the past. How is the end of your week looking? Please share your scenario.'
4. The participant responds to the question spontaneously and shares a possible, a preferable and a probable scenario of how the week could, should or will likely end.
5. The back button is used to return to the color-changing eye. The participant nominates the next player on the roll, and the game goes on until everyone has had a turn.

Customization

The Proximity Seeker game is available in English and German. It can be adapted to specific organizations or session goals. The game provides two standardized game modes, both as 'plug-and-play' options. Both have the same objective of reinforcing social ties, trust and teambuilding. Both versions can be adapted through rule variations according to the time available and purpose of the session.

The third game mode called 'made to fit' provides an easily customizable template that any team can adapt with the topics they want to use for the session. The game mechanics are the same, and include a randomizer and conversational frames. Users, team leaders and facilitators have the complete freedom to tailor the activity to best fit their needs for a specific session. A Facilitator Guide provides all the information needed for customizing a session using the different game modes and rule variations.

Patterns

The Proximity seeker game addresses the overarching challenge to create high quality, strong social dynamics and innovative conditions in remote team work. It utilizes the flow patterns of *WARM-UPS* and *AWARENESS RAISING*. These are realized using component patterns such as *HUMOUR, STORYTELLING, METAPHORS* and *DEDICATED FACILITATORS* (see Figure 11.2 for visual depiction).

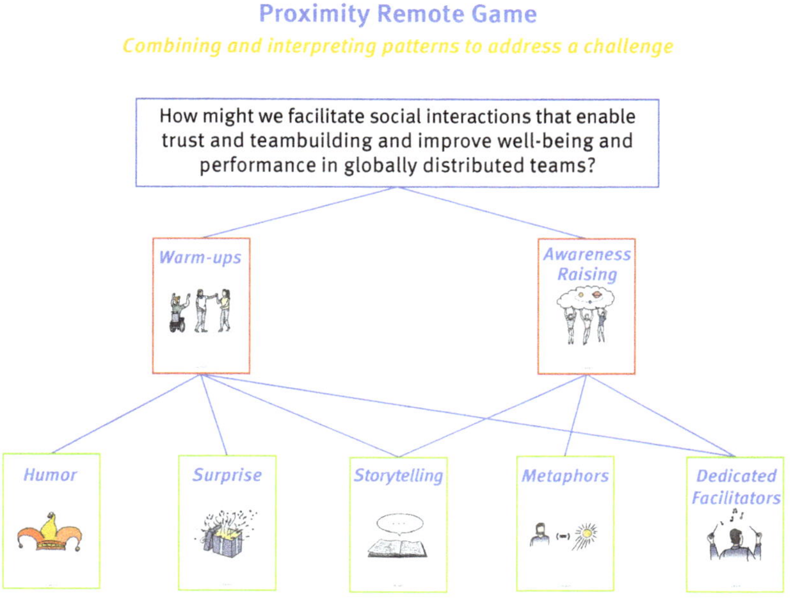

Figure 11.2: A selection of flow and component patterns contributing to the *Proximity Seeker* game and its innovation challenge.

Chapter 12
Games: Ecosystem Canvas

Jacob Thomsen & Sune Gudiksen

How can we help future entrepreneurs grasp the potential synergies in their own business ecosystem? The *Ecosystem Canvas* enhances each player's understanding of the factors influencing the entrepreneurial journey.

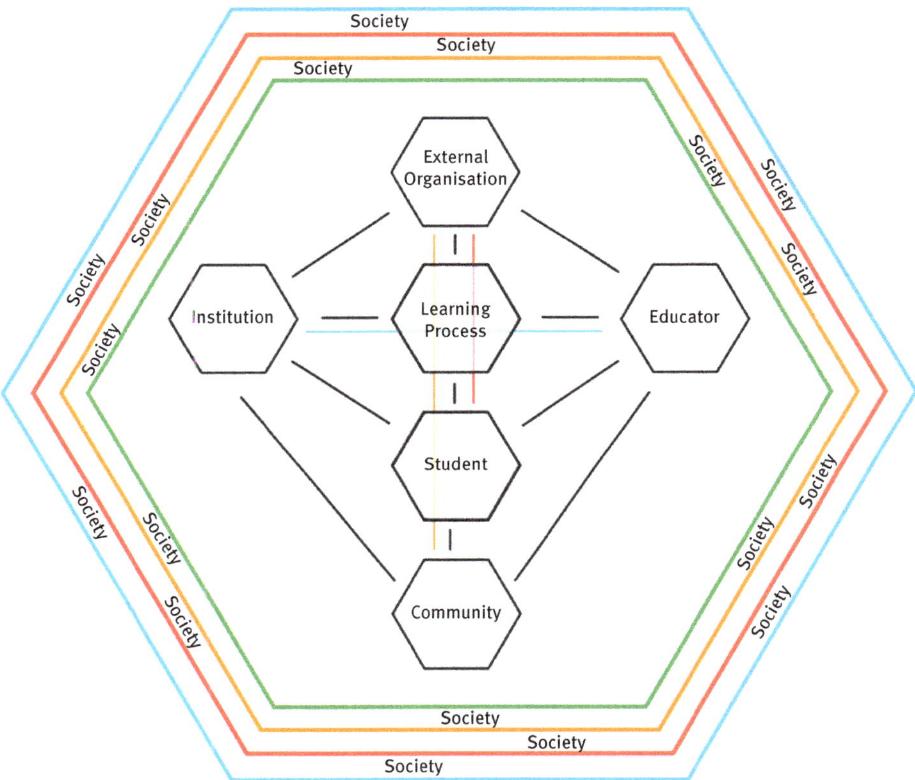

Figure 12.1: The Entrepreneurial Education Ecosystem model reveals dialogical relations between the different actors in the eco-system.[2]

https://doi.org/10.1515/9783110725582-018

The *Ecosystem Canvas* is a game that allows future entrepreneurs to become aware of and explore potential for joint value creation in networks (Figure 12.1). To build up and strengthen the relations and potential in the business ecosystem, a board game was created. It supports the co-exploration of opportunities and gives future entrepreneurs and start-ups the chance to experience how stakeholder involvement leads to better first steps in their business ventures.[1]

Challenge

The starting challenge for developing this game was the fact that actors in a business ecosystem rarely reach optimal joint value because they fail to build on relational awareness and help each other reach next levels. Recent studies confirm that entrepreneurship ecosystems are a vital factor in entrepreneurship education (EE) programs[3] and for the first steps in start-ups. There is a growing demand for students to be introduced to and learn from entrepreneurship as it is widely recognized that this would not only stimulate economic growth but also contribute to developing new skills and competencies.[4]

A business ecosystem should be built around local conditions.[5] A local university can act as the anchor organization in the process of generating knowledge and establishing relations between stakeholders,[6] which is why universities should expand their interaction with both industry and government.[7] A recent study[8] confirms that the entrepreneurial university plays a role in entrepreneurial behaviour. Other frameworks provide detailed descriptions of the relations between stakeholders in such entrepreneurial education ecosystems (EEE).[9]

Entrepreneurship research indicates that establishing a strong ecosystem around higher education institutions based on learning experiences for the stakeholders, including potential entrepreneurs (for instance innovation and entrepreneurship students) is a vital means for successful start-ups.[10] However, entrepreneurship students often do not fully understand their own role in these ecosystems, and different educators, community, external partners and the institution may each have a different understanding of (economic, enjoyment, social, harmony and influence) value for others or oneself.[11] They thus miss the bigger picture of how to exploit these roles. Stakeholders in the ecosystem tend to focus on short-term, internal views rather than open innovation that would enable new value creation with joint competencies and resources. Collaborative and dynamic stakeholder involvement methods are needed to bridge between the theoretical understandings of ecosystems and practical, direct stakeholder value creation.

Purpose

Dialogue and co-created opportunity spaces are key to greater understanding among different actors in the entrepreneurial education ecosystem. The objectives for the *Ecosystem Canvas* are to gain insights into:

- knowledge, in relation to your core curriculum and how it evolves in the EEE.
- value, as created by you and other actors in the EEE.
- learning, for the players of the game, and the ecosystem, about the different dilemmas it contains.

Methodology

The methodology builds on six propositions on how the joint value creation and learning in eco-system can be achieved:

1. Learning is a constant process in which you need to engage.
2. All learning is relearning.
3. The learning process is driven by conflicts, differences and disagreements.
4. Learning is the result of a holistic process.
5. Learning occurs in synergetic transactions between the learner and their ecosystem.
6. Learning happens by creating knowledge.[12]

These six core elements structure the facilitation process. The EEE framework brings a holistic approach to education: the questions designed for each round of the games drive and enhance different perspectives for each participating player and introduce a broader and new understanding of the other's actions.

Participants

The entrepreneurial education ecosystem model in Figure 12.1 has at its centre the learning process, to which five actors contribute: students, educators, the community, external organizations and the institution. The *students* are in a higher education programme studying to launch their first start-up or work as an intrapreneur in an exciting company. The Educator is the teacher in the core curriculum at a higher education programme, who structures the learning process, possibly in collaboration with an external organization, with support from the community and in a structure shaped by the Institution. The entrepreneurial *community* contains actors supporting the learning process and the curriculum, such as the head of the incubator or an engineer from a maker space or another lab. The External Organization can be made up of NGOs, public-sector institutions, foundations or privately-owned companies. The *external organization* is a key partner that closely collaborates with higher education institutions, who have a keen interest in collaborating with *society*,[13] as entrepreneurship stimulates economic growth and contributes to students learning new skills and competencies.[14] The role of the *institution* can be taken by a head of programme, a consultant or someone working in education.

The game should be played by a mix of the five different actors, but it can also be successfully played with one or more actors missing. Each round in the game is based on a dialogical relationship[15] between stakeholders in the team framed by a theme (and question) given by one of the four Q-piece figures on the board. The four themes are:

1. key factors including resources, skilled people and opportunities[16]
2. key determinants including regulatory framework, market conditions, access to finance, R&D technology, entrepreneurial capabilities and culture[17]
3. entrepreneurial skills, business idea, business model, environmental scanning, opportunity recognition, advisory board and networking[18]
4. ever-changing environments (society in Figure 12.1)[19]

Gameplay

The board game guides and challenges the players to reflect upon learning from and about the other participating players. The board has a hexagon shape and each represents one part (for instance an educator, a student, a community) of the EEE.[20]

First, teams are formed of 4–6 people. They take a few minutes to define a common understanding of learning, dialogical relationships, and value for oneself or others in the Entrepreneurial Education Ecosystem. In the first round, team members draw a Q-piece and discuss how they understand the question. One exemplary question is phrased: ‘What do the ever-changing environments mean for an educator?’ After some discussion they place the Q-piece on the board and draw a new Q-piece with a new question and a new discussion. After four rounds and discussions about questions from the four themes the game is over. A debriefing discussion focusses on how the participants’ understanding of learning, dialogical relationships and value in connection to the Entrepreneurial Education Ecosystem has changed.

Exemplary case

UCL University College in Denmark applies the Ecosystem Canvas as a tool for creating a strong joint understanding of value, learning and dialogic relationships between the actors in their entrepreneurial education ecosystem. Playing the Ecosystem Canvas with UCL actors and local ecosystem actors we learned that there is a large gap between the actors' individual understanding and perspectives on the four question themes in the game: key factors, key determinants, entrepreneurial skills, and ever-changing environments. The game improved the students' understanding of:

- their own role in EEE: 'I see very clearly how the dialogical relationships affect me as a student, and what influences the different actors have upon me in the matter of the learning process, but also my own role in the EEE as an active actor and not just a passive bystander.'
- value: 'I see myself being motivated to do better, so I can be of some value to those organizations [in the ecosystem]'.
- their own learning: 'Every time anyone interacts with another person, both can gain something valuable from the interaction . . . Any interaction can broaden our horizons and provide us with valuable lessons that we then incorporate into our own 'cultural backpack', which we later can share with others in our future interactions'.

Customization

The game can be customized for different local contexts.[21] It can be played several times by the same players. Each time a new Q-piece challenges the actors' (players) understanding of learning, value, and dialogical relations a new context is present. Learning is a constant process driven by conflicts, differences and disagreements. The game is designed to help, guide, move and develop the actors to gain further insights into how the other players perceive the four different factors, key factors,[22] key determinants,[23] entrepreneurial skills,[24] and ever-changing environment[25] shaping the ecosystem and affecting the learning process.

Patterns

The *Ecosystem Canvas* game addresses the overarching challenge for students and entrepreneurs to make full use of external competencies and potential in the ecosystem around them. It utilizes the flow patterns of *EXPERIENTIAL LEARNING* and *DILEMMA SOLVING*. These are realized based on component patterns such as *STORYTELLING, ROLES, CHALLENGES* and *DEDICATED FACILITATORS* (see Figure 12.2 for visual depiction).

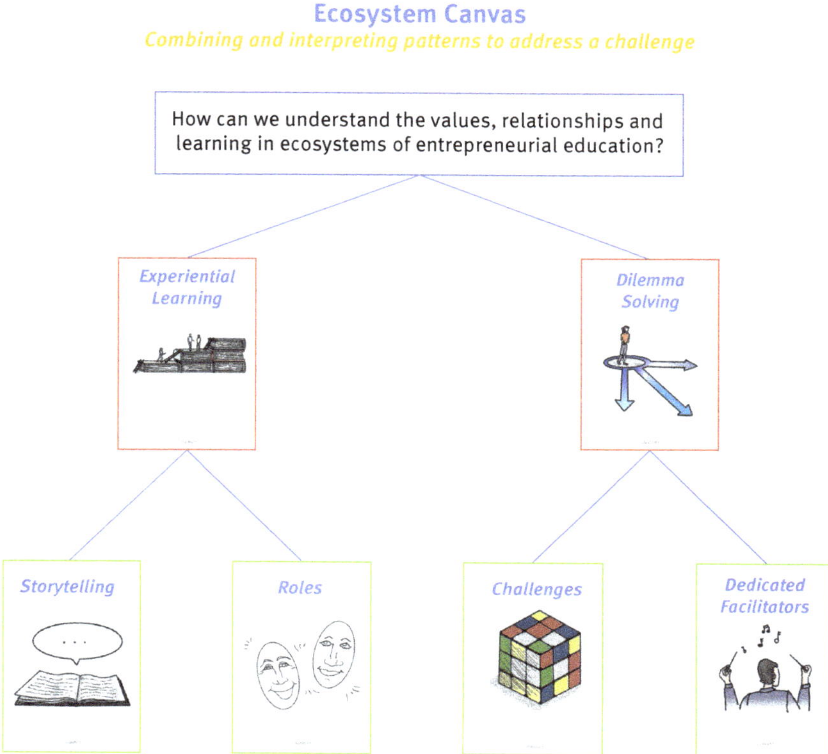

Figure 12.2: A selection of flow and component patterns contributing to the *Ecosystem Canvas* game and its innovation challenge.

Chapter 13
Games: *Lego serious play*

Sandra Dijk & Sina Plietzsch & Claudia Lehmann

How can we facilitate knowledge sharing, problem solving, strategizing and decision making among innovators and entrepreneurs? LEGO Serious Play provides workshop participants with a common medium to address innovation-related questions by building and discussing 3D models.

Figure 13.1: Example of a Lego model to open a discussion.

The LEGO *Serious Play (LSP)* method is a workshop format for group work experiences that utilize object-mediated communication to facilitate knowledge sharing, problem solving, strategy development and decision making.[1] Participants create their own models, which are then discussed and combined to create a shared vision of a solution (Figure 13.1). The goal of the exercise is to enhance creativity and communication and to improve innovation management and business performance.[2]

Challenge

A recurring business challenge is to make decisions that everyone is willing to follow, even if they do not fully agree with them. In addition, it is difficult to grasp the big picture of complex and multi-layered problems, to find connections and to explore a range of options and possible solutions. This requires a method that fosters creativity, engages all participants in the discussion and gives them the opportunity to express themselves. LEGO provides such a method. Its application fields include creation of strategy or scenarios, problem solving and conflict management, visioning, *IDEATION*, prototyping, as well as teambuilding and coaching.

https://doi.org/10.1515/9783110725582-019

Purpose

Lego Serious Play (*LSP*) is an innovative and effective method to explore complex issues without obvious answers. It enables deeper insights into problems and unlocks more creative solutions through storytelling, meaning making and experimentation. It appeals to the creativity of the participants to fully exploit the insights, ideas and imagination available in the organization by using LEGO elements.[3] This follows the goal of describing and making sense of the existing business to initiate change and improvement and even to create something radically new while including heterogeneous team members who have the opportunity to express themselves building 3D LEGO models. The combination of hand-mind coordination uncovers new knowledge and ideas through a process that is sometimes referred to as constructionism.[4] It leads to a more effective reflection process and supports an effective dialogue for everyone in the organization.

Methodology

The idea for the *LSP* methodology dates back to 1996, when professors Johan Roos and Bart Victor at the International Institute for Management Development (IMD) in Switzerland and LEGO Group CEO and owner Kjeld Kirk Kristiansen explored alternative strategic planning tools and systems. In the process, they developed a new method of strategy development, later referred to as *Lego Serious Play*, which integrated underlying theoretical notions concerning autopoiesis, complex adaptive systems, collective mind, imagination and storytelling.[5]

During the workshop, landscape models are built with *MODELLING MATERIALS*, in this case LEGO elements, which are given meaning by inventing stories and then acting out different scenarios. This process can help to deepen reciprocal understanding, generate insights and improve team spirit in a playful way.

LSP workshops are group processes designed around a relatively limited number of powerful core concepts. These conceptual modules can be configured in a variety of ways to best meet a group's needs. A workshop based on *LSP* materials and methodology varies in the number of participants and duration depending on the topic. Typically, a full-day session is effective. Short sessions last 3–4 hours. The longest sessions can extend up to three days. Organizations, whether private or public, use the *LSP* methodology when they want to unleash the full potential of their people – and to encourage everyone to participate, contribute and commit to the solution. Workshops can focus on innovation challenges or strategy development, to create a physical prototype or a tangible structure of a conceptual, intangible idea.[6]

Participants

During the workshop, all participants are asked questions about an ongoing task, project or strategy. To answer those questions, they build metaphorical or symbolic models of their experiences, insights and ideas using LEGO pieces and present them to their peers. This requires open-minded and committed participants[7] and a free-thinking, non-judgmental and playful interaction between them.[8] *LSP* – like most innovation and creativity techniques – works best with interdisciplinary and heterogeneous teams. Groups of a size between four to eight people view the problem on hand from different perspectives. Their complementary individual experiences and knowledge lead to a solution. The fact that all participants have equal rights results in a solution with which many can identify. Participants can create additional models to enrich the solution and create a network of ideas and entities.

Gameplay

The core processes of *LSP* include four steps. Normally, the questions will be posed in Step 1 (challenge) and determine the content toward step 2 (construction), then step 3 (sharing), sharing constructions with others in the group and, lastly, step 4 (reflection) where participants reflect on the overview and output of the activity.[9]

1. **Challenge.** The *DEDICATED FACILITATOR* sets a complex question that all participants then address, and sets the time for building with the LEGO bricks. Questions are considered complex if they do not allow for clear right or wrong answers and if different feelings, knowledge and experiences can lead to different answers. Often participants are asked about their personal motivation, their special skills, a vision for a better future, their ideas for new products or a perfect business strategy. The goal is to bring out the individual ideas before connecting them to a shared solution.
2. **Building.** Each participant faces the challenge and answers the question by creating their own personal model. The connection between hands and brain helps unlock existing and new ideas by activating not conscious processes. The building bricks are a tool that participants use to find and develop ideas. Usually there is a limited time, starting with approximately 20 minutes (timeboxing). Decisions made under time constraints are usually at least as good as those made without time constraints, sometimes even better, but most importantly, people are often happier when making fast decisions.

   In most cases, the participants have not used LEGO bricks for a long time or have even never used them. Therefore, it usually makes sense to plan a short warm-up exercise and let the participants build a bridge, for example, so that they can familiarize themselves with the bricks available.

3. **Sharing.** After creating their personal model, participants are asked to tell a story about the model that answers the original question. Through this *STORY-TELLING*, the others see how the model answers the question. The methodology is based on the insight that people think as they speak. Sharing allows the other participants to understand the model, gain new insights, see the problem from a different perspective and combine another person's possible solution with their own ideas. Steps 1 to 3 can be repeated several times during a session.
4. **Reflection.** The final step presents the greatest challenge to the presenter. A *DEDICATED FACILITATOR* should recap the stories without anticipating a compromise. This should be worked out by the teams. A good facilitator must be able to shift gears quickly and have plenty of experience to reflect and highlight commonalities, conflicts and irritations from a bird's eye view. It also helps to ask the participants about their feelings after each round to check their motivation, obstacles or possible reactions.

The workshop is finished when a common vision of a good solution is found. This is done by the participants combining their individual models into a common model. The most important findings or key aspects of the solution should be condensed into a statement with 3–5 simple words or key points. Sometimes the Lego models are not dismantled after the workshop, but remain in a room for weeks, months or even years while the joint strategy is elaborated upon and implemented. The model may be changed as new insights are gained as the environment changes or as hypotheses are proven correct or incorrect. For the purpose of good documentation, it is also advisable to photograph the models in detail and to label them digitally so that the numerous ideas and thoughts do not get lost.

Exemplary case

In one case an international company headquartered in Germany wanted to innovate their business model, especially with regard to their sustainability strategy. The first step towards that goal was a two-day *LSP* strategy workshop with employees from different branches. In this context, LEGO bricks were used for constructing different business model scenarios, especially to facilitate group collaboration, support a deeper level of understanding, explore relationships between different parts of the business model as well as to discuss proposed solutions. With the help of *LSP* participants were able to see and understand the project's systemwide impact. Potential problem areas were identified by the team members that were not obvious to them before the workshop.

In addition, the approach provided a sustainable learning outcome for the participants by allowing them to develop their own content and deal with the topic of business models in a detailed yet hands-on manner. Participants enjoyed the learning experience, and particularly the playful and participatory way of developing and applying knowledge.

Customization

The *LSP* methodology has been developed primarily for use in business contexts. It works across a very broad range of industries and areas. Large organizations, as well as educational institutions have benefited from the methodology. Only the nature of the problem and the beliefs of the organization seeking to solve that problem limit the method's applicability. How successful an *LSP* workshop turns out to be depends on the organization's culture. The workshop is only rewarding if the organization believes in the potential of each employee to act and think strategically[10].

LSP works for every person in any culture. There are no requirements to meet for someone to participate in the workshop. They don't need any experience with LEGO bricks, or need to consider themselves creative. The only customization *LSP* needs making the question specific to the organization and the goal being pursued in the workshop.

How can *LSP* be conducted *online*? *LSP* was made for collaborative problem solving, and thrives on interaction and joint construction. Although *LSP* was designed for hands-on modelling in the physical world, the method has made the step into the digital environment with the beginning of the home office era. A new challenge was the lack of a tactile component in the digital experience. The method remains the same while the medium changes with the creative use of digital tools. The result is not inferior to the physical model if it is appropriately prepared and moderated. The demands placed on the workshop leader have increased. In addition to a good knowledge of the *LSP* method, experience and tact in the moderation of online meetings are especially needed.

In an online setting, workshop participants receive a Lego set by mail before the meeting or use their own if available. As in traditional workshops, the goal of *LSP* online is for participants to approach a central issue through modelling creative thoughts.

At the beginning of the workshop, the participants familiarize themselves with the digital tools. As in the classic *LSP* process, the central question is formulated by the facilitator. The participants build their individual model using the LEGO bricks. Then they present their model with the webcam and share its story with the group. Once all participants have shared their models and answered all the group's questions, the next phase of the workshop begins.

The models are photographed, digitized and uploaded using digital whiteboard tools such as Miro. This step can be challenging for some participants, which is why intensive onboarding with the whiteboard tool is essential. The individual virtual models are then combined into a virtual common model. The merged whiteboard model represents the shared vision of the best possible solution to the central challenge.

Even if the process is quite different in important ways from the classic approach, online *LSP* has the advantage of allowing virtual teams to solve their problems across borders and time zones.

Patterns

The *LSP* method and language can be used to solve all kinds of problems through workshops and *WORKSHOP FACILITATION*, but it depends on *DEDICATED FACILITATORS* being trained in making the most effective use of the *MODELLING MATERIALS*. It can facilitate gamified interaction flows such as *IDEATION*, and engage participants in sharing their experiences in *STORYTELLING* exercises and taking on stakeholder *ROLES* in an innovation project (see Figure 13.2 for visual depiction).

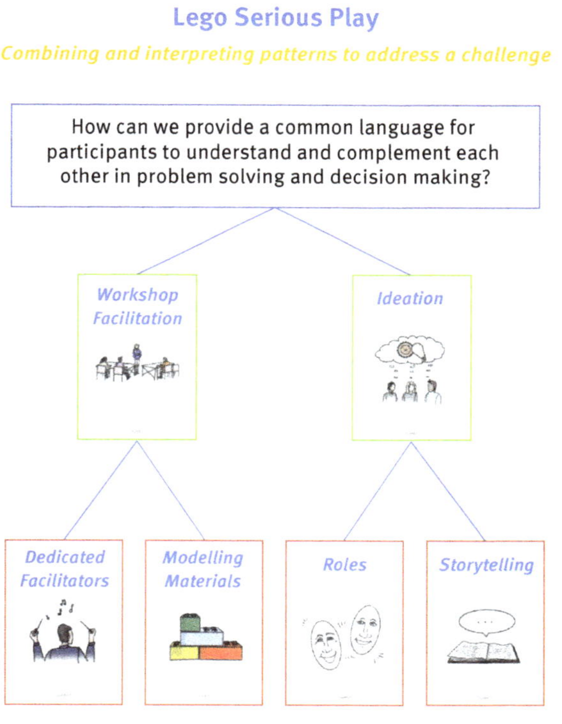

Figure 13.2: A selection of flow and component patterns contributing to the *Lego Serious Play* formats.

Part IV
Our future with games for innovation and entrepreneurship

https://doi.org/10.1515/9783110725582-020

The final part is dedicated to our future – the next generation among us and the challenges we pass on. We started with the bold claim of introducing a new *superpower*: One that enables a person to use, repurpose and create games that will help solve the great societal and organisational challenges companies, startups and public institutions are dealing with. Time will tell whether games are a 'superpower'. But if they are, then it will only be because we have found engaging ways to teach gamification, and to use it ourselves to meet the grand challenges of our time.

In this final part we look into innovations that gamification and games can bring to education, and how we empower students as future innovators and emerging entrepreneurs to use gamification. We also look into future business and organisational challenges that we need to address – with or without games – but, as we believe we have demonstrated in this book, games and gamification have an important contribution to make.

Chapter 14 focusses on education. 'Bread and circuses' is an old prejudice against games. If we don't just want to distract people from what really matters in the real world, and if we want to excite, engage and empower people to tackle the challenges they care about, we need to find out more about how games work and how they create a positive impact.

Chapter 15 gives a glimpse into what might be next in gamification for innovation and entrepreneurship: While exciting new technologies and materials are becoming available, some business challenges they address will always be with us – like aligning strategy and organizational culture or managing values for innovation – and other grand challenges – like enabling a sustainable development and preserving democracy – are becoming even more urgent. This last part is dedicated to those educational and grand societal challenges.

Chapter 16 concludes with an invitation to contribute your experience, your game design patterns and challenges to a growing community of practice.

Chapter 14
Education: Games for learning and training and teaching gamification

In educational settings gamification and games enable new forms of encounter between students, teachers and companies. Gamification design patterns can be used for professional training and education.

Games are increasingly part of the teaching, training and coaching repertoire, and teaching gamification and game development have become subjects of study on their own. This chapter shows how games are already being used to facilitate professional development, teaching and learning. In some case they are used to create new interaction architectures between students and teachers, or between companies and students. The chapter concludes with an outline on how to teach gamification and games for I&E using the design pattern approach.

14.1 Games for learning, teaching and training

There is extensive scope in a variety of contexts for using games as part of an approach to learning, from classroom or lecture theatre to workshops and beyond. Collections of games are part of the resource base used by in-company trainers, consultants and lecturers going back to the 1960s,[1] but only recently has the growth of the internet created the rich variety of material on which we can draw today.

Several drivers are pushing the popularity of games and gamification among teachers and professional development experts. Students and professionals are increasingly turned off by the rigid didactic approach of the classic lecture or leader's speech. Games, by contrast, create a two-way communication path embedded in a ludic space (see chapter 2). All parties learn from the activity, and new perspectives and knowledge generation are encouraged. Indeed, in a post-industrial society these ludic flavours have become an essential taste in learning.[2] Corporate training and coaching nowadays are guided by experiential and action-oriented formats that lead to high engagement. For leaders in organizations and for teachers in higher education this also means to some degree letting go of the full control. While they still need to prepare and give talks, these need to be complemented by experiential learning styles.

For instance, in *higher education* the shift to 'flipped classroom' models (in which students read or otherwise prepare work on concepts ahead of classroom interaction)

https://doi.org/10.1515/9783110725582-021

means that students and teachers now have more time for exploring and elaborating the concepts being learned – and games provide a powerful way of doing this.

In *companies and public sector organizations* the challenge is often one of engaging learners who may be caught up in daily routines to be able to respond to alternative, sometimes disruptive ways of moving on to new and better ways of doing things. Here games offer motivation and fun as integral parts of workshop-based approaches. From our own consulting experience, we know that basic methodologies such as modelling future scenarios based on potential future signals and assessing key influencing factors are often difficult to understand, much less to integrate on a daily basis for practitioners preoccupied with short-term operations. Gamified learning around a 'live' project with some priority on their to-do list offers a path to leave their daily routines behind.

The expansion of *online* learning helps extend the reach of educational programmes to a wider audience and the Covid-19 pandemic has accelerated this expansion. Effective distance learning thrives on a high variety of input. It can be tedious to work full-time on a screen, passively consuming content, and games provide an interactive alternative to working with course materials. At the moment there is an abundance of software options that, when combined with in-person activities and the tangibility of offline games, offer a set of both online and in-person activities that can be quite powerful.

When selecting and adapting an approach, first consider the learning contexts (see chapter 6.2). Are you dealing with small or large groups, in an online or face-to-face setting, involving participants inside or also outside the organization, experienced practitioners or less experienced students in classrooms? There are targeted applications in classrooms and training courses that focus on delivering predefined knowledge or skills. There are also emergent applications that enable an organization to learn about itself and to resolve problems or tensions (for instance, in teambuilding or strategizing). In this case, insights and concepts emerge from gamified interactions.

14.2 New forms of encounter between students and companies

For many students there is a gap between the concepts they are learning in the classrooms and their practical application in in workplaces they have yet to experience. Typically, undergraduates will not have had much direct experience of working in organizations. Many of the situations and challenges they are presented with remain somewhat abstract and theoretical. Realistic, but fictional or past cases and games can bring such situations to life, engaging players in simulations that recreate a version of 'live' experience – for example, in starting up a new venture or being a senior manager with complex responsibilities.

The reverse is also true. Students and even more so professionals who are working in organizations may find themselves too close to the day-to-day business and find it hard to distance themselves and focus on something new. Outside the traditional classroom setting, short intensive in-company programmes can be conducted as games. Games can help recreate and focus the learners' experience in an alternative world, from which they are able to transfer what they have learned from the game world to their real one.

We find that there are two ways for students to get closer to innovation activities in companies. The first one is connected to the games presented earlier in the book. For these to work in classrooms the key is to develop realistic cases that are either fictional or based on past cases. Game-based learning can be further scaled as full courses or even curricula. For example, Wilcox and colleagues have redesigned the entrepreneurship curriculum to one based on a series of games and live experiences followed by reflection and reinforcement.[3] Organizations like Venturewell provide learning resources – a significant proportion of which is game-based – to support start-up training and education.[4] Evaluation suggested that while students enrolled in the lecture-based course learned the material equally as well as the students from the game-based course, the latter students had more positive working relationships in their teams and exhibited more entrepreneurial skills.

The second way is to let students experiment in companies and organizations, and use gamified co-creation formats to challenge directions and accelerate organisational development. A Play-Based Intrapreneurship master's degree course at Design School Kolding, Denmark does exactly this.

In the development of this experimental course[5] we asked: Can we put students in the passenger's seat or even in the driver's seat of organizational development processes? Can organizations move beyond classic internship formats to integrate students more fully? And can students and organizations co-design tangible games to reach common understandings and push in new directions?

The course design pursues a vision of closing the gap between school-oriented work and professional work. For students, it creates the space and conditions to engage in processes in which something is at stake. Participants from the organizations experience that outside-in perspectives are key to challenging habitual thinking. By comparing their experiences with organizational constraints and culture, students also gain competence to review potentially unhealthy routines and underlying assumptions in organizations. Through a series of co-creation activities based on play and game principles, students shape both the processes and the component actions. They create quick design thinking games with a few tangible metaphors and process steps in order to challenge dominant perspectives and reframe directions. However, this unconventional course design challenges all involved actors – students, organizational collaborators and teachers. Teachers need to support just-in-time learning on the spot in the organization. Organizations need to onboard and work with students and allow them to run initiatives beyond the established internship tracks.

For the students, results from over the last four years show that it is through such courses that they learn to open doors to organizations, work constructively and meet challenges continuously and consider organizational constraints an incentive to be creative. Students learn to take the initiative, and prioritize a multitude of tasks. For students, this approach often leads to their first job, or connections that open doors to their next collaboration. For organizations, we see benefits not only on a project level, but also on a strategic, visionary and organizational culture level. It comes in the sometimes messy, co-creative, visual and tangible game-based way that we firmly believe gives a much richer development and learning experience for all involved.

In the master's module on Gamification for Organizations at the University of Applied Sciences for Media, Communication and Management (HMKW) in Berlin, Germany, we actively work with the Gamification Design Patterns described in the previous chapters, and experiment with different pattern configurations and designs to sketch new innovation games.

14.3 Teaching gamification with patterns

It makes sense to teach gamification for innovation and entrepreneurship (I&E) using gamified formats. This section outlines how and provides such an approach and an exemplary educational module that teachers and professional trainers are welcome to adapt to their own needs. In fact, they often appreciate the pattern collection as a compact yet lightweight resource for their courses. All the content and materials required are included in this book or available through the companion sites, and we also invite you to experiment with different designs and share your experiences and add your own materials there.

The pattern collection builds on a *research-based learning* approach that enables students to generate insights with relevance for others in a self-directed manner. Its sequence follows the phases from framing the research question (or innovation challenge) to selecting and applying methods, to generating, examining and presenting results.[6] This outline also acknowledges the difficulty that students in academic programs want to learn about games and gamification, but usually lack first-hand experience and in-depth theoretical knowledge about I&E, its essential concepts and methods and its relevance in practice. Their first challenge is often to understand what an innovation challenge is in the first place, how to source the knowledge needed to capture and formulate it, and how to address it with conventional innovation methods.

Introduction and warm-up with games

The module outline consists of three stages: *introduction, project and reflection.* The introduction covers the potential for gamification to drive innovation and entrepreneurship, basics about play, games and gamification and a core body of knowledge on innovation and entrepreneurship (roughly following part I). Discussions of case studies provide insights into the opportunities and risks of gamified approaches to tackle innovation challenges in practice. In an academic context, discussing recent research will familiarize learners with research questions and methods. A learning outcome for students is an advanced understanding of the state of the art in gamification for I&E and an ability to critically assess current research.

Practising what you preach, from the very beginning use games to facilitate interaction among the students and with the teacher or trainer. For instance, the *Proximity Seeker* game (chapter 11) can be used as a warm-up format for the module which allows the participants to get to know one another. Videos from the *Shift* game (chapter 10) help convey a better understanding of innovation-related issues and barriers.

A journey of gamified gamification (JOGG)

The second and main part of the module takes students on a *gamified journey*, a gamified gamification project addressing a real innovation challenge. This gamified journey builds itself on flow design patterns like *AWARENESS RAISING, EXPERIENTIAL LEARNING* and *IDEATION* together with component patterns like *STORYTELLING* and *CHALLENGES*, *COOPERATION* and *COMPETITION*, *MAPPING* and *PITCH*. Participants take the *ROLES* of game designers preparing a pitch to a corporate client. This is how it works:

The course participants collaborate in small groups representing innovation consulting and design agencies. They are invited to name (and later, when their project is more advanced to rename) the agency to foster team spirit and social cohesion. Their agencies may collaborate throughout the process, but in the end they compete against each other in a round of pitches in which they present their work results to a client. Their challenge is to create a game or gamified format that addresses a real innovation challenge of a corporate client. Ideally this is a real business partner who provides a real innovation challenge from their organisation. Alternatively, well-documented case materials (e.g. from the games described in part III) can be used and presented by the teacher who then slips into the client's role. The client introduces an innovation challenge, for instance, how to improve corporate sustainability (chapter 7) or how to create and manage future scenarios for a business unit. There is either one company innovation challenge for all the agency teams, or different departments of the company each request a different proposal from the agency teams but the budget is only granted to one of them after the final round of pitches.

To make their mission tangible, each team of students is equipped with a physical bag (we call *bagpack*) that contains scaffolding and *MODELLING MATERIALS* for them to master the journey: the Game Design Canvas and the patterns overview (chapter 4.3), the full deck of the *Gamification Design Pattern Cards* including cards to sketch new patterns, a joker and a progress board. The joker can be played in a critical situation to gain additional resources or options (like contributions from another group or skipping a step). The progress board (a Kanban-like board) serves as a shared playing field, sequencing the progress of the groups and depicting them on a shared map. It shows five rows of activities for each student group and three steps for each activity. Each group can only enter a new activity row when the steps from an upper row are finished (Figure 14.1). Three icons (like the flower, planet and lens below) can be used to show where each group is on the progress board.

First, each agency specifies the innovation or entrepreneurial challenge. Participants interview a contact partner of the client and as far as possible other stakeholders (roughly following the process described in section 6.1). They start to fill in the canvas before they specify the relations between its fields, dive into open issues and revise. Second, they review the flow and component patterns and select the ones they intend to work with. Once the relations are roughly mapped, they specify how each pattern should be interpreted and consider alternative combinations until they find a sound concept. Here, students should also be encouraged to develop new flow and component patterns that are missing from the current set of 26 patterns. It is usually helpful to decide on a key metaphor and storyline for the overarching gameflow. Third, the whole game or gamified format or some of its key elements are implemented into a prototype. This usually involves an iterative approach, as the pattern selection and combination and their interpretations can be revised. Fourth, the game prototype is evaluated, ideally with real players from the client organisation – as a fall-back solution, students from the other groups can take their place. Based on feedback and observation of gameplay, the prototype can be revised. Finally, each agency pitches its game or gamified format – using presentations, video demonstrations or interactive formats. Using one of these formats can also be part of the challenge.

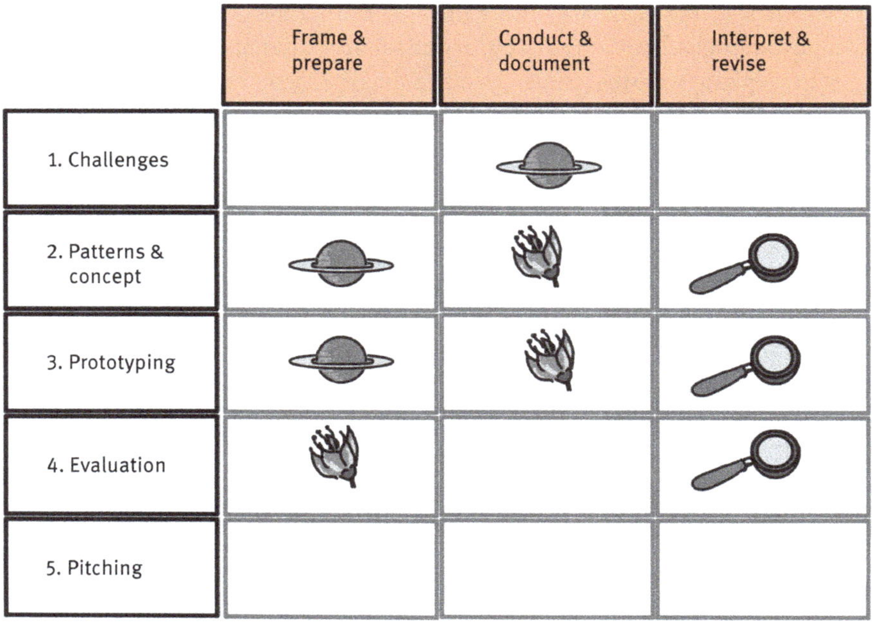

Figure 14.1: Progress board used to structure progress of student teams.

Learning outcomes include the know-how to identify and frame design challenges for gamification, skills to collaboratively sketch and iteratively develop alternative game formats, and understand how and why games work or do not work as intended, based on first-hand experiences.

Reflection

In a final round of reflections, the whole journey (not just the pitches and feedback) should be reviewed and discussed on an individual and group basis. Guiding questions will depend on the nature of the agency's innovation challenge and their reaction to the pitches. Exemplary questions for discussion are: Which insights from the introduction (and assigned literature) helped us to navigate the process? What additional knowledge would have been helpful? How did we know we had identified the right innovation challenge? How did we collaborate as a group? How did we experience collaboration and competition with the other teams? Which main hurdles did we face as a group, and what were the reasons for these? How did we or could we have overcome them? What was the most helpful thing in the *bagpack*, what would we add? What did we learn from which kind of feedback in each step? How would we redesign the process based on what we know now?

Relating the discussion of these and other questions to the cases and insights from the literature may then lead to follow-up research questions. A short reflection paper together with the documented pitches serve as an additional reference for grading or follow-up projects. To wrap up the module try a discussion of recent trends and the future potential of games to tackle some of the grand innovation challenges described in the next and final chapter.

Chapter 15
What's next? Future challenges and chances for gamification

Tracking and sustaining impact of games is a difficult and constant effort.Technological and material developments create new opportunities to deal with our future and grand innovation challenges.

We have covered a wide range of challenges for innovators and entrepreneurs that can be addressed by means of gamification and games developed explicitly for this purpose. In this chapter we look ahead into the future. We point to some of the persisting challenges for gamification and speculate about the potential of games. We discuss how to validate the positive impact of games, and review some technology-based developments. We end like we started the book – by pointing to enduring innovation challenges for innovators and entrepreneurs and to those that are trending.

15.1 Tracking and sustaining impact

One key aspect of validating games is tracking their impact, that is, determining what exactly happens during the game so that new insights can inform future iterations in game design. Researchers will want to compare alternative designs or different combinations of design patterns in order to optimize a game for a particular innovation challenge. Researchers (and practitioners) will want to know, using qualitative and quantitative data, whether a gamified intervention has a positive impact. Experimental research could compare the quality of results produced by groups working with different ideation games. However, it is largely impossible to conduct a longitudinal study tracking the effects of a single activity in a complex innovation process. Instead we can focus on limited timeframes and look into pivotal moments of interaction when dialogue and content move in novel directions, create tension or result in radical new viewpoints. This makes it easier to detect a game's impact in a particular context, and aggregate findings from different contexts. For instance, in a research setting one researcher focusses on their role as game facilitator while the other observes, with both switching roles during the game. The use of video allows live experiences and interpersonal interactions to be recorded[1] – even micro-interactions that are happening simultaneously. Ethnography[2] provides a suitable methodology for such an assessment.

https://doi.org/10.1515/9783110725582-022

As we saw in our first cases in chapter 1, we can focus on immediate 'after-action' responses to evaluate a game's impact. Although this is impractical over long periods of time, immediate after-actions can often be observed, at least to a degree. After the *ACT Dilemma* game (chapter 5.3) was played in a FinTech company, the use of values was observed in everyday work conversations after the gamified intervention. When games focus on specific strategic actions, follow-up inquiries can reveal whether participants chose to follow new paths or not, and discover the reasoning behind these choices. For games designed for training purposes, the focus would be on how well the participants grasp the learning content of the game.

Table 15.1 describes four ways of capturing data from game activities. In-action data can be captured on video, if this is acceptable to all participants. It is the best way to have a second look at interactions and analyse the complex micro-interactions that occur in very short periods of time. Photos can be taken of all outcomes. Notes and a brief report should be written up immediately after the game. Focus group reflections provide participant feedback on the game, and follow-up interviews provide insights into what longer term impact the game has had.

Table 15.1: Four ways of capturing data from game activities.

Type	Capturing complex interactions	Capturing outcomes	Capturing reflection on action immediately after game	Capturing reflection on action sometime after game
How	Using video cameras to capture interaction, dialogue and content	Using camera to capture visual outcomes and displays; taking notes on observations	Focus group session to discuss content and outcomes	In-depth interviews to determine long-term impact
Why	Fine-grain analysis of interactions reveals attitudes and thought processes: root causes of problems and novel solutions	A timely brief illustrated report provides decision-makers with needed and fresh input.	Debriefing and a focus group session aid participants to reflect on their experiences	The impact of a gamification intervention can only be determined by its long-term impact

15.2 Technological developments and embodiment

As we have seen, games are a powerful device to engage stakeholders and provide new perspectives to explore different topics. Not surprisingly they have become a key resource for professional development, with a sizeable industry built around designing games. One feature of this development is the application of innovation to games themselves. Whether it is the use of new technologies to enable new kinds of interaction and gameplay, the use of portable devices and interactive spaces to set out on radically new directions, or the development of novel game rules and procedures – there is plenty of activity along this moving frontier.

The widespread adoption of new technologies is changing the ways in which games are created and delivered. New augmented realities, advanced personal platforms and artificial intelligence applications create new application formats and new possibilities for future games. Online collaboration platforms (like Mural, Miro, Conceptboard or Jamboard) combine visual overviews, simple navigation and interaction techniques which infuse play and game triggers. Other digital platforms are focused on game-based learning content for students and organizations with the goal of constructing a repository of options for users to customize their own games.

With virtual and augmented reality (VR/AR) becoming more widely available, delivery technologies provide new experiences. The potential for interactive gameplay in virtual space is increasing as major players like Facebook reconfigure their business model around the 'metaverse' – a collective three-dimensional space where physical and virtual reality converge. New versions of existing games can be 'ported' into virtually enhanced environments, opening up new interactive possibilities. Massive multiplayer games like *Warcraft* have been around for some time, and *Second Life* demonstrated an early version of a metaverse in which online interaction – using avatars, virtual locations and such – took place in parallel with the real world. This trend is likely to accelerate and open up increasing opportunities for remote access to gaming worlds, raising the possibility for large and globally distributed organizations to build interactive communities. In the field of I&E this could lead to more cross-border collaboration, asynchronous participation, content generation and increasingly more realistic environments. Serious digital games have been around for a while, but they are still costly to develop. Online simulation software will bring down these costs and provide a platform allow the rapid creation and customization of games for specific needs – creating a digital sandbox where different shapes can be easily created.

The availability of simple tools to build apps and websites can be used as elements in building new games experiences. The *60-Minute MVP* building game developed by an Experiential Entrepreneurship programme in the USA is a good example of such an approach.[3] It uses online tools such as website builder templates and Facebook adverts in much the same way as LEGO bricks or *Post-It notes* play a role in today's games toolbox.

Increasing use of personal and wearable platforms, devices equipped with new sensors, pedometer and location-based services, and the continuing rise of mobile gaming on hand-held devices boost the potential of 'pocket' games which can be quickly accessed and played in many different locations. In the I&E space, portable devices are increasingly used to generate game content and to quickly and easily document outcomes. They can also be used to quickly capture a scenario developed in-game, which can then be acted out or simulated from diverse and surprising perspectives. At the same time advances in machine learning and artificial intelligence are likely to mean that agent-based games become increasingly lifelike with interactions and outcomes driven by sophisticated and adaptive algorithms rather than the simple roll of a dice. The potential here is breath-taking: it was some ago that AlphaGo beat the best *chess* player in the world and it has now mastered the much more complex game of *Go*. The likelihood of simulated *ROLES* approximating the actions of real people is increasing. In many online simulations each choice and move made by the participants can be saved and stored, leading to datasheets that facilitate self-reflection and that allow comparison with the choices made by other participants, groups and even competing companies.

While these technological developments will increasingly create new forms of communication, the isolated 'arenas' during the covid-19 pandemic clearly show that reliance on online media entails a loss of social interaction and tangibility that severely reduces the possibility of reaching deep mutual understanding in cross-disciplinary settings. The future of innovation games must therefore also lead to the exploration and creation of tangible games where materials, space and roleplay are used as means to bring to the surface tacit knowledge and bring forward those perspectives and ideas that are not otherwise easily communicated. Many of the games described in this book embody affordances and build on the importance of highly tangible and visual boards and maps. For instance, *Business Model Branching* relies on a bigger 'branch model' where participants write on bricks and move them around. The *Lego Serious Play* approach has at its core tangible bricks that promote metaphorical, strategic thinking, while the *Shift* game also uses floor space to invite bodily movement and positioning. New frontiers for these tangible games include moving away from materials reliant on playing cards and tables to make use of the full location space, including the floor, walls and furniture. The use of embodiment, enactment and role-play are powerful ways to engage participants in games.

Alongside developments in technology and embodiment, we are likely to see a broader range of application contexts for games. Whereas games were often confined to classroom or workshop settings in the past, we have already seen an extension of their application to contexts where they can form part of the innovation agenda itself. Many of the games in part III operate in this fashion as part of the day-to-day work experience, facilitating exploration and innovation in 'live' organizational contexts.

15.3 Foundational challenges and trending application contexts for games

While it would clearly be impossible to make a complete list of future application contexts, we can have a brief look at those basic innovation-related business challenges that are particularly tough and won't go away. Instead they are likely to become even more relevant in the near future. First we will outline three basic challenges, then three trending challenges.

Basic challenge 1: Organizational ambidexterity & rethinking organizational structures

Organizational ambidexterity as a response to the innovator's dilemma[4] continues to heavily influence how strategy and innovation processes are organized, launched and managed – in particular, who from the organization should participate in such processes. In today's markets characterized by a high degree of complexity and temporary competitive advantages, it is a tough challenge for leaders to take on an ambidextrous mindset – one that spans on-going operations and innovation – and to establish it in the broader culture of the organisation. Games can play a significant role in pushing more employees and stakeholders to think beyond day-to-day operations and develop a range of future scenarios which help them tackle needed radical changes.

We just need to stretch our imagination a little bit to take the next step here – to rethink the *organization as a serious game* that blurs the boundaries between the safe space of the game and the unsafe adventure of taking consequential decisions in the real world. *Innovation markets* already point in that direction when the bets of participants on different product and service design options are taken as stage-gate decisions that determine which option receives further funding.

Basic challenge 2: Aligning culture & strategy

'Culture eats strategy for breakfast', the famous slogan of Peter Drucker formulates another enduring challenge that is highly relevant for innovators and entrepreneurs. Actions speak louder than words and plans. But both strategic plans and the values constituting an organization's culture are subject to re-interpretation. New viewpoints can be explored in gamified excursions off the beaten track and otherwise overlooked team members and stakeholders can find their voice. The safe space games provide makes it easier for participants to speak up, to articulate their interpretations and to consider more or less appropriate actions to take. This can help everyone reach a shared understanding. By engaging and acting in alternative worlds, by working their way through scenarios, dilemmas and stories, players become familiar with what influences their actions, and what the consequences are. Playful encounters leave them better prepared to align corporate strategy with organizational culture.

Basic challenge 3: Managing values for innovation

Revising and realizing organisational values are often difficult to handle in a repeatable, engaging and action-oriented manner. Games are an excellent way to raise awareness of this challenge and to support these activities. They can be used to explore the systems of priorities that values represent, making implicit values explicit, determining the values of different stakeholder groups, and finding individual and organisational ways to translate them into action and repeatable practices. Easily accessible and scalable formats enable large numbers of diverse stakeholders to contribute to this integration process. Digital tools (like the one IBM used for its values and innovation jams) and gamification can be used to crowdsource and aggregate contributions for values-based innovation management.[5]

Trending challenge 1: Sustainability & circularity

While politicians and policymakers are increasingly prioritizing sustainability and circularity in their agendas, innovation managers are looking for approaches that would help them reach the triple-bottom line of economic, social and environmental value creation.[6] Gamification and games already play a role here. However, they can and need to do better, for instance to encourage a creativity as a counter to common sense solutions that foreclose the very potential for innovation they set out to explore. An example of this is found in a critical analysis of social imaginaries in six serious computer games addressing the energy transition – which revealed a fundamentally reductionist design approach.[7] The overarching narratives, the mechanics and the audio-visual design all treated renewable energy as an add-on to the current fossil fuel system, and prioritized technological developments over the potentials of social change, thereby stifling the development of radically new ideas. The challenge we see for game design is how to incorporate niches for true innovation and radical change in the imaginaries (and player actions and decision-making) so that games do not reproduce outdated socio-technical regimes.

Trending challenge 2: Entrepreneurial skill development

Beyond the immediate benefits of establishing a culture of innovation and entrepreneurship, gamified formats can enhance an experience-based development of 21st century skills such as managing non-routine interpersonal tasks,[8] and intrapreneurship or entrepreneurship.[9] Games play an important role where conventional language and concepts are unavailable or unhelpful. They provide access to tacit knowledge and allow the exploration of concepts without calling on formal or explicit knowledge. Instead they offer an experiential route to learning and entrepreneurial skill development. A case in point would be working with refugee entrepreneurs where the potential for providing a sense of identity as well as a livelihood is significant. Training the skills of entrepreneurship using conventional tools like books and spreadsheets may not be possible or appropriate but game-based simulations and other learning experiences can communicate the key concepts and help develop needed skills.[10] Other contexts include early year school programmes and skills development for people without business backgrounds – for example, arts-based entrepreneurship and social entrepreneurship.

Trending challenge 3: Democratizing innovation and sustaining democracy

Games can contribute to 'democratizing innovation'[11] by making complex issues accessible to a broad range of stakeholders in and outside organisations. Gamification has the potential to provide a unique approach to non-formal education, motivating young people and engaging diverse stakeholders in the future development of products, services, business models, work processes and new firms. Conversely, democratic institutions themselves can be strengthened through gamified applications such as election support systems which help voters with their decision-making[12] and make complex information easily accessible – also in thought-provoking ways. In countries like Germany, interactive tools like Wahl-o-mat[13] have already become an essential source of information for voters before elections, and for civic education.

For both basic and trending innovation challenges, there are endless opportunities to develop game formats that are enriching for all of us and pave the way to a desirable future. Now it's up to you to accept the challenge and go for it!

Chapter 16
Outlook: What's your future with games?

Before we close we invite you to reflect on how you might work with games in the future. Is there a role for games in your work as a teacher, trainer or coach? Or do you already work with games – if so we hope this book has given you some fresh insights, structures and techniques to revitalize your work with games. Or it may be that you are still at an early stage – and just dipping your toes in the water. What we've tried to do is to offer a pathway along which you might travel. As shown in chapter 6 there's a spectrum games that you can plug and play, you can adapt and configure, or you can design and make your own. Whatever you do, think of games as 'spices' that can enrich how you now teach, coach or consult.

You can use games as ways of bridging theory and practice in a classroom with students lacking practical experience, simulating different worlds to provide input to the learning cycle. You can use them as ways of recreating experiences from the world of practice – and then explore them in a 'safe space'. Set up a factory simulation – and let it crash. Your business doesn't really go bankrupt. Or try out 'off the wall' financial decisions in a start-up simulation – and see if they work. If not, the bailiffs won't be knocking on your door to repossess your home. Games allow you to freely experiment in life-like simulations – where the real-world consequences are learning what works, and what doesn't.

You can use games to deal with sensitive issues, bringing them to the surface in disguised form to recreate the tricky reality that players in the innovation world have to navigate. Eric Berne applied the concept of psychological scripts to games – patterns of human interaction which have structure and pay-offs and where the stakes may be high.[1] Thomas Harris and others developed this into a form of therapy based on the idea of 'transactional analysis' – in which the relationships between roles is played out as game scripts which can be reviewed and adapted.[2] Similarly, some of the games in this book allow players to learn to deal with tensions and experiment with alternative strategies so they can be resolved in a win-win fashion.

In games we can push the frontiers of innovation. After all, innovation management is about creating new routines – something we've seen games are very good at – so that 'the way we do things around here' becomes a culture of 'the way we innovate around here'. Innovation management is by definition a never-ending quest – because organizations are constantly being confronted with new and complex challenges posed by the ever-changing environments they operate in.

https://doi.org/10.1515/9783110725582-023

Some of the challenges we are now facing include remote working and redistributing the locus of interaction. Others involve fostering diversity, especially across generational and other identity boundaries, learning to work at a systems level, playing roles in networks where power is unevenly distributed, learning to be platform players and last but not least making innovation more values-based, responsible and inclusive. If we are to meet these challenges we will need to experiment with proto-routines – and strengthen the dynamic capability to do so. Games offer a powerful way of trying things out and prototyping behaviours, as we saw in part III, which surveyed how new games are developed and tested to help organizations surmount the challenges they are facing.

So, as we saw in part I, games have a key role to play in learning about innovation and entrepreneurship. What's next for you? We suggest you simply continue to explore games in a playful fashion and experiment with some of the ideas put forward in this book – including using our framework presented in part II to develop your own games for innovation and entrepreneurship.

Towards a community of practice

We also invite you to join us. Help us build a library of games by contributing your ideas and experiences with using and developing them. After all, the work on this book began in a collaborative knowledge alliance, creating a small-scale community of practice that built the prototype version. Now we want to grow that community on the companion sites. Take a look at www.gamify.site and www.uxberlin.com/gamification.

One of the most valuable assets we have is being able to draw on our collective experience of using games. What works? And why and how does it work? How can we best select and recombine flows and components to create games that will make a difference? How can we best make these games to provide reusable solutions to recurring challenges? There are numerous design patterns, games and gamified formats which might help foster innovation and entrepreneurship. We can help each other learn more about their potential. This is *our* innovation challenge.

We'd like to see this community of practice create a curated online library of games for I&E, and how we can access them. We're keen to tap into your experience so we can build a kind of travel website for games, one that gathers information about games, posts reviews and opinions about game-related content and helps us engage in interactive game forums. This would allow us to build on what we have already accomplished and identify gaps where something is needed.

What you'll find on the websites

On the companion sites to this book you'll find additional materials to support your gamification journey. First and foremost, our collection of gamification design patterns – both as a card deck and in a more detailed version that provides you with some of the theory and research that went into their development. You will find the games discussed in part III along with guidelines on how to customize them. You will also find more details about the original project, including videos, webinars, presentations. We have assembled links to many of the games currently available and, where possible, provide a brief summary with comments. There's already a rich set of resources awaiting you. The appendices will give you a taste of what to expect.

What we want you to do

Help us build this community of practice. Share the games you've already used. And please send us new ones you consider helpful in fostering innovation. Tell us whether they are free of charge or what the costs and conditions of use are. And let us know about your experiences with gamification design patterns we've included in the appendix (and in the extended version on the companion sites). Our collection of 36 patterns is far from complete – some may need further details or modification and there are more to add. We want this to be an open community, a shared resource from which we all can benefit. Your experiences could be invaluable to others. Like leaving a review on a travel website, tell us which games you would recommend? And which games you would steer clear of? Make a wish list. What kinds of games would you love to see developed? You never know – someone might just take up the challenge. Become a part of our community of practice. See you there!

Appendix 1
Gamification design patterns

Henning Breuer & Kiril Ivanov

https://doi.org/10.1515/9783110725582-024

Following this overview, we present a short version of the gamification design pattern collection introduced in chapter 4.3 (see companion site to download the card deck and an elaborate version including further references and examples).[1]

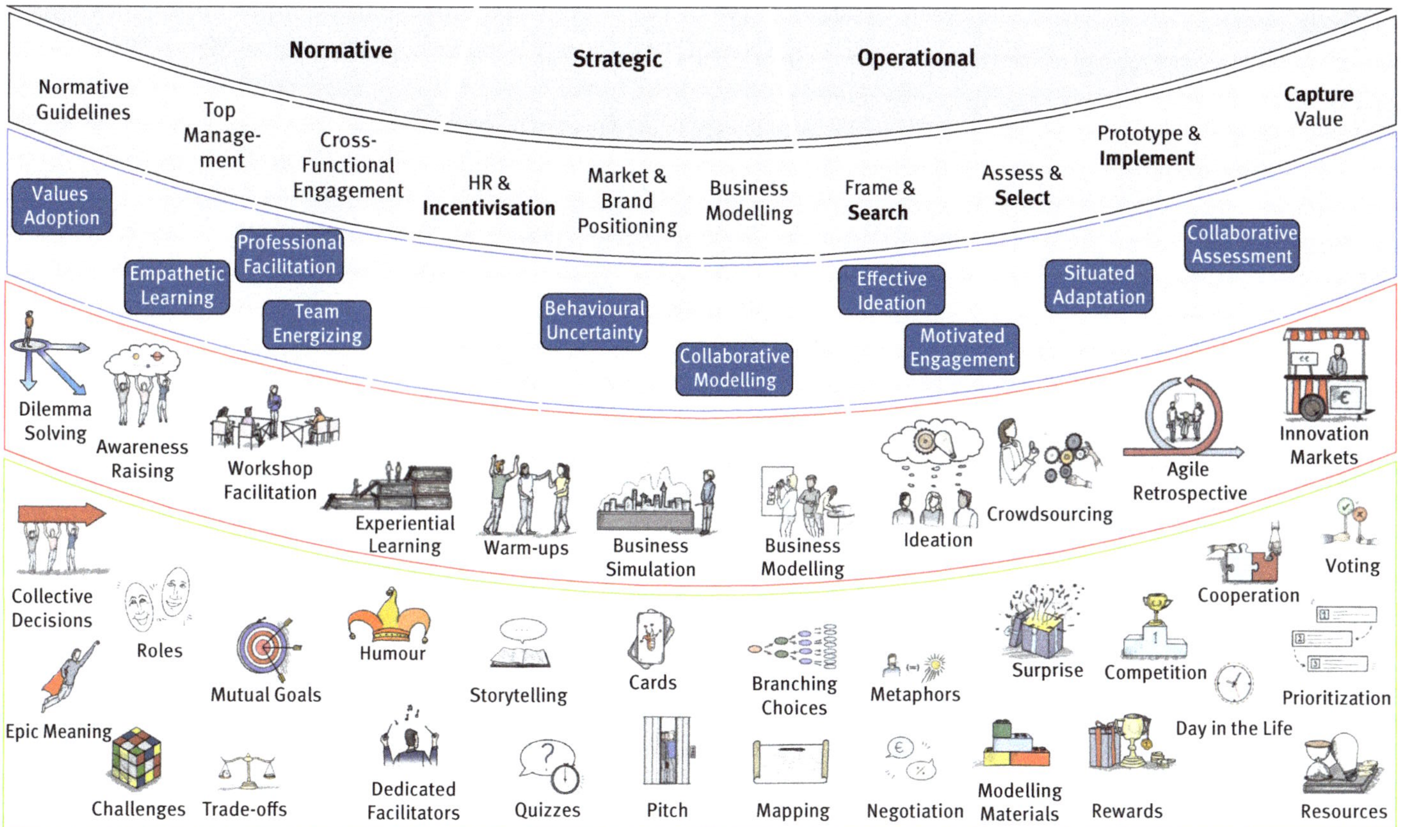

Figure A.1: Overview of innovation challenges and gamification design flow and component patterns to address them.

Flow Patterns

Agile Retrospective

Challenge: **How can we structure team reflection in order to improve agile collaboration?**
Solution: Use *agile retrospective* in meetings to reflect on and improve iterations over the course of a project. These games are designed with only one or a few game components (e.g. takingon *roles* of a shopper or vacationer to provide feedback, or *mapping* what each participant is mad, sad, or glad about). They improve team motivation and interaction.

Business Modelling

Challenge: **How can we facilitate collaborative business modelling that will provide a common reference point and generate new ideas?**
Solution: Gamified *business modelling* formats provide a framework and the methods to create and evaluate alternative business models. The flow provides a self-explanatory sequence of activities and reduces preparation time.

Dilemma Solving

Challenge: **How should we understand organisational values and turn them into actionable heuristics?**
Solution: *Dilemma solving* games help people interpret values – often in mission and vision statements – and their implications. By clarifying networks of beliefs, attitudes and intentions, they help align individual and organizational values and sensitize individuals to potential conflicts.

Experiential Learning

Challenge: **How can we best convey the knowledge and skills necessary for innovation?**
Solution: *Experiential learning* flows provide practicable means for conveying knowledge and developing innovation competencies. They promote experience, reflection, knowledge transfer and experimentation in a safe space.

Awareness Raising

Challenge: **How can we raise awareness for the practical implications of organisational values?**
Solution: Experiential workshops can *raise awareness* and foster the adoption of values, strategies and related practices. They allow participants to experience, apply, interpret and better understand a value or strategy, its implications and importance for their organization's culture.

Business Simulation

Challenge: **How can we anticipate challenges to innovation and prepare alternative courses of action?**
Solution: *Business simulations* can be used to explore plausible and/or desirable future scenarios, by taking anticipatory perspectives, reducing uncertainty and revealing innovation potential. Players advance their knowledge, skills and behaviors, such as collaboration or leadership, in a safe and realistic environment.

Crowdsourcing

Challenge: **How can we mobilize the problem-solving potential of a crowd?**
Solution: Gamified *crowdsourcing* flows and innovation tournaments enhance the motivation of all stakeholders in contributing to the innovation process by providing rewards or encouraging cooperation (e.g. feedback through likes and comments). They can also enhance contribution quality.

Ideation

Challenge: **How can we foster idea generation?**
Solution: The *ideation* flow creates a playful atmosphere and a safe space where participants explore diverse perspectives and approaches to a problem. Game rules and tangible symbols and activities provide a solid structure that balances freedom and constraint in the creative process.

Innovation Markets

Challenge: **How can we promote participation in assessing market potential?**
Solution: Participants in *innovation markets* invest virtual currency to screen, select and promote innovative ideas. Ideas meeting a predefined investment threshold move from the ideation to the implementation phase. This competitive scenario stimulates emotions such as joy, curiosity, ambition and commitment among players.

Warm-ups

Challenge: **How can we prepare for engaged collaboration?**
Solution: *Business simulations* can be used to explore plausible and/or desirable future scenarios, by taking anticipatory perspectives, reducing uncertainty and revealing innovation potential. Players advance their knowledge, skills and behaviors, such as collaboration or leadership, in a safe and realistic environment.

Workshop Facilitation

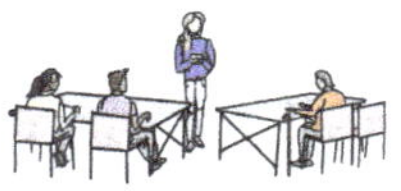

Challenge: **How can we facilitate workshops flexibly and efficiently to convey knowledge and methods?**
Solution: Semi-standardized *Workshop facilitation* formats and toolkits structure sequences of collaborative activities in different fields of innovation. Cards impart knowledge as needed and allow participants to learn while doing.

Component Patterns

Branching Choices

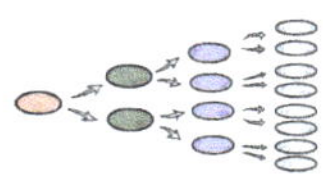

Challenge: **How can we cultivate the anticipation of alternative courses of action and their consequences?**
Solution: *Branching choices* enable players to choose from alternative courses of action and face their consequences. Employees learn to reflect on the consequences of their choices and acquire competencies for dealing with uncertainty and dilemmas in their daily work.

Cards

Challenge: **How can we flexibly provide knowledge and guidelines when needed?**
Solution: *Cards* contain a written and visual presentation and/or guidelines that make abstract or complex information easier to understand. They provide a just-in-time overview of needed knowledge or insights that inform ideation, co-creation or a shared understanding.

Challenges

Challenge: **How can we foster learning and skill development, and facilitate flow rather than frustration in dealing with innovation challenges?**
Solution: *Challenges* create motivational tension, foster learning and skill development and facilitate flow by matching a participant's skills to a challenge's level of difficulty. Complex innovation challenges are broken down into achievable tasks that are then addressed in an engaging and practice-oriented way.

Collective Decisions

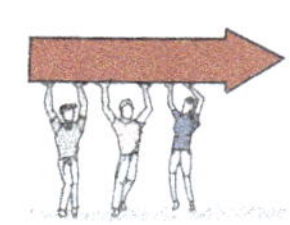

Challenge: **How can we practice making and reflecting upon decisions made by project groups?**
Solution: *Collective decisions* simulate the dynamics of collective decision-making in conventional teamwork. Innovation teams learn to negotiate alternatives in a low conflict safe space and derive practice-oriented insights from their discussions.

Competition

Challenge: **How can we motivate individuals or teams to find the best solutions?**
Solution: Gamified *business modelling* formats provide a framework and the methods to create and evaluate alternative business models. The flow provides a self-explanatory sequence of activities and reduces preparation time.

Day in the Life

Challenge: **How can we frame and communicate workshop results in a customer-centric manner that cultivates empathy?**
Solution: *A Day in the Life* frames storytelling sessions around typical events occurring during a single day. It cultivates empathy among the participants and promotes understanding of their daily problems, needs, attitudes and values.

EpicMeaning

Challenge: **How can we convey the impact and meaning of innovation efforts?**
Solution: *Epic meaning* allows you to design games with a compelling narrative, often with players identifying as the 'heroes' of the story. Such narratives create a sense of meaning among players that enhances their intrinsic motivation to act.

Mapping

Challenge: **How can we build shared understanding and collaboration in an interactive, creative and action-oriented manner?**
Solution: In *mapping* players use visual templates to gamify brainwriting activities. Players map their ideas (often written on post-its) to predefined matrixes or spatially related clusters.

Cooperation

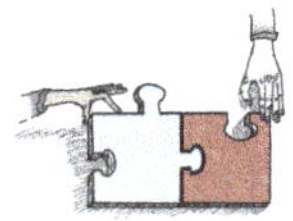

Challenge: **How can we encourage the effective exchange of knowledge across organizational and functional boundaries?**
Solution: Competition specifies game rules to select a winner among two or more individuals or teams. It provides players with clear goals and incentivizes them to outperform others, be more proactive and improve the quality of their work.

Dedicated Facilitators

Challenge: **How can we manage the complex workflows and diverse participants in collaborative settings?**
Solution: *Dedicated facilitators* maintain and update the game in response to on-going situations and interactions. They provide instructions, background information and feedback. They ensure focus and help order tasks. They can also provide warm-up, relax or engage participants, or introduce them to the narratives or other content.

Humour

Challenge: **How can we create a fun work environment that enhances team members' experiences and performance?**
Solution: *Humour* has emotional, social and cognitive functions that mediate and stimulate fun in games. It helps players share critical feedback and accept failure, intensifies social bonding and plays an important role in enhancing attentiveness, comprehension, memory and creativity.

Metaphors

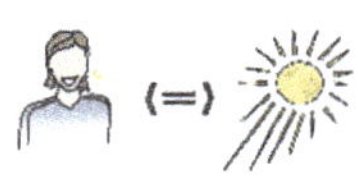

Challenge: **How can we facilitate understanding among group members engaging in unfamiliar tasks?**
Solution: *Metaphors* introduce unfamiliar concepts in familiar terms and so lower cognitive barriers to new tasks. Integrating *metaphors* into the rules, narratives or other contents of a game helps establish an informal atmosphere and mutual understanding among participants.

Modelling Materials

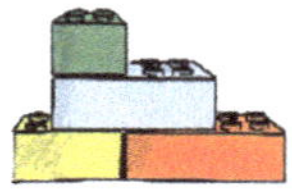

Challenge: **How can we trigger unconventional thinking and spur creative collaboration in mixed groups?**
Solution: Combinations of different *modelling materials,* such as craft paper, cardboard, toys or building blocks are used to build simple representative models or other objects that help participants respond to a question or task. They promote attentiveness, knowledge sharing, interaction, consensus building and creative thinking among players.

Negotiations

Challenge: **How can we create common ground for cooperation and knowledge exchange?**
Solution: The *negotiation* pattern provides participants with practical experience in handling typical negotiation situations. It allows them to experiment with various approaches – tools, techniques, strategies – to understand the perspectives of different stakeholders and reach a mutually acceptable agreement.

Prioritization

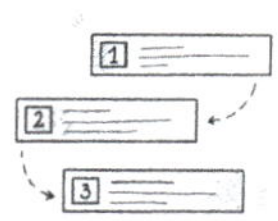

Challenge: **How can we ensure a shared sense of direction in innovation projects with uncertain outcomes?**
Solution: *Prioritization* asks players to arrange a number of items in order of their relative importance. This allows stakeholders from different hierarchical levels and functional backgrounds to participate in defining what is more valuable to the company and translating those priorities into cues for follow-up action.

Resources

Challenge: **How can we sensitize and train innovation managers to optimize resource efficiency and productivity?**
Solution: *Resources* prompts organizational members to recognize the challenges, restrictions and priorities related to finance and the use of limited resources. In games, players increase investing or exchanging in-game resources, such as money, land, natural resources, human resources or simply points.

MutualGoals

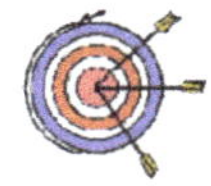

Challenge: **How can we facilitate effective collaboration?**
Solution: Multiple participants pursue mutual *goals* in a game that provides them with incentives to exchange information and collaborate more effectively.

Pitch

Challenge: **How can we generate attention and enthusiasm for innovative ideas and concepts?**
Solution: *Pitch* requires players to vividly and concisely describe something – a concept, project, product – in a limited timeframe. *Pitch* rules break speaking habits and unleash creativity, spurring an audience's interest and persuading them of the advantages of a proposition.

Quizzes

Challenge: **How can we convey basic knowledge and facilitate learning to further innovation processes?**
Solution: *Quizzes* provide a light-handed approach to learning by challenging players through series of questions. They can be used to impart and test knowledge, sensitize innovation teams about a topic or allow them to develop a nuanced understanding of a problem.

Rewards

Challenge: **How can we increase participant engagement in projects?**
Solution: Rewards are used to promote competitive engagement and a sense of accomplishment among players, motivating them to contribute ideas or other input to innovation.

Roles

Challenge: **How can we facilitate empathy and the taking on of different viewpoints?**
Solution: *Role* playing participants enact the goals and behaviors of fictional agents in a playful manner, acquiring a deeper understanding of their emotions and motivations. *Roles* allow desired behaviors to be practiced in a safe space.

Surprise

Challenge: **How can we encourage unconventional thinking and sensitize people for unexpected developments?**
Solution: *Surprise* introduces unexpected events or pieces of information into a game flow that deviates from an expected course of action. *Surprise* can be stimulated by predefined content (e.g. drawing wild cards), by prompting players to generate radical scenarios or by providing them with special capabilities or unexpected rewards.

Voting

Challenge: **How can we facilitate decision making?**
Solution: *Voting* prompts players to allocate votes, points, fictitious money or other tokens to different alternatives. Innovation project participants prioritize alternatives in a collaborative, engaging and transparent way, while avoiding lengthy discussions and conflicts.

Storytelling

Challenge: **How can we make knowledge, empirical insights and values explicit in an engaging manner?**
Solution: *Storytelling* makes knowledge and values explicit, while promoting engagement and enhancing ideation. Narrative features like engagement, conflict, characters, emotions, meaning, causal relationships and time-space constraints create larger and more meaningful constructs that support participants' comprehension and interpretation.

Trade-offs

Challenge: **How can we prepare innovation managers for taking difficult decisions?**
Solution: *Trade-offs* prompts players to compare and choose among several options that lead to different negative or positive consequences. They simulate decision-making between conflicting alternatives and allow participants to experiment with different approaches in a safe space.

Appendix 2
Overview of games discussed in the book

https://doi.org/10.1515/9783110725582-025

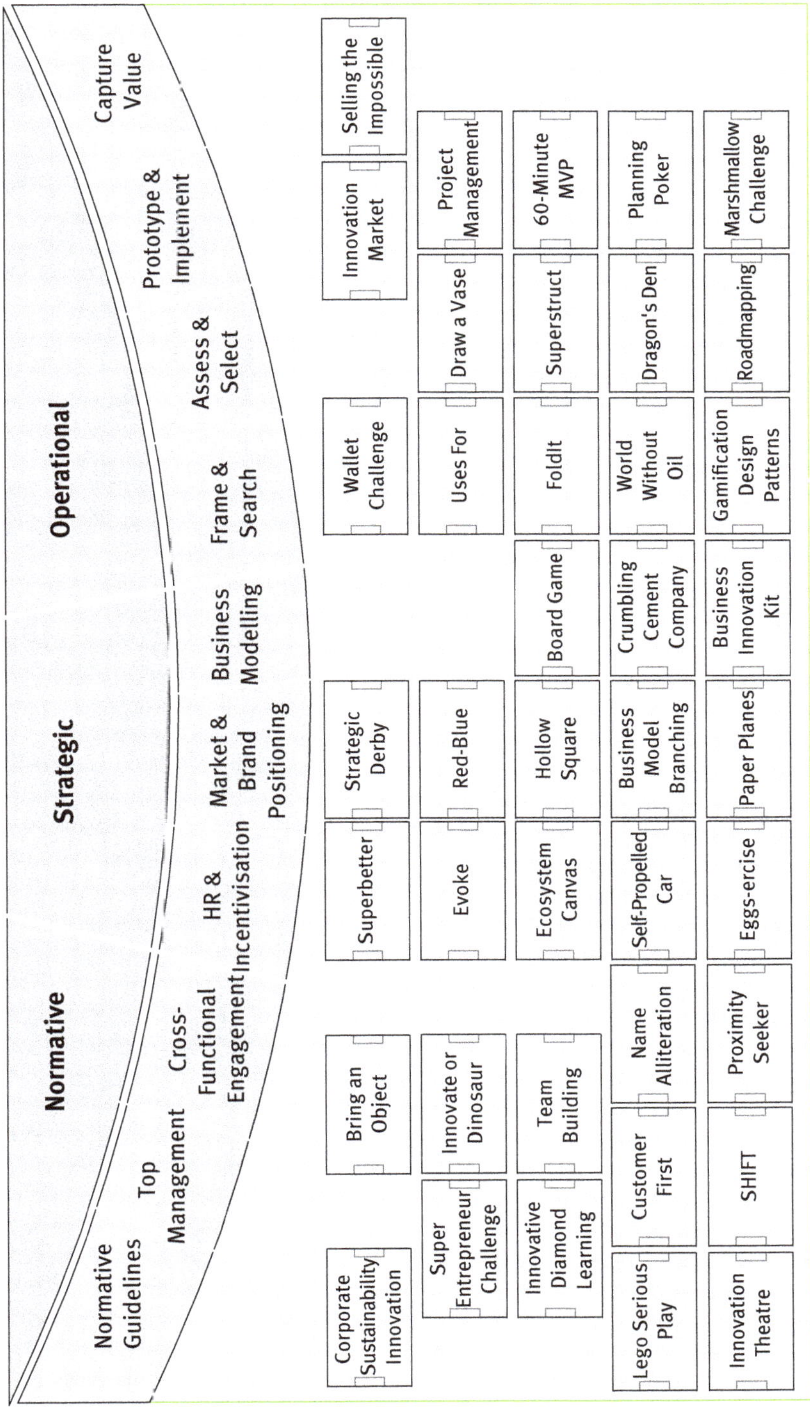

Figure A.2: Overview of games and gamified formats to drive innovation and entrepreneurship discussed in the book.

No.	Game	Innovation Challenge	Solution
1	*60-Minute MVP*[1]	Developing new offerings – products and services – requires focused team-based activity. This high intensity experience allows fast learning about early stage prototyping. How can we quickly test early stage innovation concepts and value propositions?	This simple experience challenges teams to come up with ideas and create an app to communicate the essence of an idea as a prototype. It is a high energy experience which can be used as the basis of a reflective activity to distil key principles. It forms part of an experience-based entrepreneurship programme.
2	*Board game for co-creating ecosystem based circular economy business models*[2]	Diverse stakeholders with complementary or divergent skills and knowledge need to create a shared understanding and vision of their ecosystem. How can we create a strategic vision for an ecosystem an its circular economy business models?	The *Board game* uses cards with descriptions of terms related to circular economy strategies and blank cards to be filled in. Participants are taken through initiation, ideation, integration and implementation stages of business model development.
3	*Bring an Object*[3]	People inevitably bring different preconceptions of a topic to open ended workshops, and want to see them reflected in the process. How can we ensure everyone's perspective is acknowledged right from the beginning?	*Bringing an Object* asks workshop participants to bring an object they associate with the topic or objective of the workshop. Telling others about the object's associations with the topic reveals different viewpoints among the participants and provides reference points for subsequent discussions.
4	*Business Innovation Kit*[4]	Entrepreneurs with their teams, startups and innovation teams face recurring business modelling challenges: How to collaboratively develop business models aligned with what we care about? How to explore and understand the range and depth of business model design options for an already existing business or a new business idea?	The *Business Innovation Kit* is a self-explanatory workshop format to model values-based business with collaborative and interactive exercises. It involves puzzles to convey basic knowledge about business models and to review and discuss different good practice cases. It facilitates ideation, prioritization and future challenges to guide teams to develop alternative business models for a new business idea.

5	***Business Model Branching (chapter 9)***[5]	As companies grow they become increasingly better at repeating and optimizing what is already in the portfolio of the company and slower at developing completely new branches to the company. How can we provide an overview and facilitate considerations whether it is the right time to reconfigure existing portfolios and put resources into development of new branches?	*Business Model Branching* works with visual mapping models to systematically create strategies for when to reconfigure existing business branches, and to prepare and ramp up new ones before it is too late. It is based on insights on resource allocation, the pros and cons in various ambidexterity models, and building up innovation portfolios.
6	*Crumbling Cement Company*[6]	Innovation often involves conflicts over strategic resource allocation. And there is no 'right' answer, only a negotiated outcome. How can we best learn to appreciate different strategic viewpoints in the innovation process?	This is a role-playing game designed to give participants a sense of the underlying tensions in a resource allocation conflict and challenge them to find a negotiated solution.
7	***CSI (Corporate Sustainability Innovation, chapter 7)***[7]	Companies need new processes, products, services and business models to improve their sustainability. How can we turn sustainability challenges in the workplace into seeds for innovation?	Through a sequence of moderated activities, the *CSI* game conveys basic knowledge and raises awareness for corporate sustainability. It taps into the participants' experience to help them generate and illustrate ideas for sustainability-oriented innovation.
8	***Customer First (chapter 8)***[8]	Some companies have good ideas for optimizing their business model. However, implementation often fails if focus on the customer gets lost. How can we introduce and adapt change processes with a customer first orientation?	*Customer First* runs through various implementation steps in a web-based simulation showing what effects these have on various stakeholders, including the customer. Participants learn to improve decision making, strategic thinking and change management processes.
9	*Dragon's Den*[9]	Innovating teams face many situations where they need to pitch their ideas in order to win support, finance, etc. This game develops skills in both pitching and judging innovative ideas. How can we best develop and present an engaging narrative around our innovation project?	This game is based on the popular UK TV series *Dragon's Den* (Shark Tank in the USA). Contestants pitch their business idea to investors who question the business idea and then decide whether to invest in exchange for equity in the new business.

(continued)

(continued)

No.	Game	Innovation Challenge	Solution
10	***Draw a Vase***[10]	Different ways of framing innovation challenges have far reaching implications for ideation and resulting proposals. How can we sensitize workshop participants to the impact of framing challenges, for instance from a user point of view?	*Draw a Vase* is a simple design thinking exercise. Participants are asked to either draw an object (like a vase), or a context of experience (like a way to enjoy flowers). The following discussion then sensitizes them to the implications of framing problems, and helps them approach a design task from different perspectives.
11	***Ecosystem Canvas (chapter 12)***[11]	Start-ups have difficulties trying to understand and extract the benefits they could get from stakeholders and the entrepreneurial ecosystem around them. How can we help future entrepreneurs grasp the potential synergies in their own business ecosystem?	The *Ecosystem Canvas* game enhances each player's understanding of the factors influencing the entrepreneurial journey. It explores opportunities for co-creation of benefits, dialogical relations and learning about entrepreneurial education ecosystems.
12	*Eggs-ercise*[12]	Much innovative activity involves shared creativity, often under time and resource pressures. Effective teams understand the underlying group dynamics around team roles, psychological safety and conflict resolution. How can we best learn about different team roles and dynamics in innovation?	These *eggs-ercises* are a series of creativity challenges based on coming up with solutions to a variety of egg-related problems in a competitive time-based game.
13	*Evoke*[13]	Understanding grand challenges requires advanced skills and confidence. How can young people acquire skills and gain confidence needed to address global challenges such as displacement, hunger, poverty and water scarcity?	*Evoke* is a multi-player online game that uses social networking, storytelling and other game design patterns to teach social innovation skills.

14	*FoldIt*[14]	The mass of citizen scientists can contribute distributed human abilities to solving great scientific problems. How can we enable non-experts to contribute to scientific research?	*FoldIt* is a crowdsourcing computer game that leverages human puzzle-solving and pattern recognition abilities. Players compete to fold the best proteins that can help to prevent or treat diseases.
15	*Gamification Design Pattern Cards*[15]	Numerous design patterns are available to create gamified responses to innovation challenges. How can we facilitate the design process by comparing different combinations of design patterns and games?	*Gamification Design Pattern Cards* convey basic knowledge about the challenges addressed by patterns, the solutions they provide and related patterns. Students or designers can play with different combinations to create new or modify existing games.
16	*Hollow Squares / Jigsaw Puzzles*[16]	This type of game is designed to highlight the importance of communication and collaboration within and between teams in innovation projects. It is difficult to solve the core problem without sharing information and the game provides a powerful experience, which stimulates reflection. How can we best improve collaboration within and between teams?	Two teams, a planning team and an implementing team, work together to solve a puzzle as fast as possible. If there are more than 6–8 players, you can make it a contest by letting several pairs of teams compete to solve the puzzle. Each team receives its own briefing: one team knows the solution from the start, and they explain it to the other team, who then has to build it. This means that communication is key to winning, but the briefings are written in such a way that the teams invariably misinterpret them and fail to communicate during the exercise.
17	*Innovate Or Dinosaur*[17]	Innovate or die. Do more with less. This is what individuals and teams are being pushed to do if they want their business to survive and thrive. How can we avoid people getting stuck by fixed thinking based on past experiences, and enable them to get unstuck?	*Innovate or Dinosaur* is an unconventional collaborative innovation game that helps teams, businesses and organizations think creatively and critically, generate new ideas for real work activities, products and services, and move those ideas to action.

(continued)

(continued)

No.	Game	Innovation Challenge	Solution
18	*Innovation Markets*[18]	First and second impressions, emotional responses, social dynamics and temporal aspects impact the implementation and market potential of new ideas. But they are difficult to anticipate. How can companies prospectively evaluate ideas, concepts and prototypes in a collaborative manner?	*Innovation Markets* asks participants to decide which product and service concepts to invest in and devise key indicators for their future market success. Crowdsourcing estimates and beliefs over future outcomes is used to evaluate ideas, concepts or prototypes.
19	*Innovation Theatre*[19]	Innovation as a process relies on people relating to one another in novel ways that are difficult to anticipate and often blocked by habitual interaction patterns. How can we explore and improve social dynamics in the context of innovation?	*Innovation Theatre* prompts participants to create and act out aspects of innovation-related activities and processes as improv theatre. They explore different viewpoints and dynamics and find potential for improvement.
20	*Innovative Diamond Learning*[20]	Innovation leaders need to practice more than one leadership approach to prevail. Research shows that the early stages of innovation processes (sometimes labelled as 'preject'), can be improved dramatically if teams repeatedly shift between different modes of inquiry and their expectations and visions for the project. How can we get insights into vital roles in prejects?	The *Innovation Diamond Learning* game enables participants to develop and acquire four leadership roles associated with the early stages of innovation. By working on 16 different tasks, participants gain hands-on experience with the four leadership roles: the knowledge detective, the jester, the conceptualizer and the gardener.
21	***Lego Serious Play (Chapter 13)***[21]	Due to cultural differences, diverging perspectives or limited means of expression, workshop participants often lack a common language. Not all participants speak up, and ideas cannot be easily discussed. How can we provide a common medium for participants to learn how to understand and complement each other in new ways?	*Lego Serious Play* provides workshop participants with a common language medium to address innovation-related questions by building 3D models. These form the basis for subsequent knowledge sharing, discussions, problem solving and decision making.

22	*Marshmallow Challenge*[22]	Innovation-related challenges are difficult to grasp especially for students who have never confronted them. How can we convey basic knowledge about innovation and entrepreneurship in an experiential, action-oriented and self-reflexive manner?	Using basic materials and carefully described instructions, the *Marshmallow Challenge* provides an entertaining group experience to reflect upon innovation and entrepreneurship issues like teamwork, collaboration and leadership, creativity, ideation and prototyping.
23	*Name Alliteration*[23]	Often team members collaborating on an innovation challenge do not know one another in advance. How do we ensure that they get to know each other quickly and easily and remember the names and affiliations of other team members?	By introducing all team members to each other with a *Name Alliteration* at the beginning of the meeting, participants learn each other's name as well as a specific characteristic of the person. This guarantees a fun start to the meeting and that all participants get to know each other.
24	*Paper Planes*[24]	Novices in innovation and entrepreneurship should understand key concepts and aspects of innovation, including product and process innovation, strategy, marketing and learning. How can we teach the language of innovation through a simple hands-on exercise?	This is a simple exercise and introductory game designed to provide a competitive and fun experience from which participants derive some key concepts and language around innovation.
25	*Planning Poker*[25]	New software or product development teams need to estimate efforts in ways that are sufficiently accurate and consensual. How can we benefit from different individual experiences and agree on shared estimates?	*Planning Poker* prompts participants to contribute and reflect upon their individual estimates for a workpackage in order to come up with a shared estimation.
26	*Project Management*[26]	Innovation inevitably requires careful management of resources over time and against a background of uncertainty. Simply trusting to luck is not enough. Instead there is a need for some form of structured project planning and review. How can we best develop an understanding of the importance of project planning and the basic elements in project management?	This game involves teams carrying out a project under time and resource constraints. Reflection helps identify some of the key issues in project management and the need for a structured but flexible approach.

(continued)

(continued)

No.	Game	Innovation Challenge	Solution
27	***Proximity Seeker (chapter 11)***[27]	Some teams work in remote mode, often times without group members having any previous acquaintance. How can we promote trust and empathy to cooperate effectively and efficiently?	The *Proximity Seeker* game facilitates sharing experiences and knowledge of the team's members by randomly posing different questions as an opening of remote meetings. Questions are broad, fun and engaging and they are related to current work projects as well as provide personal insights.
28	*Red-Blue (Prisoners Dilemma)*[28]	Many innovation activities involve working with other groups or organizations. Effective collaboration depends on trust and shared risk taking. How can we best learn the value of trust and strategic collaboration between teams?	This is a version of the prisoner's dilemma game which provides a powerful demonstration of the value of inter-group trust and co-operation and the negative effects of treating innovation issues as a zero-sum game.
29	*Roadmapping*[29]	Working with future scenarios and projections can help identify innovation opportunities but these need to be linked to an action plan to move from today's context towards realising those opportunities. How can we work with images of the future to best develop practical present-day actions that enable innovation development?	This is a structured game to develop skills in roadmapping as a strategic planning tool. It involves techniques such as backcasting, consensus building in order to provide direction for strategic and technology innovation management.
30	*Self-Propelled Car*[30]	Much innovative activity involves group problem solving under resource and time constraints. How can we best learn about the different challenges in the agile implementation of innovation projects?	This game and its many variants provide experience in meeting challenges of shared creativity under time and resource pressure, which can then be reflected upon to identify key insights about effective team work and agile innovation.

31	*Selling the Impossible*[31]	Pitching skills are about storytelling, and how to weave the elements of a value proposition into a coherent narrative. This game explores the skills in creative storytelling. How can we best develop an engaging narrative around innovation projects?	This game involves developing pitches for 'impossible' value propositions and provides an entertaining way of setting up a competition to demonstrate the value of storytelling as a pitching skill.
32	***SHIFT Game (Chapter 10)***[32]	New product development teams and innovation managers usually encounter high innovation barriers when they grow as a company – as growth can prevent radical thinking. How can we overcome typical barriers in full scale innovation processes?	*SHIFT* is a is floor-based game with stakeholder roleplay as participants work through a number of innovation barriers and develop strategies to overcome them. Barriers are for instance related to user and employee perspectives, business models, organizational structure and culture, as well as regulation.
33	*Strategy Derby*[33]	Strategizing is difficult because while a company can make their own moves it is hard to anticipate how other companies in the market will react. How can we improve our awareness of alternative strategies and anticipate our competitors' likely reactions?	Strategic Derby is a table-based game that lets teams play the roles of their own company and its competitors in a fiercely competitive market. By investing resources into more or less radical strategic moves, and reflecting on the reasoning behind them, managers learn how alternative strategies unfold.
34	*Super Entrepreneur Challenge*[34]	Successful entrepreneurship requires the ability to apply a variety of different skills. This simple game involves players in identifying the various key skills that make up a 'super-entrepreneur'. How can we best convey an understanding of what it takes to be an entrepreneur?	Participants are invited to create an understanding – a picture, description or model – of a 'super-entrepreneur' who has all the necessary skills to be successful.
35	*Superbetter*[35]	Not just entrepreneurs face great personal challenges in starting up a company. How can people be empowered to deal with their personal challenges?	*Superbetter* works with life hacks or techniques such as daily quests, power ups to gain strengths and 'bad guy' obstacles to improve mental health and resilience.

(continued)

(continued)

No.	Game	Innovation Challenge	Solution
36	*Superstruct*[36]	If grand challenges and wicked problems are to be addressed, a variety of people with different experiences will be required to contribute. How can we generate and share ideas about how to deal with future challenges?	The online game *Superstruct* confronts players with an end-of-the-world scenario and a call to save the world. It crowdsources ideas for the future of energy, food, health, security and social safety.
37	*Team Building*[37]	Much innovation activity relies on teams to deliver creativity by bringing together different knowledge sets. How can we best learn about team dynamics, roles, conflict resolution and shared creativity?	This set of games is designed to explore the make-up of effective innovation teams through a series of fun competitive activities.
38	*Uses For*[38]	Creativity is something everyone has – the ability to solve open-ended problems. But group creativity enhances both the number of solutions generated and their variety. How can we best learn to appreciate the value of diversity in innovation?	This simple game quickly demonstrates the power of shared creativity in terms of fluency (number of ideas generated) and flexibility (the range of ideas generated).
39	*Wallet Challenge*[39]	Developing a solution requires understanding the users and what they value. Developing the ability to empathise is at the heart of the design thinking approach. How can we best enable design thinking?	A simple exercise (with several variants) provides a powerful learning experience. It is available with extensive support documentation and a facilitator's guide.
40	*World Without Oil*[40]	How can we generate and share ideas about how to adapt to environmental changes, and motivate people to reflect upon and adapt their behaviour?	*World Without Oil* is a future scenario game that prompts players to share ideas about how to adapt to an oil shortage. Participants immerse themselves in the scenario, explore and share how they would change their lives, and actually take up some new ideas from the game.

Appendix 3
Overview of games to facilitate values-based innovation

https://doi.org/10.1515/9783110725582-026

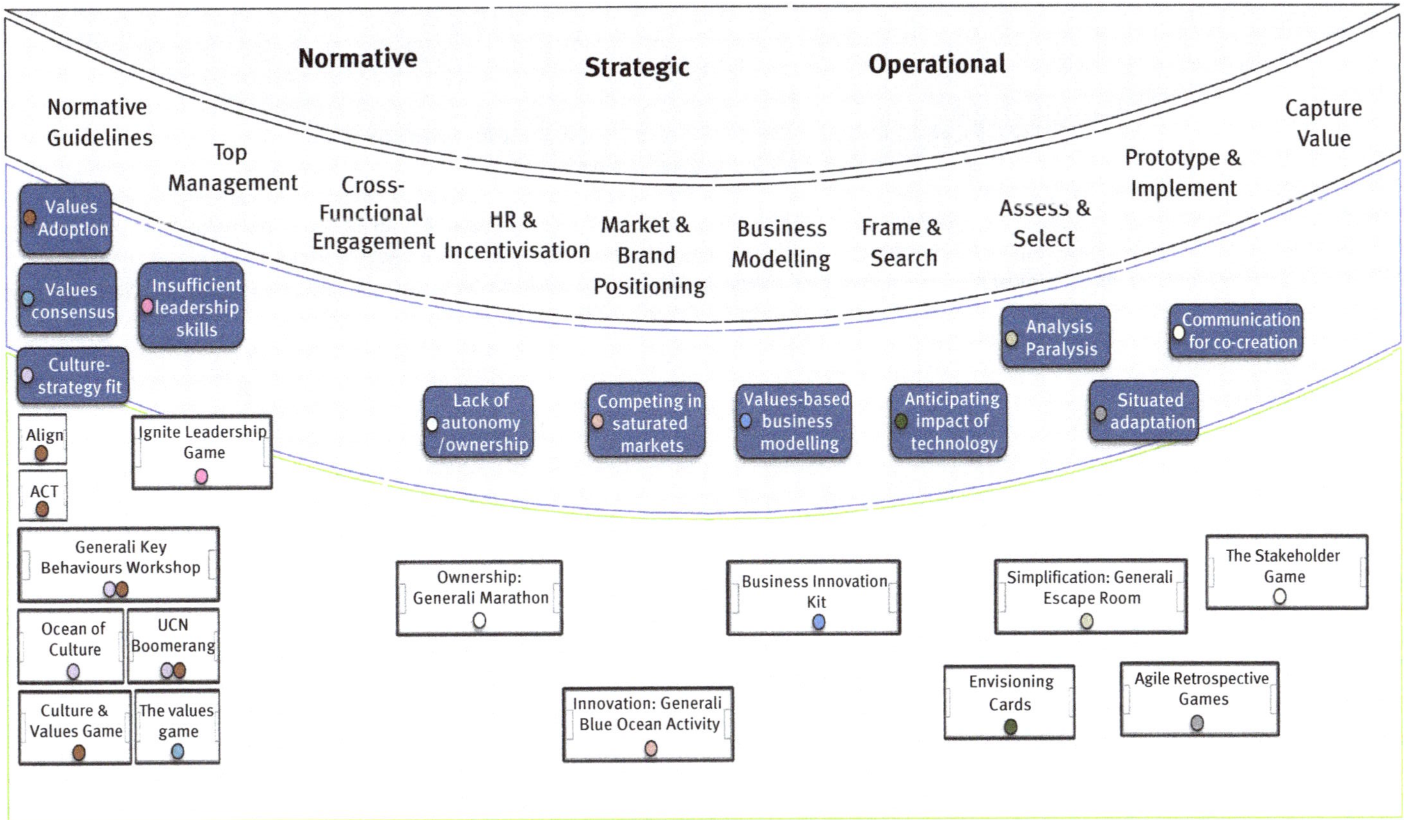

Figure A.3: Overview of publicly available games and gamified formats to facilitate values-based innovation and entrepreneurship.

No.	Game	Innovation Challenge	Solution
1	Align[1]	Rapidly growing companies often struggle with their employees' disconnection from the corporate culture and core values and the lack of intrinsic motivation to act in accordance with them. How can we motivate employees to act in accordance with formal organizational values and clarify the impact of deviating from them?	*Align* allows employees to explore organizational values and experience the link between daily challenges, core values and success. Players apply core values to deal with 'dilemmas', 'challenges', 'events' and 'assignments' while the system keeps track of their choices and scores (or 'karma') to generate new obstacles.
2	ACT (Rekindling organizational values)[2]	Formal organisational values are often abstract and detached from employees' daily practices, which hinders their incorporation in everyday work situations, customer interactions and their potential to drive innovation. How can we facilitate employee comprehension of formal organizational values and foster their integration in daily practice?	*ACT* was developed to rekindle organizational values among employees of the Danish company NETS so they would be 'accountable', 'customer driven' and 'together'. Players give scores on how much different dilemmas would affect the three core values, and suggest ways to deal with the dilemmas and then evaluate their different approaches.
3	The Values Game[3]	Enhancing corporate strategy and innovation may be limited due to the lack of clear communication and/or consensus among decision makers or their limited awareness about group values and norms. How can we trigger discussion about organizational values and help decision makers to reach an agreement about shared values?	*The Values Game* increases understanding and builds consensus on values and norms that reflect both individual and group perspectives. Participants follow different variants of gameplay to discuss and prioritize cards depicting different values, subject matters and group norms.
4	Generali Key Behaviours Gamified Workshop[4]	When newly introduced values serve as a basis for defining a new innovation strategy, the integration of those values to operations can be challenging because employees perceive them as abstract notions, detached from their daily work. How can we facilitate understanding of unfamiliar values and foster their integration in daily practice?	The *Generali Key Behaviours Gamified Workshop* aids the adoption of newly introduced values defined as 'ownership', 'human touch', 'innovation' and 'simplification'. Separate rooms are allocated for each value and a corresponding game. The players take turns visiting each room and formulate their key takeaway message.

5	Ocean of Culture[5]	Modern firms face constant demands to develop, renew and enhance external and internal systems. They also face difficulties in balancing between market, strategy, culture and leadership when their strategic focus is shifting. How can we clarify the interdependence between culture and strategy and facilitate organizational transformation?	*Ocean of Culture* is a dialogue tool that motivates players to harness their corporate culture as a business driver by developing a shared understanding of, and commitment to, the alignment between culture and strategy. The Ocean Board features 17 culture fields that contain cards, inspiration materials and tasks.
6	UCN Boomerang[6]	Organizational change processes, such as rebranding, often introduce new values and principles to increase engagement with external stakeholders, but their success largely depends on effective communication among stakeholders about those values. How can we facilitate communication about new values among stakeholders?	*UCN Boomerang* was designed to aid an educational institution's rebranding and transition towards reflective practice methods for teaching and learning. It is based on dilemmas crowdsourced from university teachers and a card deck that enables students and teachers to exchange perspectives through roleplay.
7	Culture and Values Game[7]	The vagueness of value statements and poor communication about their practical relevance poses a challenge to companies that want to integrate organizational values into operations. How can we facilitate understanding of formal organizational values and foster communication about their practical relevance?	*Culture and Values* facilitates communication about core values with customers and employees. Quizzes and dilemmas provoke intense group discussions and increase awareness of how to apply core values in practice, while live data on dashboards shows how players interpret and feel about the values.
8	Ignite Leadership Game[8]	Although effective leadership is vital for the success of any project, the diverse strategies involved in innovation projects may not be compatible with traditional leadership styles and skills. How can we encourage employees to develop innovation leadership skills?	The *Ignite Leadership* game was developed to promote critical leadership skills and behaviours among NTT Data employees. Challenges based on realistic scenarios and award points given to the best players help employees to connect with their co-workers and stand out as potential leaders while staying engaged with the work at hand.

(continued)

(continued)

No.	Game	Innovation Challenge	Solution
9	Ownership: Generali Marathon[9]	Teams may fail to optimise their performance due to the lack of autonomy and ownership among their members, who often hesitate to take initiative based on their skills and in response to the team's needs. How can we encourage ownership and initiative among team members?	The *Generali Marathon* sensitizes players to ownership-related themes, such as distribution and sequencing of responsibilities, teamwork and coordination. Players on a field try to bring a set of disorganized cards into a sequence at the same time, while other players give hints from outside the field.
10	Innovation: Generali Blue Ocean Activity[10]	Traditionally, innovations are differentiated as being less costly or technologically superior to standard offerings. Still, they tend to fail in gaining traction if they enter saturated markets, instead of creating or capturing new markets. How can we encourage an innovative mindset and the generation of radical ideas?	The *Generali Blue Ocean Activity* motivates players to go beyond traditional innovation strategies and generate disruptive ideas. Players act as a small ice cream retailer that competes against a retail chain. They use Blue Ocean Strategy templates to define their business model and learn from critical insights shared by others.
11	Envisioning Cards[11]	Designers need to anticipate the uses, benefits and harms of a new technology and integrate these considerations into the product development process. This may be challenging given the divergence of values among stakeholder groups. How can we adopt diverse stakeholder perspectives to anticipate the impact of new technology?	*Envisioning Cards* facilitate exploration of design themes related to stakeholders, time (short- and long-term implications), values (and how they are impacted by technology) and pervasiveness (technology diffusion) to provoke idea generation for value sensitive design.
12	Simplification: Generali Escape Room[12]	Innovation teams need to adopt a multitude of perspectives and approaches to dealing with a problem but in doing so they often fall into the trap of overanalysing, even to the point of analysis paralysis. How can we increase awareness about the importance of simplification for efficient problem solving?	The *Generali Escape Room* provides an analogy of overanalysing a problem to make participants aware of the power of simple reasoning. Players deal with puzzles that have both complicated and simple solutions. Most players overanalyze and take the difficult way instead of taking a step back to find the simpler one.

13	Agile Retrospective Games[13]	When multiple innovation criteria are defined at the beginning of a project, there is little room for reflection, revision and changing direction if requirements change or if something does not work as expected. How can we enable more agile and reflexive approaches to managing innovation projects?	*Agile Retrospective Games* address technical or human related factors in the innovation process that could affect the final product quality or the work environment. One example is Circles and Soup where players map their ideas onto 3 circles that represent the things they can control, influence or cannot change.
14	The Stakeholder Game[14]	Users' emotional values and experiences with regard to a product are implicit and difficult to verbalize, which hinders communication and collaboration between them and product developers. How can we facilitate communication about emotional values between users and designers?	*The Stakeholder Game* aids designers in establishing a dialogue with users about soft and non-verbal issues, such as emotional values in textile design. Players map a set of statements and images with design trends to four zones of pleasure reflecting emotional values (physio-pleasure, socio-pleasure, psycho-pleasure and ideo-pleasure.

Appendix 4
Overview of games to facilitate sustainability-oriented innovation

https://doi.org/10.1515/9783110725582-027

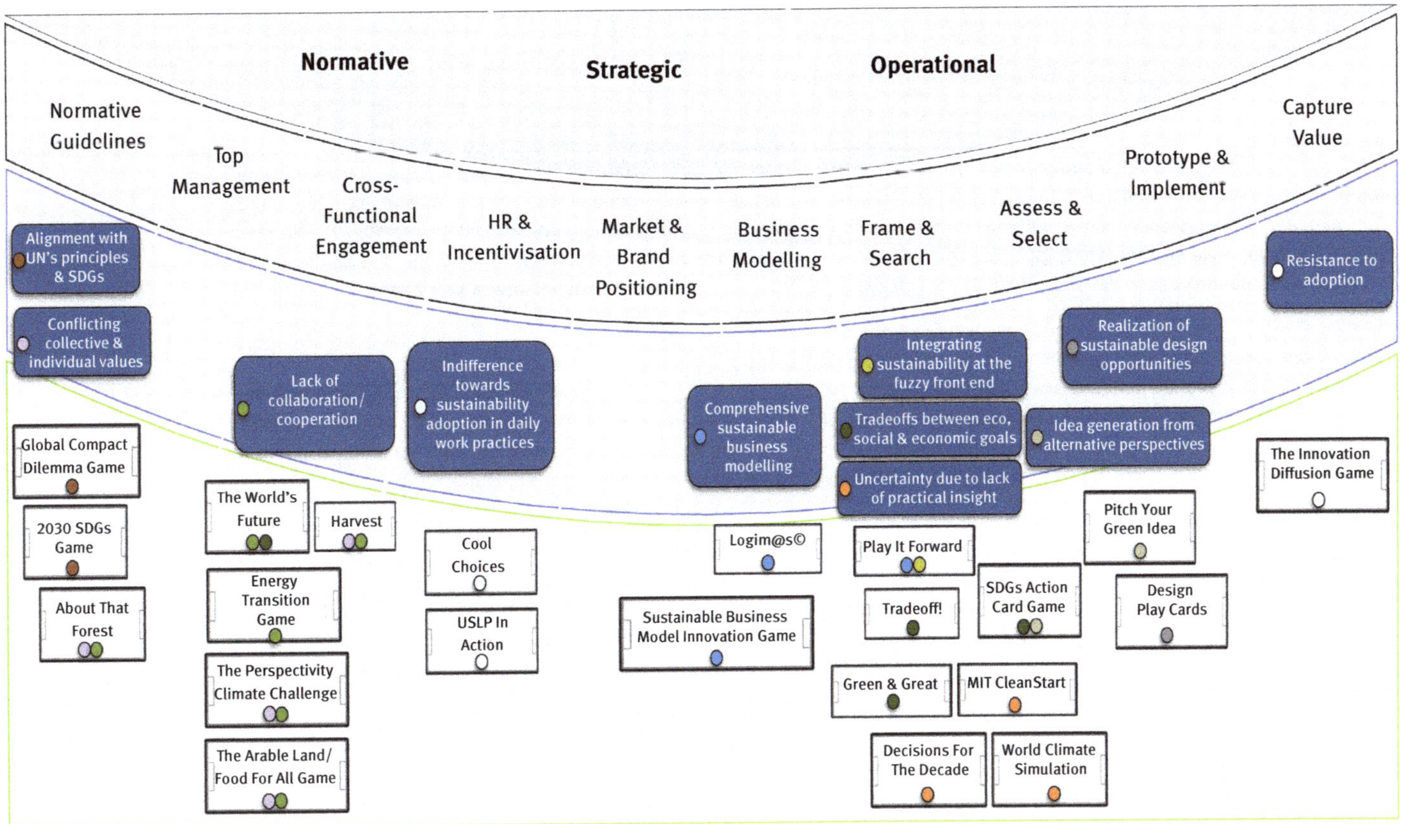

Figure A.4: Overview of publicly available games and gamified formats to facilitate sustainability-oriented innovation and entrepreneurship.

No.	Game	Innovation Challenge	Solution
1	Global Compact: Dilemma Game[1]	Innovators and entrepreneurs need to be aware of the ten principles of the UN Global Compact and how to apply them in making difficult decisions relating to human and labour rights, the environment and anti-corruption. How can we convey knowledge and raise awareness about the Global Compact and its impact on decision making?	The *Global Compact: Dilemma Game* confronts players with dilemmas and real-case experiences of social and environmental issues in order to create awareness and facilitate consideration of different stakeholder values in organisational decision making.
2	2030s SDGs Game[2]	To manage business endeavours in line with UN's Agenda 2030, innovators and entrepreneurs need to build a shared understanding of the SDGs and a common ground for collaboration, also with stakeholders, based on related values and priorities. How can we establish common ground for values-based collaboration?	The *2030s SDGs Game* provides participants with the experience of co-creating a sustainable world in a simulative environment. Players gain deeper understanding of the business impacts of the SDGs and acquire an increased sense of personal and shared responsibility towards sustainability issues.
3	About That Forest[3]	The effectiveness of sustainable resource management can be undermined due to conflicting values, short-term focus and reluctance towards imposed regulations. How can we improve decision-making for the common good?	*About That Forest* gives insights into the challenges that arise while making collective decisions for the common good. Players roleplay members of a village community, living off the jointly managed forest and facing dilemmas that serve as metaphors for social, economic and cultural processes behind sustainability issues.
4	The World's Future[4]	Businesses want to adopt strategies that support sustainability but unknowingly impede each other as they lack awareness of the overall picture and focus on short term goals that benefit one business at the cost of another. How can we improve sustainability-oriented cooperation?	*The World's Future* empowers players to cooperate on solving complex issues, deal with trade-offs and experience the consequences of their decisions. Players develop creative strategies to manage energy and industrial investments while advancing social and environmental sustainability.

5	Harvest[5]	Sustainable use of resources needs the whole community to be aware of and acknowledge resource limitations and that we need to work together and not against each other to make profit. How can we improve resource management and community collaboration?	*Harvest* helps players to realize the long-term consequences of using a limited common resource (like fish) for maximizing an individual's short-term gain, and practice co-planning. Each team roleplays a fishing company aiming to make the highest possible catch although the stock of fish is limited.
6	Energy Transition Game[6]	The urgency of a transition towards renewable energy requires being prepared for socio-economic impacts, such as price fluctuations, harsh competition and financial shortfalls. How can we facilitate coordination and cooperation among the many actors involved?	The *Energy Transition* game presents the general challenges of system-wide change and has an energy producer, energy provider, technology start-up, governmental representative and an NGO member to propose innovative solutions for the energy system's adaptiveness and potential to mitigate climate change.
7	The Perspectivity Climate Challenge[7]	Divergent interests and increasing complexities in social, environmental, economic and technological dynamics require greater awareness and the adoption of 'coopetitive' approaches to deal with the world's commons in different fields. How can we foster coopetition among stakeholders with divergent interests?	*The Perspectivity Climate Challenge* provides insights into the dynamics of sustainable development and stimulates reflection on competition and collaboration between stakeholders with divergent interests. Players negotiate and address trade-offs between long-term sustainability and short-term economic growth.
8	Cool Choices[8]	Due to some employees' indifferent or adverse attitudes towards sustainability, it is often challenging for business to bring about positive change that contributes to the achievement of sustainable goals. How can we encourage and support employees to adopt sustainability-oriented behaviours?	*Cool Choices* engages workers in an action-oriented program that offers a fun, sociable and easy way to practice sustainability-oriented behaviours. Colleagues organise themselves in teams and earn points and badges by practising so-called cool choices that save resources and waste in every context of their lives.

(continued)

(continued)

No.	Game	Innovation Challenge	Solution
9	USLP In Action[9]	Translating various facets of sustainability into everyday corporate practices is challenging as the workforce needs to learn how to establish such habits in their daily lives by thinking and planning ahead. How can we promote deliberation on and adoption of corporate sustainability practices among employees?	Unilever Polska launched the intranet platform *USLP in Action* to educate employees and engage them in a discussion about its sustainability strategy, the "Sustainable Living Plan". Each week, employees address a new sustainability challenge, earn points (e.g. by answering quiz questions) and compete for a final award.
10	The Arable Land/ The Food For All Game[10]	Limited resources create pressure on their distribution. This calls for long term planning and management with collaborative decision making so that everyone benefits and resources are not wasted. How can we ensure fair and sustainable distribution of common goods?	*The Arable Land* provides a metaphor and a shared experience of the consequences of overexploitation of resources. It is a simple game of elimination (like musical chairs), which encourages players to adopt basic systems thinking and long-term thinking as well as more openness to new plans and policies.
11	Logim@s©[11]	The development of sustainable solutions requires managers to translate research-based insights into actions and design policies and business models that can cope with the risks of natural disasters, especially in large cities. How can we anticipate and prevent negative impacts when developing sustainable solutions?	Logim@s© was designed to aid managers in introducing sustainability measures that could mitigate the impact of a highway interchange project. Players use a business model canvas to explore and discuss their common project at a higher level of abstraction that also considers social consequences and benefits.
12	Sustainable Business Model Innovation Game[12]	Conventional business modelling approaches hinder the implementation of sustainability strategies across all business model components and from the very early stages of business model development. How can we address sustainability concerns when designing new business models in a systematic way?	The *Sustainable Business Model Innovation Game* equips players with knowledge about sustainable business modelling through real-world examples using a Business Model Canvas. Participants see the positive and negative impacts typical to business model components in the respective sections of the canvas.

13	Play It Forward[13]	Dealing with sustainability in the fuzzy front end of innovation is complex due to the multitude of factors at play and the scarcity of tools that promote learning about and fulfilment of sustainability goals in this stage of the innovation process. How can we facilitate and inform sustainability-oriented ideation at the fuzzy front?	*Play It Forward* facilitates description, analysis, discussion and design of sustainable products and services in the early stages of innovation. It is based on the Business Model Canvas, which it extends with two new building blocks: 'Societal Costs' and 'Societal Benefits' and a set of STEEP (Social, Technological, Economic, Environmental, Political) cards for evaluating ideas.
14	Tradeoff[14]	The multifaceted, geopolitical nature of sustainability issues can obstruct the balance between environmental, social and economic goals, as specific values and resources have to be prioritised in different regions. How can we sensitize decision makers about the typical trade-offs that occur in different geographic regions?	*Tradeoff!* introduces the concept of ecosystem services, explores trade-offs across multiple services and demonstrates how spatial data can inform decision making. Players interact and seek synergies between traditional development and natural capital values while gaining awareness of ecosystems around the globe.
15	SDGs Action Card Game[15]	Making with wise trade-offs is a major challenge for achieving sustainable development goals, as solutions to one problem may give rise to another problem and conventional solutions often fail to reconcile contradictory goals. How can we encourage the development of solutions that can alleviate trade-offs between sustainability goals?	The *SDGs Action Card* game enhances players' skills for dealing with trade-offs related to sustainability by encouraging idea generation. It consists of Trade-off cards with stories of people struggling to achieve an SDG and Resource cards with people or products that might be helpful to solve sustainability challenges.
16	Green & Great[16]	Growing interest in sustainable development requires going beyond business as usual, introducing innovative thinking in daily operations and making the interconnectedness between profit and sustainable business more visible. How can we sensitize decision makers about the advantages of a sustainability-oriented approach to innovation?	*Green & Great* is a simulation game that aims to provide clarity about the risks and benefits of sustainability as well as to aid transformative learning and decision making towards sustainability in business. It allows players to experience the importance of sustainability as a source of competitive advantage.

(continued)

(continued)

No.	Game	Innovation Challenge	Solution
17	MIT CleanStart[17]	Sustainability-oriented innovators and entrepreneurs face uncertainty, exacerbated by the limited availability of visualised challenges in real-time scenarios and practical learning resources. How can we prepare business actors to anticipate and address typical challenges to sustainability-oriented entrepreneurship?	*MIT CleanStart* is a web-based simulation that allows participants to experience the learning curve entrepreneurs in the clean energy sector face as they deal with challenges of business development in a competitive environment. Players learn about key entrepreneurial concepts through the lense of different roles in a startup company.
18	Decisions For The Decade[18]	Climate change is associated with many uncertainties that require knowledge and experience in using coordinated, well-informed and long-term approaches to risk management and strategic decision making. How can we prepare business actors to manage risks and coordinate efforts in the face of climate change threats?	*Decisions For The Decade* supports group decision-making regarding uncertain events and helps players to be more alert and vigilant about risk management and planning for extremes related to the impacts of climate change. Each round, players decide how to prepare for an extreme event, such as a flood or drought.
19	World Climate Simulation[19]	There are limits to learning from experiences and experiments, especially when it comes to climate change impacts because the time scales involved are decades to millennia and many climate impacts are irreversible. How can we enable experiential learning about the complex dynamics of climate change in real-time?	The *World Climate Simulation* helps players to learn about the policy-relevant science of climate change, viscerally experience international politics and explore solutions to the challenges of shaping a green economy. Players take the roles of various nations as they negotiate a global agreement to mitigate CO2 emissions.
20	Pitch Your Green Idea[20]	Sustainable development is associated with multilateral challenges that need to be addressed from different perspectives and through the generation and evaluation of alternative business ideas. How can we encourage open-mindedness and thinking from alternative perspectives when generating ideas for sustainable value creation?	*Pitch Your Green Idea* encourages idea generation from different perspectives while conveying knowledge about sustainable management. Players develop their own ideas to solve current sustainable problems, design their company and solve knowledge questions in the fields of start-up development and sustainability.

21	Design Play Cards[21]	When pursuing sustainable design opportunities, product developers often lack an overview and comprehensive understanding of potential pitfalls and proven pathways to success. How can we inform designers about the typical approaches for and challenges to sustainability-oriented design?	*Design Play Cards* use fun and engaging exercises to convey complex approaches to design problem solving taken from the eco-design and sustainable product design communities. Players use Design Strategy cards (with case studies) and Design Inspiration cards (with eco-design approaches) to solve design problems.
22	Innovation Diffusion[22]	Companies have to anticipate resistance from stakeholders involved in the diffusion of sustainability innovations and understand the dynamics of such diffusion in order to meet users' needs in the most sustainable manner possible. How can we anticipate potential barriers to the widespread adoption of sustainable innovations?	*The Innovation Diffusion Game* demonstrates principles of innovation diffusion theory through role-playing of change agents, laggards, mainstreamers and iconoclasts, each with their unique attitudes and ambitions. Players are sensitized about the complex dynamics of culture change and commercialization.

References

Preface

1 In fact, it builds on a sequence of three EU Erasmus+ projects. The first explored alternative complementary approaches to learning about innovation and entrepreneurship (I&E) beyond the traditional classroom model (www.tacitproject.org). One strand of that work began exploring the use of games in enabling learning about IE and this led to a second major project – GAMIFY – which is a second-generation project specifically aimed at exploring this question (www.gamify.site). GAMIFY builds on the on-going work and strong partnership of the ERASMUS+ Project TACIT and the ISPIM Special Interest Groups for Teaching & Coaching Innovation and Values-Based and Sustainable Innovation. The third project is IMPACT (www.impact-project.site). Crucially, all three projects created a 'knowledge alliance' with the purpose of engaging innovation professionals as well as coaches, teachers and learning designers in a wide range of contexts – classrooms, training workshops, online, etc. – and to equip them with extensions to their repertoire, helping them add games to their resources. Different authors were responsible for different chapters (Henning for this preface and chapters 1, 4, 5 and 6, John for chapters 2 and 16, and Henning, Sune and John together for chapters 3, 14 and 15). Additional co-author teams are listed in part III (chapters 7–13) and the appendices.

2 Breuer, H., Ivanov, K., Abril, C., Dijk, S., Monti, A., Rappaccini, M., & Kasz, J. (2021). Building Values-based Innovation Cultures for Sustainable Business Impact. Proceedings of ISPIM Innovation Conference 2021, Berlin.

Chapter 1

1 Pelling, N. (2015). Gamification past and present. GWC14. Retrieved from https://www.youtube.com/watch?v=XZ4AbQvUGho

2 Deterding, S. (2011). Situated motivational affordances of game elements: A conceptual model. In Gamification: Using game design elements in non-gaming contexts, a workshop at CHI (Vol. 10, No. 1979742.1979575).

3 Kapp, K. M. (2012). The Gamification of Learning and Instruction. Game-Based methods and Strategies for Training and Education. San Francisco: Pfeiffer / Wiley; also see Kapp, K. M. (2011). Another proposed definition of 'game'. Retrieved from http://karlkapp.com/a-proposed-definition-of-game-2/

4 Ferrara, J. (2013). Games for persuasion: Argumentation, procedurality, and the lie of gamification. *Games and Culture*, 8(4), 289–304.

5 Perrotta, C., Bailey, C., Ryder, J. Haggis-Burridge, M. & Persico, D. (2020). Games as (not) culture: A critical policy analysis of the economic agenda of horizon 2020. *Games and Culture*, Vol. 15(8), 902–922.

6 Werbach, K., & Hunter, D. (2012). For the win: How game thinking can revolutionize your business. Philadelphia, PA: Wharton Digital Press.

7 Cooper, R. (1990). Stage-gate systems: A new tool for managing new products. *Business Horizons*, Vol. 33, No. 3, 44–54.

8 Ries, E. (2011). *The lean startup*. New York, NY: Crown Business.

9 Following Jane McGonigal, games can be a training for extreme self-motivation, which she calls 'urgent optimism': 'Urgent optimism is the desire to act immediately to tackle an obstacle, combined

https://doi.org/10.1515/9783110725582-028

with the belief that we have a reasonable hope of success. Gamers always believe that an epic win is possible, and that it's always worth trying, and trying now' (McGonigal, J. (2011). Gaming can make a better world. TED Talk retrieved from https://www.ted.com/talks/jane_mcgonigal_gaming_can_make_a_better_world).

10 Inspired by the well-known quote from Søren Kierkegaard: 'It is perfectly true, as the philosophers say, that life must be understood backwards. But they forget the other proposition, that it must be lived forwards.'; Kierkegaard, S. (1843/1949). Die Tagebücher [Journals] 1834–1855, Auswahl und Übertragung von Theodor Haecker. Koesel: Munich.

11 See von Schlippe, A. & Schweitzer, J. (2003). Lehrbuch der systemischen Therapie und Beratung [Textbook of systemic therapy and consulting]. Vandenhoeck & Ruprecht.

12 For instance, playing video games can positively impact social cooperation and flow, and help to reduce in-group bias among youngsters; Adachi, P. J., & Willoughby, T. (2012). Do video games promote positive youth development? *Journal of Adolescent Research, 28*(2), 155–165.

13 Jullien, F. (2017). *Une seconde vie* [A second life]. Editions Grasset & Fasquelle (German edition 2020 by Passagen Verlag), 15.

14 A yet unsolved challenge with great potentials for gamification is the promotion of futures literacy, responding to the call from UNESCO (2021).

15 Musk Foundation (XPrize Carbon Removal). (2021). One recent example is the carbon removal challenge issued by the Musk Foundation. Retrieved from https://www.xprize.org/prizes/elonmusk.

16 Rittel, H. & Webber, M. (1973). Dilemmas in a general theory of planning. *Policy Sciences*, Vol. 4, No. 2, 155–169; Waddock, S. (2013). The wicked problems of global sustainability need wicked (good) leaders and wicked (good) collaborative solutions. *Journal of Management for Global Sustainability*, Vol. 1, No. 1, 91–111.

17 In this aspect, they resemble the early military use of war simulations where decision-makers were using giant maps, scenario techniques and role-play to play out specific scenarios before they might occur on the battlefield.

18 Gudiksen, S., & Inlove, J. (2018). *Gamification for business: Why innovators and changemakers use games to break down silos, drive engagement and build trust.* Kogan Page Publishers.

19 The UN Global Compact Dilemma Game was created and distributed by Global Compact Network Germany. Retrieved from https://www.globalcompact.de/en/about-us

20 In countries like Germany, interactive tools like *Wahl-o-mat* (https://www.bpb.de/politik/wahlen/wahl-o-mat) have developed into an essential source of information for voters before elections and for civic education. In Switzerland, Projekt CH+ develops Games for Democracy that provides voters with information and supports their decision making for upcoming elections (https://projektchplus.ch/en/).

21 Peterson, J. (2012). *Playing at the World: A History of Simulating Wars, People and Fantastic Adventures, from Chess to Role-playing Games.* Unreason Press.

22 Strategic Derby was created by Sune Gudiksen and Jake Inlove in collaboration with the consultancy company Dansk Produktion Univers and refined in use with different companies; see: Inlove, J. & Gudiksen, S. (2017). Strategic Derby: a game tool approach to strategic foresight and agility. In Proceedings of The International Society for Professional Innovation Management. ISPIM conference Vienna June 2017

23 Kapp, K. M. (2012). *The Gamification of Learning and Instruction. Game-Based Methods and Strategies for Training and Education.* San Francisco: Pfeiffer / Wiley.

24 Gudiksen, S., & Inlove, J. (2018). *Gamification for Business: Why Innovators and Changemakers Use Games to Break Down Silos, Drive Engagement and Build Trust.* Kogan Page Publishers.

25 Gray, D., Brown, S., & Macanufo, J. (2010). *Gamestorming: A Playbook for Innovators, Rulebreakers, and Changemakers.* Cambridge: O'Reilly.

26 Thomas Malone investigates sources of fun in games and identifies challenge, fantasy and curiosity as the three key motivational components; Malone, T. (1981). *Toward a theory of intrinsically motivating instruction*. Cognitive science, 4, 333–369.
27 Elgood, C. (1981). *Handbook of Management Games*. Gower Publishing: Aldershot, Hampshire.
28 Hohmann, L. (2006). *Innovation Games: Creating Breakthrough Products Through Collaborative Play*. Addison-Wesley: Boston, Mass, USA.
29 Patrício, R., Moreira, A. C., & Zurlo, F. (2018). Gamification approaches to the early stage of innovation. *Creativity and Innovation Management*, 27(4), 499–511.
30 Gudiksen, S. (2015). Business model design games: Rules and procedures to challenge assumptions and elicit surprises. *Creativity and Innovation Management*, *24*(2), 307–322.
31 Vijay Kumar complied a rich collection of 101 design methods including ideation game design – however, most of the methods can also become flows or components of gamified responses to innovation challenges. See: Kumar, V. (2011). *101 Design Methods: A Structured Approach for Driving Innovation in Your Organization*. Wiley, 222–227; Schulz, K. P., Geithner, S., Woelfel, C., & Krzywinski, J. (2015). Toolkit-based modelling and serious play as means to foster creativity in innovation processes. *Creativity and Innovation Management*, 24(2), 323–340.
32 Roth, S., Schneckenberg, D., & Tsai, C. W. (2015). The ludic drive as innovation driver: Introduction to the gamification of innovation. *Creativity and Innovation Management*, 24(2), 300–306; Kavaliova, M., Virjee, F., Maehle, N., Kleppe, I. A., & Nisar, T. (2016). Crowdsourcing innovation and product development: Gamification as a motivational driver. *Cogent Business & Management*, 3, 1128132; Morschheuser, B., Hamari, J., Koivisto, J., & Maedche, A. (2017). Gamified crowdsourcing: Conceptualization, literature review, and future agenda. *International Journal of Human-Computer Studies*, 106, 26–43.
33 Grenning, J. (2002). Planning Poker or How to avoid analysis paralysis while release planning. Retrieved from https://wingman-sw.com/papers/PlanningPoker-v1.1.pdf
34 Jovanović, M., Mesquida, A. L., Radaković, N., & Mas, A. (2016). Agile retrospective games for different team development phases. *Journal of Universal Computer Science*, 22(12), 1489–1508.
35 Mosleh, W. S., & Leue-Bensch, C. (2017, June). How Games can Address Organisational Innovation Challenges. In ISPIM Innovation Symposium, 1. The International Society for Professional Innovation Management (ISPIM).
36 Shi, V. G., Baines, T., Baldwin, J., Ridgway, K., Petridis, P., Bigdeli, A. Z., . . . & Andrews, D. (2017). Using gamification to transform the adoption of servitization. *Industrial Marketing Management*, 63, 82–91.
37 Breuer, H. & Ivanov, K. (2020). Gamification to address cultural challenges and to facilitate values-based innovation. In: Proceedings of ISPIM Virtual Innovation Conference 2020.
38 See e.g. McGonigal, J. (2011). *Reality is Broken: Why Games Make Us Better and How They Can Change the World*. New York: Penguin.
39 *Games for Change* is a non-profit organisation founded in 2004. It 'empowers game creators and social innovators to drive real-world impact through games and immersive media'; retrieved from https://www.gamesforchange.org/who-we-are
40 *World Without Oil*, created 2007, prompt players to share ideas how to adapt to an oil shortage. *Superstruct* crowdsources ideas for the future of energy, food, health, security and social safety; McGonigal, J. (2011). Gaming can make a better world. TED Talk retrieved from https://www.ted.com/talks/jane_mcgonigal_gaming_can_make_a_better_world

Chapter 2

1 Gray, P. (2018). Evolutionary Functions of Play: Practice, Resilience, Innovation, and Cooperation. In: P. Smith & J. Roopnarine (Eds.), *The Cambridge Handbook of Play: Developmental and Disciplinary Perspectives* (Cambridge Handbooks in Psychology, 84–102). Cambridge: Cambridge University Press.
2 Gray, D., Brown, S., & Macanafu, J. (2010). *Gamestorming: A Playbook for Innovators, Rulebreakers and Changemakers*. New York: O'Reilly Media Inc.
3 He also wrote that 'play is a free activity standing quite consciously outside "ordinary" life as being "not serious" but at the same time absorbing the player intensely and utterly'. However, his idea of Huizinga as 'free' play was widely criticized, since play is always triggered by surroundings, materials, objects, interactions and comes in a space with constraints. In our context, 'safe ludic space' also comes with heavy organizational constraints and conditions; Huizinga, J. (2016). *Homo Ludens: A Study of the Play-Element in Culture*. New York: Angelico Press.
4 'Games . . . can also be placed on a continuum between two opposite poles. At one extreme an almost indivisible principle, common to diversion, turbulence, free improvisation, and carefree gaiety is dominant. It manifests a kind of uncontrolled fantasy that can be designated by the term *paidia*. At the opposite extreme, this frolicsome and impulsive exuberance is almost entirely absorbed or disciplined by a complementary, and in some respects inverse, tendency to its anarchic and capricious nature: there is a growing tendency to bind it with arbitrary, imperative, and purposely tedious conventions, to oppose it still more by ceaselessly practicing the most embarrassing chicanery upon it, in order to make it more uncertain of attaining its desired effect. This latter principle is completely impractical, even though it requires an ever greater amount of effort, patience, skill, or ingenuity. I call this second component *ludus*' (Caillois, R. (2001). *Man, Play, and Games*. Champaign, Illinois: University of Illinois Press; 13).
5 Dautovic, G. (2021, June 21). The Rise of Virtual Empire: Video Game Industry Statistics for 2021. Retrieved from https://fortunly.com/statistics/video-game-industry-statistics/
6 Clement, J. (2021, May 3). Number of monthly active players of Minecraft worldwide as of March 2021. Retrieved from https://www.statista.com/statistics/680139/minecraft-active-players-worldwide/
7 Getzels, J. W., & Csikszentmihalyi, M. (1976). *The Creative Vision: A Longitudinal Study of Problem Finding in Art*. New York, NY: John Wiley & Sons.
8 Dyson, J. (1997). *Against the Odds: An Autobiography*. London: Orion Publishing Co.
9 Steven Johnson exemplifies such fertile environments in the natural history of innovation through the eyes of Charles Darwin near the Keeling Islands in the Indian ocean: 'Darwin's Paradox: so many different life forms, occupying such a vast array of ecological niches, inhabiting waters that are otherwise remarkably nutrient-poor. Coral reefs make up about one-tenth of one percent of the earth's surface, and yet roughly a quarter of the known species of marine life make their homes there'; Johnson, S. (2010). *Where Good Ideas Come From: The Seven Patterns of Innovation*. Penguin Books: London.
10 Dyson (1997)
11 Schrage, M. (1999). *Serious Play: How the World's Best Companies Simulate to Innovate*. Boston: Harvard Business School Press.

Dodgson, M., & Gann, D. (2019). Book review: 'The Playful Entrepreneur', *International Journal of Innovation Management* (IJIM), World Scientific Publishing Co. Pte. Ltd., vol. 23(05), pages 1–2, June.

Thomke, S. H. (2002). *Experimentation Matters: Unlocking the Potential of New Technologies for Innovation*. Boston: Harvard Business School Press.
12 Allen, T. and Henn, G. (2007). *The Organization and Architecture of Innovation*. Oxford: Elsevier.
13 Fritzsche, A., Jonas, J. M., Roth, A., & Möslein, K. M. (eds.). (2020). *Innovating in the Open Lab: The New Potential for Interactive Value Creation Across Organizational Boundaries* (Vol. 1). Walter de Gruyter GmbH & Co KG.

14 Gray, D., Brown, S. & Macanufo, J. (2010). *Gamestorming. A Playbook for Innovators, Rulebreakers, and Changemakers*. O'Reilly: Cambridge.
15 Breuer, H. & Ivanov, K. (2020). Gamification to address cultural challenges and to facilitate values-based innovation. In: Proceedings of ISPIM Virtual Innovation Conference 2020.
16 For instance, in his work, Dewey positions knowledge as experience-based and socially constructed, which suggests teachers should facilitate real-life experiences and generate transferable learning outcomes. Dewey, J. (1938). *Experience and Education*. New York: MacMillan.
17 Piaget, J. (1972) *Psychology of The Child*. London: Basic Books. Retrieved from https://www.pentagonplay.co.uk/news-and-info/psychology-learning-through-play
18 Vygotsky, L. S. (2016). Play and its Role in the Mental Development of the Child. *International Research in Early Childhood Education*, *7*(2), 3–25.
19 Scaffolding 'refers to the steps taken to reduce the degrees of freedom in carrying out some task so that the child can concentrate on the difficult skill she is in the process of acquiring' (Bruner, 1978, p. 19); Bruner, J. S. (1978). The role of dialogue in language acquisition. In A. Sinclair, R., J. Jarvelle, and W. J.M. Levelt (eds.) *The Child's Concept of Language*. New York: Springer-Verlag.
20 Kolb, D. A. (1984). *Experiential learning: Experience as the source of learning and development* (Vol. 1). Englewood Cliffs, NJ: Prentice-Hall, 38.
21 Bessant, J. (2021). NPD car activity: Managing Innovation. Retrieved from https://johnbessant.org/activities
22 Kolb, A.Y. and Kolb, D.A. (2010). Learning to play, playing to learn: A case study of a ludic learning space. *Journal of Organisational Change Management*, 23 (1), 26–50.
23 Kolb & Kolb (2010), 46–47
24 Caillois, R. (1958). Théorie des jeux. *Revue de Métaphysique et de Morale*, *63*(1), 83–102.
25 From Kolb & Kolb (2010), 46

Chapter 3

1 ISO 56002: 2019. Innovation Management – Innovation Management System – Guidance. Retrieved from https://www.iso.org/standard/68221.html
2 https://johnbessant.org/2020/05/28/sweeping-the-floor-with-innovation/
3 Lüdeke-Freund, F., Bohnsack, R., Breuer, H., & Massa, L. (2019). Research on sustainable business model patterns: status quo, methodological issues, and a research agenda. In *Sustainable Business Models* (25–60). Palgrave Macmillan, Cham
4 Berkun S. (2013). The Best Definition of Innovation. Retrieved from https://scottberkun.com/2013/the-best-definition-of-innovation/
5 Gemünden & Salomo (2004, 505) combine process and results in their widely recognized definition: 'Innovations are the results of a creative process involving different actors from one or more organizations, which leads to a qualitatively new means-end combination that is introduced to the market or the operations of a firm for the first time'; Gemünden, H.G. & Salomo, S. (2004) Innovationsmanagement. In: von Werder A. & Schreyögg, G. (Eds.), *Handwörterbuch der Organisation* [Dictionary of the organisation], 4th edition, 505–514. Stuttgart: Schäffer-Poeschel.
6 Breuer, H. & Lüdeke-Freund, F. (2019). Values-Based Stakeholder Management – Concepts and Methods. In: Wunder, T. (ed.): *Rethinking Strategic Management: Competing Through a Sustainability Mindset*. Berlin: Springer.
7 Baumol, W. J. (2014). *The Free-Market Innovation Machine*. Princeton University Press. Joseph Alois Schumpeter already found that 'carrying out innovations is the only function which is fundamental

in history'; Schumpeter, J.A. (1934). *Theory of Economic Development. An Inquiry into Profits, Capital, Credit, Interest, and the Business Cycle*. Harvard University Press: Cambridge.

8 This is based on a quote by Peter Drucker (2014, 19): 'Innovation is the specific tool of entrepreneurs, the means by which they exploit change as an opportunity for a different business or a different service. It is capable of being presented as a discipline, capable of being learned, capable of being practiced. Entrepreneurs need to search purposefully for the sources of innovation, the changes and their symptoms that indicate opportunities for successful innovation. And they need to know and to apply the principles of successful innovation; Drucker, P. (2014). *Innovation and Entrepreneurship*. Routledge. London: New York.

9 Schumpeter, J. A. (1939). *Business Cycles*, Vol. 1, 161–174. New York: McGraw-Hill.

10 OECD (2018). Oslo Manual 2018. Guidelines for Collecting, Reporting and Using Data on Innovation, 4th Edition. Retrieved from www.oecd.org/science/oslo-manual-2018-9789264304604-en.htm

11 Breuer, H. & Lüdeke-Freund, F. (2017). *Values-Based Innovation Management: Innovating by What We Care About*. Hampshire, GB: Palgrave Macmillan.

12 Bleicher, K. (2011). *Das Konzept Integriertes Management* [The integrated management concept], 8th edition. Frankfurt a.M.: Campus; also see Wikipedia (2022). Integrated Management Concept. Retrieved from https://en.wikipedia.org/wiki/Integrated_Management_Concept.

Breuer, H., & Lüdeke-Freund, F. (2017). Values-based network and business model innovation. *International Journal of Innovation Management*, *21* (03), 1750028.

13 March, J. G. (1991). Exploration and exploitation in organizational learning. *Organization Science*, *2* (1), 71–87.

14 Bessant, J. (2021). New Product Development Game. Managing Innovation: Creating Value from Ideas. Retrieved from https://johnbessant.org

Chapter 4

1 Alexander, C., Ishikawa, S., Silverstein, M. (1977). *A Pattern Language: Towns, Buildings, Construction*. Oxford University Press, New York.

2 Alexander et al. 1977, XXXV

3 Gamma, E., Helm, R., Johnson, R., Vlissides, J. (1995). *Design Patterns: Elements of Reusable Object-Oriented Software*. Addison-Wesley.

4 Tidwell, J., Brewer, C. & Valencia, A. (2020). *Designing Interfaces: Patterns for Effective Interaction Design* (3rd edition). O'Reilly.

5 Breuer, H., Zurita, G., Baloian, N., & Matsumoto, M. (2008). Mobile learning with patterns. Proceedings of the 8th IEEE International Conference on Advanced Learning Technologies (ICALT), Santander, Spain, 626–630.

6 Gassmann, O., Frankenberger, K., & Choudury, M. (2020). *The Business Model Navigator: The Strategies Behind the Most Successful Companies* (2nd ed.). FT Publishing.

7 Lüdeke-Freund, F., Breuer, H. & Massa, L. (2021). *Sustainable Business Model Design – 45 Patterns*. Berlin: Self-Publishing; see www.sustainablebusiness.design

8 Alexander, C. (1979). *The Timeless Way of Building*. Oxford University Press.

9 Gimenez-Fernandez, E., Abril, C., Breuer, H., Gudiksen, S. (2021). Gamification approaches for open innovation implementation: A conceptual framework. *Creativity and Innovation Management*, Vol. 30, Issue 3, Sept. 2021, 455–474.

10 Breuer, H. & Ivanov, K. (2020). Gamification to address cultural challenges and to facilitate values-based innovation. In: Proceedings of ISPIM Virtual Innovation Conference 2020.

11 Deterding and colleagues refer to these as game elements; Deterding, S., Dixon, D., Khaled, R., & Nacke, L. (2011). From game design elements to gamefulness: defining gamification. In: Proceedings of the 15th international academic MindTrek conference: Envisioning future media environments, 9–15. ACM.
12 Rüegg-Stürm, J., Grand, S., & Grand, S. (2017). *Das St. Galler Management-Modell*. Bern: Haupt; Bleicher, K. (1994). Integrative management in a time of transformation. *Long Range Planning*, Vol. 27, No. 5, 136–144; Bleicher, K. (2011) *Das Konzept Integriertes Management. Visionen, Missionen, Programme*. [The integrated management concept. Visions, missions, programs], 8th edition. Frankfurt a.M.: Campus.
13 Cooper, R.G. & Edgett, S.J. (2012). Best practices in the idea-to-launch process and its governance. *Research-Technology Management*, Vol. 55, No. 2, pp. 43–54; Cooper, R. (1990). Stage-gate systems: A new tool for managing new products. *Business Horizons*, Vol. 33, No. 3, pp. 44–54.
14 Tidd, J., & Bessant, J. R. (2020). *Managing Innovation: Integrating Technological, Market and Organizational Change*. Hoboken: John Wiley & Sons; Breuer & Lüdeke-Freund (2017).
15 Initial research on this dyad was later extended to recognize a troika of roles critical to success: The technology promoter – an individual that possesses the technical knowledge or input for the innovation process; a power promoter – an individual typically from higher management that would 'protect' the idea, win over reluctant colleagues and help overcome psychological barriers to innovation, and the process promoter – who translates the technical know-how into a language understood by the entire organization. The 'troika of promoters' model provides a heuristic to think about and manage the roles required for innovation in mid-sized and larger firms; Hauschildt, J. & Kirchmann, E. (2001). Teamwork for innovation – the 'troika' of promotors. *R&D Management* Volume 31, Issue 1, 41–49.
16 Also see examples of 'innovation time-off' in Breuer & Lüdeke-Freund 2017, Chapter 4.
17 Kim, W.C. & Mauborgne, R. (2015). *Blue Ocean Strategy, Expanded Edition: How to Create Uncontested Market Space and Make the Competition Irrelevant*. Boston, MA: Harvard Business Review Press.
18 Breuer, H. (2013). Lean venturing: Learning to create new business through exploration, elaboration, evaluation, experimentation, and evolution. *International Journal of Innovation Management*, *17*(03).
19 Tidd, J. & Bessant, J. (2014). *Strategic Innovation Management*. Chichester: Wiley, 281–286.
20 See chapter 1.2 and Breuer & Ivanov (2020)
21 In this case gamified activities are oriented to solving innovation challenges, with flows of interactions that are realized by component-related operations. 'Activities are oriented to motives, that is the objects that are compelling by themselves. Each motive is an object, material or ideal that satisfies a need. Actions are processes functionally subordinated to activities; they are directed at specific conscious goals . . . Actions are realised through operations'; Kaptelinin, V. (1996). Activity Theory: Implications for Human-Computer Interaction. In: Nardi, B. (Ed.). *Context and Consciousness. Activity Theory and Human-computer Interaction*. Cambridge, MA: MIT Press, 108.
22 Breuer & Ivanov (2020)
23 Björk, S. & Holopainen, J. (2004). *Patterns in Game Design*. Charles River Media; Chou, Y. K. (2019). *Actionable Gamification: Beyond Points, Badges, and Leaderboards*. Packt Publishing Ltd; Kapp, K. M.; Blair, L., Mesch, R. (2014). *The Gamification of Learning and Instruction Fieldbook: Ideas into Practice*. John Wiley & Sons; Marczewski, A. (2015). *Even Ninja Monkeys Like to Play*. CreateSpace Indep. Publish Platform, Charleston, Chapter User Types, 69–84; Gudiksen, S., & Inlove, J. (2018). *Gamification for Business: Why Innovators and Changemakers Use Games to Break Down Silos, Drive Engagement and Build Trust*. Kogan Page Publishers.
24 Breuer, H. & Ivanov, K. (2022). Gamification Design Pattern Cards. 46 Cards. GAMIFY. Retrieved from www.gamify.site and www.uxberlin.com.
25 Mackey, J. & Sisodia R. (2015). Foreword. In: Freeman, R. E., & Auster, E. R. Bridging the values gap: How authentic organizations bring values to life. Berrett- Koehler Publishers.

26 Schwartz, S.H. (2012). An overview of the Schwartz theory of basic values. Readings in Psychology and Culture, Vol. 2, No. 1, http://dx.doi. org/10.9707/2307-0919.1116.
27 Feather, N. T. (1996). Values, deservingness, and attitudes toward high achievers: Research on tall poppies. In C. Seligman, J. M. Olson, & M. P. Zanna (Eds.), *The psychology of values: The Ontario symposium*, Vol. 8, pp. 215–251). Lawrence Erlbaum Associates, Inc.
28 Gudiksen, S., & Sørensen, L. (2017). Value-based leadership: Game tool as bridge maker. In ISPIM Conference Proceedings (pp. 1-13). The International Society for Professional Innovation Management (ISPIM).
29 Breuer, H., Gudiksen, S., Abril, C. & Lehmann, C. (2019). Gamification and Games as Facilitation Methods for Innovation and Entrepreneurship. In Bitran, I., Conn, S. et al. Proceedings of XXX ISPIM Innovation Conference 2019 in Florence.
30 Björk, S. & Holopainen, J. (2004) Patterns in Game Design. Charles River Media. ISBN1-58450-354-8.
31 Van der Meer, A. (2022). How role-playing games can help teach business and leadership. Retrieved from https://aestranger.com/role-playing-experiences-leadership/
32 Swailes, S., & McIntyre-Bhatty, T. (2002). The ‚Belbin' team role inventory: Reinterpreting reliability estimates. Journal of Managerial Psychology, 17(6), 529–536.
33 Darsø, L. (2010). Innovation in the Making. Samfundslitteratur, Frederiksberg.
34 Gudiksen, S., & Inlove, J. (2018). Gamification for business: Why innovators and changemakers use games to break down silos, drive engagement and build trust. Kogan Page Publishers.
35 De Bono, E. (1985). *Six Thinking Hats*. London: Penguin Books.

Chapter 5

1 Wujek, T. (2010). Build a tower, build a team. Retrieved from https://www.ted.com/talks/tom_wujec_build_a_tower_build_a_team?language=en; Anthony, S. D. (2014, December 09). Innovation Leadership Lessons from the Marshmallow Challenge. Retrieved from https://hbr.org/2014/12/innovation-leadership-lessons-from-the-marshmallow-challenge
2 For ideation games see the book on 'gamestorming' (Gray et al 2010); for customer integration and design thinking techniques see for instance *101 Design Methods* (Kumar 2013); for 'agile retrospective games' to improve a shared understanding of values and project-related objectives in small group development, see Jovanović et al. (2016).
3 For example in a series of training workshops within the utility provider SWK the problem was that participants in one workshop could 'leak' information about the game (a creativity and problem-solving challenge) to future participants who could then use this to win. The *Eggs-Ercises* game involved coming up with solutions to operate on an egg in such a way as to stop it breaking when it was released under various conditions. The trainers adapted the same basic game structure to present a different version of the challenge (for instance being suspended from the ceiling by strings which were then cut, dropped from a high window, thrown across the room). Each case would require a different solution – but the underlying learning and core concepts remained the same.
4 Innovation Bazar (2021): 3 Warm-Ups to Ignite Your Design Thinking Workshop. Retrieved from https://www.innovationbazar.com/warm-ups /
5 For instance, the values-based kickbox format is described with further references at: UXBerlin (2022). Wertebasiertes Intrapreneurship mit der Kickbox. Retrieved from https://www.uxberlin.com/values-based-kickbox/
6 The programme is described in Bessant, J. (2022). Managing Innovation. Case Studies: J-L. Retrieved from https://johnbessant.org/casesjl

7 Changing content versus structure of the game should not be confused with the distinction between structural gamification (embedding existing content in a gamified structure using points and leaderboards, badges and levels, progress tracking to motivate learners) and content gamification making the content itself more game-like in educational settings (Kapp et. al. 2014, 224).
8 The *ACT Dilemma* game was created by Sune Gudiksen in collaboration with the consultancy company Relation Technologies. See: Gudiksen, S. & Sørensen, L. (2017). Value-based leadership: Game tool as bridge maker. In Proceedings of The International Society for Professional Innovation Management. ISPIM conference Vienna June 2017
9 The World Bank (2021). EVOKE – An online alternate reality game supporting social innovation among young people around the world. Retrieved from https://www.worldbank.org/en/topic/edutech/brief/evoke-an-online-alternate-reality-game-supporting-social-innovation-among-young-people-around-the-world
10 McGonigal, J. (2015). *SuperBetter: A Revolutionary Approach to Getting Stronger, Happier, Braver and More Resilient–Powered by the Science of Games*. London: Penguin Press. For the game itself see: https://www.superbetter.com/ and https://www.gamesforchange.org/game/superbetter/
11 Bessant, J. (2021).
12 Morgan, G. (1975). *Images of organization*. Sage Books, New York.
13 Bessant, J. (2022). The paper aeroplane exercise. Retrieved from https://ae44e96f-9228-4cfc-8b1a-cc1349890204.filesusr.com/ugd/6ba33a_8b93b22dabfb479481ea41df70fe5bdc.pdf
14 Bessant, J. (2022). The red-blue exercise. Online https://ae44e96f-9228-4cfc-8b1a-cc1349890204.filesusr.com/ugd/6ba33a_6bcc3fc281f1476b824d68a7c5daa161.pdf
15 Bessant, J. (2021).
16 Breuer, H. & Lüdeke-Freund, F. (2018). Values-Based Business Model Innovation: A Toolkit. In: Moratis, L., Melissen, F. & Idowu, S.O. (eds.). *Sustainable Business Models*, 395–416. Springer; also see https://www.uxberlin.com/businessinnovationkit/
17 Bessant, J. (2021).
18 An Introduction to Design Thinking: The Wallet Challenges. Institute of Design at Stanford. Retrieved from https://hci.stanford.edu/dschool/resources/wallet/Wallet%20Facilitators%20Guide.pdf
19 IfM Engage. University of Cambridge (2021). Retrieved from https://engage.ifm.eng.cam.ac.uk/roadmapping/
20 FoldIt. (2022). The Science behind FoldIt. Retrieved from https://fold.it/portal/info/about; also Kapp et al. (2014), 57
21 McGonigal, J. (2011). Gaming can make a better world. TED Talk retrieved from https://www.ted.com/talks/jane_mcgonigal_gaming_can_make_a_better_world
22 McGonigal, J. (2011).
23 Breuer, H., Gudiksen, S., Abril, C. & Lehmann, C. (2019). Gamification and Games as Facilitation Methods for Innovation and Entrepreneurship. In Bitran, I., Conn, S. et al. Proceedings of XXX ISPIM Innovation Conference 2019 in Florence.
24 Bessant, J. (2021).
25 Winkel, D., Wilcox, J., & Mammano, F. (2020). Teaching Entrepreneurship: Experiences Teach Skills. Retrieved from https://www.teachingentrepreneurship.org/60-minute-mvp/

Chapter 6

1 Breuer & Lüdeke-Freund (2017), 187–189; retrieved from https://www.uxberlin.com/wp-content/uploads/2012/12/2016_Ethnographic_Exploration.pdf
2 You may download an interactive PDF template from the companion sites to this book.

3 Clark, R. E. (1994). Media will never influence learning. *Educational Technology Research and Development*, *42*(2), 21–29.
4 Caillois, R. (2001). *Man, Play, and Games*. University of Illinois Press: Champaign, Illinois.
5 'Design is a journey of discovery' is a saying by Derek Parker, British Writer & Broadcaster.
6 See Kapp et al. 2014, 103ff. for storytelling basics for the design of interactive learning environments
7 Bessant, J. (2021). For the paper aeroplane activity, see Managing Innovation: Creating value from ideas. Retrieved from https://johnbessant.org
8 An Introduction to Design Thinking: The Wallet Challenge. Institute of Design at Stanford. Retrieved from https://hci.stanford.edu/dschool/resources/wallet/Wallet%20Facilitators%20Guide.pdf
9 Bessant, J. (2021).
10 Bessant, J. (2021).
11 Bessant, J. (2021).
12 TACIT Knowledge alliance (2016–2018). Erasmus+ Programme of the European Union. Storytelling, innovation theatre and several other activity-based inputs are described in detail at the TACIT project. Retrieved from https://www.tacit-project.org/
13 There are a variety of workshop games based on using eggs as a fragile (high risk) component.
14 Lakoff, G., & Johnson, M. (1980). Conceptual metaphor in everyday language. *The Journal of Philosophy*, *77*(8), 453–486.

Part III

1 Developing such games to address major challenges – from solving the great societal sustainability challenges, to redesigning the business model and overcoming innovation barriers, or the daily need to empathize with colleagues – was a core activity of the GAMIFY project. Each game and companion materials are available to use and/ or customize for specific challenges from the companion sites.

Chapter 7

1 Breuer, H., & Ivanov, K. (2020). Gamification to address cultural challenges and to facilitate values-based innovation. In *ISPIM Conference Proceedings* (1–18). The International Society for Professional Innovation Management (ISPIM).
2 Both game formats were developed in close collaboration with the Social Engagement Group, the Sustainability Management Group and the Design Gallery of Deutsche Telekom. From initial conversations we learned that imparting knowledge and raising awareness for a broad audience were ongoing challenges for both groups, who were focussing on the three areas of climate action, circular economy and human rights & digital inclusion. We agreed that it was essential to encourage participants to interpret and reflect on their own impact if we were to achieve high impact learning experiences. In addition, the Design Gallery as well as the GAMIFY project explicitly stressed the need to reach beyond analysis and awareness into creating seeds for innovation and action. The third objective for gamification was a nice-to-have objective. How could ideas be better implemented in everyday work routines? In hindsight it appears a bit naïve, but we took on the complex task to pursue all three objectives with one gamified format.

Chapter 8

1 The game, which was developed with and for Generali, was also based on problem framing conversations with 3M. After these first tests, Customer First Change has been used in shorter workshops and webinars, and is openly available on the Actee platform as one of its many games on organizational change.
2 Siggelkow, N., & Terwiesch, C. (2019). *Connected strategy: Building continuous customer relationships for competitive advantage*. Harvard Business Press.
3 Maurer, R. (2010). *Beyond the wall of resistance: Why 70% of all changes still fail–and what you can do about it*. Bard Press.
4 Maurer, R. (2021). *Seizing moments of possibility: Ways to trigger energy and forward momemtum on your ideas*. Parzival Publishing.
5 Siggelkow, N., & Terwiesch, C. (2019). *Connected strategy: Building continuous customer relationships for competitive advantage*. Harvard Business Press.
6 Siggelkow & Terwiesch (2019)
7 Related to the theory from Maurer, R. (2010). *Beyond the Wall of Resistance – Why 70% of All Changes Still Fail– And What You Can Do About It*. Bard Press.

Chapter 9

1 McGrath, R. G. (2013). *The end of competitive advantage: How to keep your strategy moving as fast as your business*. Harvard Business Review Press, 31.
2 The game was developed for specific organizations and to work as an innovation method in a series of masterclasses and continuing education modules in the years 2017–2020. In an updated version with more practical elements and business model design scenario thinking it became part of the GAMIFY project for use in partner and other organizations.
3 Gibson, C. B., & Birkinshaw, J. (2004). The antecedents, consequences, and mediating role of organizational ambidexterity. *Academy of Management Journal*, *47*(2), 209–226; Birkinshaw, J., Hamel, G., & Mol, M. J. (2008). Management innovation. *Academy of Management Review*, *33*(4), 825–845; Raisch, S., & Birkinshaw, J. (2008). Organizational ambidexterity: Antecedents, outcomes, and moderators. *Journal of Management*, *34*(3), 375–409; McGrath, R. G. (2013). *The end of competitive advantage: How to keep your strategy moving as fast as your business*. Harvard Business Review Press; Govindarajan, V., & Trimble, C. (2013). *Beyond the idea: How to execute innovation in any organization*. St. Martin's Press; McGrath, R. (2019). *Seeing around corners: How to spot inflection points in business before they happen*. Houghton Mifflin Harcourt.
4 Govindarajan, V., Trimble, C. (2013). The Other Side of Innovation: Solving the Execution Challenge. Harvard Business Review Press, p.10.
5 McGrath, R. (2019). *Seeing around corners: How to spot inflection points in business before they happen*. Houghton Mifflin Harcourt.
6 McGrath, R. (2019). *Seeing around corners: How to spot inflection points in business before they happen*. Houghton Mifflin Harcourt.
7 Sinek, S. (2011). *Start with why: How great leaders inspire everyone to take action*. Penguin.
8 Sinek, S. (2011). *Start with why: How great leaders inspire everyone to take action*. Penguin.
9 McGrath (2013). Continuous reconfiguration in the transient advantage economy. *Strategy & Leadership* VOL. 41 NO. 5 2013, 17–22 (17).
10 McGrath (2013). The *end of competitive advantage: How to keep your strategy moving as fast as your business*. Harvard Business Review Press, p. 37.

Chapter 10

1 The game was developed with and for Lufthansa Systems to be included in its opening of the 'Flying Lab' space at the Frankfurt headquarters. Concept development of the game is credited to Emilie Bech Jespersen, Klara Birgisdóttir, Léa Chénot, Sune Gudiksen, and Carina Leue-Bensch. *Shift* has since been used in a series of shorter master classes and was further validated in workshops with Danish Companies Kamstrup, Danske Bank, and Arla Foods and received highest evaluation scores.
2 Christensen, C. (1997). Patterns in the evolution of product competition. *European Management Journal*, *15*(2), 117–127.
3 Gibson, C. B., & Birkinshaw, J. (2004). The antecedents, consequences, and mediating role of organizational ambidexterity. *Academy of Management Journal*, *47*(2), 209–226; Birkinshaw, J., Hamel, G., & Mol, M. J. (2008). Management innovation. *Academy of Management Review*, *33*(4), 825–845; Raisch, S., & Birkinshaw, J. (2008). Organizational ambidexterity: Antecedents, outcomes, and moderators. *Journal of Management*, *34*(3), 375–409; Govindarajan, V., & Trimble, C. (2013). *Beyond the idea: How to execute innovation in any organization.* St. Martin's Press; Tidd, J., & Bessant, J. (2018). Innovation management challenges: From fads to fundamentals. *International Journal of Innovation Management*, *22*(05).
4 Hines, A. (2008). *Thinking about the Future: Guidelines for Strategic Foresight.* Hinesight publisher.

Chapter 11

1 Ford, R. C., Piccolo, R. F., & Ford, L. R. (2017). Strategies for building effective virtual teams: Trust is key. *Business Horizons*, *60*(1), 25–34; Wilson, J. M., Boyer O'Leary, M., Metiu, A., & Jett, Q. R. (2008). Perceived proximity in virtual work: Explaining the paradox of far-but-close. *Organization Studies*, *29*(7), 979–1002; Jarvenpaa, S. L., & Leidner, D. E. (1999). Communication and trust in global virtual teams. *Organization Science*, *10*(6), 791–815.
2 Its development started off with a challenges and opportunities workshop with members of the company 3M in Madrid. Several participants mentioned the challenges of working in cross-cultural and cross-disciplinary teams. As a global organization, most of the work includes communication and collaboration with virtual team members they have little familiarity with. The perception of only engaging in transactional relationships appeared to be an important factor influencing their motivation and satisfaction with their work. When asked about the biggest difference between working with a co-located team and a remote team from the same organization, one of the participants expressed that 'there is no we feeling and the team faces a community split where efforts being made feel short-term oriented and objective focused'. Additional research was then conducted to become familiar with the challenges of remote teams through a literature review and a look into existing methods for team building and social ice breakers, previous to conceptualizing the game and its design. The game supports remote workers bridge gaps in virtual collaboration projects and kickstart discussions on new social protocols that make a positive difference in a team's work culture.
3 Gudiksen, S., & Sørensen, L. (2017, June). Value-based leadership: Game tool as bridge maker. In *ISPIM Innovation Symposium*. The International Society for Professional Innovation Management (ISPIM).

Chapter 12

1 The *Ecosystem Canvas* game is research based, using qualitative data from teaching entrepreneurial students and working in an ever-changing university sector. By applying these findings (as presented in published articles) to the core curriculum and structure of bachelor programmes, we could see there was an enhanced demand for evolving the toolbox for teaching and developing entrepreneurial education and understanding among the actors in the entrepreneurial education ecosystem. The concept development of the game is credited to Jacob Thomsen and Sune Gudiksen. The *Ecosystem Canvas* game is a core element in developing and enhancing the entrepreneurial ecosystem in Odense and Denmark.

2 Wraae, B., & Thomsen, J. (2019). Introducing a New Framework for Understanding Learning in an Entrepreneurship Education Ecosystem. *Journal of Higher Education Theory and Practice*, 19(2), 171.

3 Maritz, A. (2017). Illuminating the black box of entrepreneurship education programmes: Part II. *Education+ Training*.

4 Pilinkiene V, Maciulis P (2014). Comparison of different ecosystem analogies: the main economic determinants and levels of impact. *Procedia – Social and Behavioral Sciences*, 156, 365–370.

5 Isenberg, D.J. (2010). *How to Start an Entrepreneurial Revolution*. Harvard Business Review.

6 Clarysse, B., Wright, M., Bruneel, J., Mahajan, A. (2014). Creating value in ecosystems: Crossing the chasm between knowledge and business ecosystems. *Research Policy* 43(7), 1164–1176.

7 Etzkowitz, H. (2014). The Entrepreneurial University Wave: From Ivory Tower to Global Economic Engine. *Industry and Higher Education* 28(4): 223–232.

8 Guerrero, M., Urbano, D., Gajón, E. (2017). Higher Education Entrepreneurial Ecosystems: Exploring the Role of Business Incubators in an Emerging Economy. *International Review of Entrepreneurship* 15(2): 175–202.

9 Wraae & Thomsen (2019)

10 Foss, L., Gibson, D.V. (Eds.). (2015). *The Entrepreneurial University. Context and Institutional Change*. Routledge; Wraae & Thomsen (2019).

11 Lackéus, M. (2018), '"What is value?" – A framework for analyzing and facilitating entrepreneurial value creation', *Uniped*, 41(1), 10–28.

12 Kolb, A.Y., Kolb, D.A. (2005). Learning Styles and Learning Spaces: Enhancing Experiential Learning in Higher Education. *Academy of Management Learning & Education* 4, 193–212.

13 Ratten, V. (2017). Entrepreneurial universities: the role of communities, people and places. *Journal of Enterprising Communities: People and Places in the Global Economy* 11(3): 310–315.

14 Carvalho, L. C., Costa, M. T., & Dominguinhos, P. (2010). Creating an entrepreneurship ecosystem in higher education. In S. Soomro (ed.). New Achievements in Technology. Vukuvar, Croatia: InTech.

15 Jones, C., & Matlay, H. (2011). Understanding the heterogeneity of entrepreneurship education: going beyond Gartner. *Education + Training*, 53(8/9), 692–703.

16 Ahmad, N., Hoffmann, A. (2008). A framework for addressing and measuring entrepreneurship. OECD. Entrepreneurship Indicators Steering Group, OECD Statistics Working Paper Series.

17 Isenberg, D. (2011). The entrepreneurship ecosystem strategy as a new paradigm for economic policy: principles for cultivating entrepreneurship. The Babson entrepreneurship ecosystem project. Retrieved from http://entrepreneurial-revolution.com/2011/05/11/the-entrepreneurship-ecosystem-strategy-as-a-new-paradigm-for-economic-policy-principles-for-cultivating-entrepreneurship/

18 Chang, J., & Rieple, A. (2013). Assessing students' entrepreneurial skills development in live projects. *Journal of Small Business and Enterprise Development* 20 (1): 225–241.

19 Gibb, A.A., Haskins, G. (2013). The University of the Future. An Entrepreneurial Stakeholder Learning Organisation? In: Fayolle, A., Redford, D.T. (Eds.), *Handbook of Research in Entrepreneurial Education* Volume 4 –Entrepreneurial University Handbook. Cheltenham, UK; Northampton, MA: Edward Elgar Publishing Ltd.

20 Wraae & Thomsen (2019)
21 A limited version can be downloaded from the companion site: https://www.gamify.site/ecosystem-canvas. It can be customized with the game's developers.
22 Ahmad, N., Hoffmann, A., 2008. A framework for addressing and measuring entrepreneurship. OECD. Entrepreneurship Indicators Steering Group, OECD Statistics Working Paper Series.
23 Isenberg (2011)
24 Chang & Rieple (2013)
25 Gibb, A.A., Haskins, G., 2013. The University of the Future. An Entrepreneurial Stakeholder Learning Organisation? in: Fayolle, A., Redford, D.T. (Eds.), *Handbook of Research in Entrepreneurial Education Volume 4 –Entrepreneurial University Handbook.* Northampton, MA: Edward Elgar Publishing Ltd.

Chapter 13

1 Roos J., Said R. (2006). Object-Mediated Communication. In: *Thinking from Within.* Palgrave Macmillan, London. https://doi.org/10.1057/9780230597419_5
2 Lear, E., Dann, S., & John, P. K. (2020, April). Using Lego® Serious Play™ Processes to Build Responsible Professionals. In *2020 IEEE Global Engineering Education Conference (EDUCON)* (1770–1774). IEEE.
3 Lear, E., Dann, S., & John, P. K. (2020, April). Using Lego® Serious Play™ Processes to Build Responsible Professionals. In *2020 IEEE Global Engineering Education Conference (EDUCON)* (1770–1774). IEEE.
4 Dann, S. (2018). Facilitating co-creation experience in the classroom with Lego Serious Play. *Australasian Marketing Journal, 26*(2), 121–131.
5 Together they founded a company called Executive Discovery, which developed and implemented the *LSP* methodology. In 2004, Executive Discovery Ltd. became part of the LEGO Group, which took over ownership, methodology and distribution of *LSP* materials. In 2010, LEGO offered the methodology as an open source method; Roos, J., & Victor, B. (2018). How it all began: the origins of LEGO® serious Play®. *International Journal of Management and Applied Research*, 5(4), 326–343.
6 Mosig, T., Said, W., Lehmann, C. (2021): Designing Smart Cities: A Participatory Approach to Business Model Teaching. *Journal of Business Models* (Vol. 9, No.3, 33–49).
7 Kristiansen, P., Hansen, P. H. K., & Nielsen, L. M. (2009, May). Articulation of tacit and complex knowledge. In *13th International Workshop of the IFIP WG* (Vol. 5, 77–86).
8 Gauntlett, D. (2007). *Creative explorations: New approaches to identities and audiences.* Routledge.
9 Freeman, L. (2003). Simulation and role playing with LEGO® Blocks. Journal of Information Systems Education; Inthrface (2021) THE LEGO® SERIOUS PLAY® METHOD https://inthrface.com/en/lego-serious-play/
10 Kristiansen, P., & Rasmussen, R. (2014). *Building a better business using the LEGO serious play method.* John Wiley & Sons.

Chapter 14

1 For example, *A Handbook of Structured Experiences for Human Relations Training*, Volume IX, Pfeiffer, J. William, John Wiley & Sons, 1986
2 Zimmerman, E. & Chaplin, H. (2013). The 21st Century Will Be Defined by Games. Retrieved from https://kotaku.com/manifesto-the-21st-century-will-be-defined-by-games-1275355204
3 Winkel, D., Wilcox, J., & Mammano, F. (2020). Teaching Entrepreneurship: Experiences teach skills. Retrieved from https://www.teachingentrepreneurship.org/60-minute-mvp/
4 https://venturewell.org/
5 This course was developed by Sune Gudiksen, Pia Schytz, Mathias Poulsen and Keila Quinones, and described in the paper: Gudiksen, S., Schytz, P., Poulsen, M., & Quinones, K. (2020). Play-based intrapreneurship: Challenging innovation processes and underlying cultural understanding. In *ISPIM Innovation Management Conference.*
6 Huber, L. (2009). Warum Forschendes Lernen nötig und möglich ist. [Why research-based learning is necessary and possible.] In: Huber, L., Hellmer, J., Schneider, F. (eds.): *Forschendes Lernen im Studium*. Bielefeld: Universitätsverlag Webler, 9–35.

Chapter 15

1 Jordan, B. & Henderson, A. (1995). Interaction Analysis: Foundations and Practice. *Journal of the Learning Sciences* 4(1), 39–103.
2 Breuer & Lüdeke-Freund (2017), 187–189; retrieved from https://www.uxberlin.com/wp-content/uploads/2012/12/2016_Ethnographic_Exploration.pdf
3 https://www.teachingentrepreneurship.org/60-minute-mvp-instructions/
4 Christensen, Clayton M. (1997). *The Innovator's Dilemma: When New Technologies Cause Great Firms to Fail*. Harvard Business Review Press.
5 Breuer & Lüdeke-Freund 2017, 77–82; for IBM InnovationJam see https://www.ibm.com/products/innovation-jam
6 45 business model design patterns for sustainable value creation are documented in Lüdeke-Freund, F., Breuer, H., Massa, L. (2022). *Sustainable Business Model Design – 45 Patterns*. Berlin: Self-Publishing; www.sustainablebusiness.design
7 Wagner, A. & Galuszka, D. (2020). Let's play the future: Sociotechnical imaginaries, and energy transitions in serious digital games. *Energy Research & Social Science* 70 (2020), 1–22.
8 Autor, D. and B. Price (2013), The Changing Task Composition of the US Labor Market: An Update of Autor, Levy, and Murnane (2003), MIT Mimeograph.
9 Bacigalupo, M., Kampylis, P., Punie, Y. and Van Den Brande, L. (2016). EntreComp: The Entrepreneurship Competence Framework. EUR 27939 EN. Luxembourg (Luxembourg): Publications Office of the European Union; 2016. JRC101581; retrieved from https://publications.jrc.ec.europa.eu/repository/handle/JRC101581
10 See Diversity Business Incubator (2022). Catapulting business success in the minority communities. Retrieved from http://dbi.org.uk/; also see the Evoke game described in chapter 5.3 and retrieved from https://www.worldbank.org/en/news/feature/2018/01/18/new-mindset-increased-profits-lessons-from-an-innovative-entrepreneurial-training-in-togo
11 von Hippel, E. (2005). *Democratizing Innovation*. Cambridge, MA: MIT Press.
12 ProjektCh+ (2022). Projekt CH+. Games for Democracy. Retrieved from https://projektchplus.ch/en/
13 Bundeszentrale für Politische Bildung. (2022). Wahl-O-Mat; retrieved from https://www.bpb.de/politik/wahlen/wahl-o-mat

Chapter 16

1 Berne, E. (1964). *Games People Play. The Psychology of Human Relationships*. New York: Penguin.
2 Harris, T. (1995). *I'm OK, You're OK*. Arrow Paperbacks, New York.

Appendix 1

1 Breuer, H. & Ivanov, K. (2022). Gamification Design Pattern Cards. Card Deck and Full Version available from www.gamify.site and www.uxberlin.com/gamification

Appendix 2

1 Teaching Entrepreneurship. (2022). Prototyping Lesson Plan: Building 1-Hour No-Code Apps. Retrieved from https://www.teachingentrepreneurship.org/1-hour-no-code-app-exercise
2 Santonen, T., Purola, A. and Nevmerzhitskaya, J., 2020. Board game for co-creating ecosystem based circular economy business models. In: ISPIM Conference Proceedings (pp. 1–17). The International Society for Professional Innovation Management (ISPIM).
3 Alternatively, a personal object representing the participant, or a photo or short film showing more complex objects or those that are not portable.
4 Breuer, H. & Lüdeke-Freund, F. (2018). Values-Based Business Model Innovation: A Toolkit. In: Moratis, L., Melissen, F. & Idowu, S.O. (eds.). *Sustainable Business Models*, pp. 395–416. Springer; also see https://www.uxberlin.com/businessinnovationkit; Breuer, H., Fichter, K., Lüdeke-Freund, F., Tiemann, I. (2018). Sustainability-Oriented Business Model Development: Principles, Criteria and Tools. *International Journal of Entrepreneurial Venturing*. Special Issue Creating Solutions with Sustainable Entrepreneurship, 10(2):256–286.
5 GAMIFY. (2022). Business Model Branching. Retrieved from https://www.gamify.site/business-model-branching
6 Bessant, J. (2022). The Crumbling Cement Company. A role play activity around innovation strategy. Retrieved from https://ae44e96f-9228-4cfc-8b1a-cc1349890204.filesusr.com/ugd/f6594a_fa048d30b6794b05af96476a6f6de4f1.pdf
7 GAMIFY. (2022). Corporate Sustainability Innovation Game. Retrieved from https://www.gamify.site/corporate-sustainability
8 GAMIFY. (2022). Customer First Change Online Game. Retrieved from https://www.gamify.site/customer-first
9 Bessant, J. (2022). Activity: Dragons' Den. Retrieved from https://ae44e96f-9228-4cfc-8b1a-cc1349890204.filesusr.com/ugd/f6594a_1a04d043c80d4c2b902d18e596e1bc59.pdf
10 Innovation Bazar (2021). 3 Warm-Ups to Ignite Your Design Thinking Workshop. Retrieved from https://www.innovationbazar.com/warm-ups /
11 GAMIFY. (2022). Ecosystem Canvas. Retrieved from https://www.gamify.site/ecosystem-canvas
12 Bessant, J. (2022). Eggs-ercises. Simple innovation games designed to help groups explore shared creativity. Retrieved from https://ae44e96f-9228-4cfc-8b1a-cc1349890204.filesusr.com/ugd/f6594a_f27a2a3b8b594b1b8571c5154092f4b0.pdf
13 The World Bank (2021). EVOKE – An online alternate reality game supporting social innovation among young people around the world. Retrieved from https://www.worldbank.org/en/topic/edutech/brief/evoke-an-online-alternate-reality-game-supporting-social-innovation-among-young-people-around-the-world

14 FoldIt (2022). The Science Behind FoldIt. Retrieved from https://fold.it/portal/info/about
15 Breuer, H. & Ivanov, K. (2022). Gamification Design Pattern Cards. GAMIFY Project. Retrieved from www.gamify.site or www.uxberlin.com/gamification
16 SilkeC2. (2022). Hollow Square Contest. Retrieved from https://www.instructables.com/Hollow-Square-Contest/
17 Traction Toolbox (2022). Innovate or Dinosaur. A collaborative innovation game to generate new ideas! Retrieved from https://tractiontoolbox.ca/innovate-or-dinosaur/
18 Breuer, H., Gudiksen, S., Abril, C. & Lehmann, C. (2019). Gamification and Games as Facilitation Methods for Innovation and Entrepreneurship. In Bitran, I., Conn, S. et al. Proceedings of XXX ISPIM Innovation Conference 2019 in Florence.
19 Larsen, H. and Strøbech, E. (2018). Innovation Theatre. TACIT Teaching Materials. Kolding. Retrieved from https://www.johnbessant.org/toolsgi
20 Brilliant Innovation (2019). Innovation Diamond. Retrieved from https://www.behance.net/gallery/25165139/Brilliant-Innovation-Innovationsdiamantspillet
21 LEGO (2022). Serious Play. Retrieved from https://www.lego.com/en-us/seriousplay
22 Wujek, T. (2010). Build a tower, build a team. Retrieved from https://www.ted.com/talks/tom_wujec_build_a_tower_build_a_team?language=en; Anthony, S. D. (2014, December 09). Innovation Leadership Lessons from the Marshmallow Challenge. Retrieved from https://hbr.org/2014/12/innovation-leadership-lessons-from-the-marshmallow-challenge
23 UCSD Sixth College (2022). Icebreakers, Team, Building Activities, and Energizers https://sixth.ucsd.edu/_files/_home/student-life/icebreakers-teambuilding-activities-energizers.pdf
24 Bessant, J. (2022). The paper aeroplane exercise Retrieved from https://ae44e96f-9228-4cfc-8b1a-cc1349890204.filesusr.com/ugd/6ba33a_8b93b22dabfb479481ea41df70fe5bdc.pdf
25 Grenning, J. (2002). Planning Poker or How to avoid analysis paralysis while release planning. Retrieved from https://wingman-sw.com/papers/PlanningPoker-v1.1.pdf
26 Bessant, J. (2022). Project management. Retrieved from https://ae44e96f-9228-4cfc-8b1a-cc1349890204.filesusr.com/ugd/f6594a_65ec900bde15495e99d3d7fd119bb73a.pdf
27 GAMIFY. (2022). Proximity Remote Game. Retrieved from https://www.gamify.site/proximity-remote-game
28 Bessant, J. (2022). The red-blue exercise. Retrieved from https://ae44e96f-9228-4cfc-8b1a-cc1349890204.filesusr.com/ugd/6ba33a_6bcc3fc281f1476b824d68a7c5daa161.pdf; https://www.investopedia.com/articles/investing/110513/utilizing-prisoners-dilemma-business-and-economy.asp
29 IfM Engage. University of Cambridge (2021). Retrieved from https://engage.ifm.eng.cam.ac.uk/roadmapping/
30 Bessant, J. (2022). New product development game (NPD game). Retrieved from https://ae44e96f-9228-4cfc-8b1a-cc1349890204.filesusr.com/ugd/f6594a_45cd0735c77a43eaada615297a811d8d.pdf
31 Bessant, J. (2022). Activities. Retrieved from https://www.johnbessant.org/activities
32 GAMIFY. (2022). Shift – overcoming innovation barriers. Retrieved from https://www.gamify.site/shift
33 Inlove, J. & Gudiksen, S. (2017). Strategic Derby: a game tool approach to strategic foresight and agility. In Proceedings of The International Society for Professional Innovation Management. ISPIM conference Vienna June 2017
34 Bessant, J. (2022). Activities. Retrieved from https://www.johnbessant.org/activities
35 McGonigal, J. (2015). *SuperBetter: A Revolutionary Approach to Getting Stronger, Happier, Braver and More Resilient–Powered by the Science of Games*. London: Penguin Press. For the game itself see: https://www.superbetter.com/ and https://www.gamesforchange.org/game/superbetter/
36 McGonigal, J. (2011). Gaming can make a better world. TED Talk retrieved from https://www.ted.com/talks/jane_mcgonigal_gaming_can_make_a_better_world

37 Bessant, J. (2022). Games for team building. Retrieved from https://ae44e96f-9228-4cfc-8b1a-cc1349890204.filesusr.com/ugd/f6594a_fe73330a97c9478eb3411e29a8b9b24f.pdf
38 Bessant, J. (2022). Activity Uses for .. Retrieved from https://ae44e96f-9228-4cfc-8b1a-cc1349890204.filesusr.com/ugd/6ba33a_c28d8d392c644a4fb612019e6d4f7204.pdf
39 Hasso Plattner Institute of Design at Stanford. (2022). An introduction to Design Thinking. Retrieved from https://hci.stanford.edu/dschool/resources/wallet/Wallet%20Facilitators%20Guide.pdf
40 McGonigal, J. (2011). Gaming can make a better world. TED Talk retrieved from https://www.ted.com/talks/jane_mcgonigal_gaming_can_make_a_better_world

Appendix 3

1 Gudiksen, S., & Sørensen, L. (2017). Value-based leadership: Game tool as bridge maker. In ISPIM Conference Proceedings (pp. 1–13). The International Society for Professional Innovation Management (ISPIM).
2 Gudiksen, S., & Sørensen, L. (2017). Value-based leadership: Game tool as bridge maker. In ISPIM Conference Proceedings (pp. 1–13). The International Society for Professional Innovation Management (ISPIM).
3 P. Gerrickens, M. Verstege and Z. V. Dun (2021). The Values Game. The Values Game Manual. Retrieved from https://www.kwaliteitenspel.nl/images/HIKASHOP/Inkijkpaginas_pdf/Handleiding WaardenNormenspelEngelsInkijkpaginas.pdf
4 Ivanov, K., & Breuer, H. (2021). Design Patterns to Teach and Learn About Gamification for Innovation. In ISPIM Conference Proceedings (pp. 1–22). The International Society for Professional Innovation Management (ISPIM).
5 Gudiksen, S., & Inlove, J. (2018). *Gamification for business: Why innovators and changemakers use games to break down silos, drive engagement and build trust*. Kogan Page Publishers.
6 Gudiksen, S., & Sørensen, L. (2017). Value-based leadership: Game tool as bridge maker. In ISPIM Conference Proceedings (pp. 1–13). The International Society for Professional Innovation Management (ISPIM).
7 Greenhatpeople.com (2021). Core Values Game. Retrieved from https://www.greenhatpeople.com/uk/core-values-implementation/core-values-game
8 Jeanne, M. (2013). Ignite Leadership Game. Gamification in leadership development: How companies use gaming to build their leader pipeline. Retrieved from https://www.forbes.com/sites/jeannemeister/2013/09/30/gamification-in-leadership-development-how-companies-use-gaming-to-build-their-leader-pipeline/?sh=269e67d55a57
9 GAMIFY Erasmus+ Project. (2020). Expert Interview with Generali staff member.
10 GAMIFY Erasmus+ Project. (2020). Expert Interview with Generali staff member.
11 Friedman, B., & Hendry, D. (2012, May). The envisioning cards: a toolkit for catalyzing humanistic and technical imaginations. In Proceedings of the SIGCHI conference on human factors in computing systems (pp. 1145–1148).
12 GAMIFY Erasmus+ Project. (2020). Expert Interview with Generali staff member.
13 Jovanović, M., Mesquida, A. L., Radaković, N., & Mas, A. (2016). Agile retrospective games for different team development phases. *Journal of Universal Computer Science*, 22(12), 1489–1508; Gray, D. (2015). Circles and Soup. Accessed July 06, 2020, from https://gamestorming.com/circles-and-soup/
14 Bang, A. L. (2011). Emotional Value of Applied Textiles: Dialogue-oriented and participatory approaches to textile design. Available at https://adk.elsevierpure.com/en/publications/emotional-value-of-applied-textiles-dialogue-oriented-and-partici

Appendix 4

1 Global Compact (2021). Global Compact Dilemma Game. Retrieved from https://www.globalcompact.de/en/shop/produkte/Global-Compact-Dilemma-Spiel.php
2 Imacocollabo (2018). 2030 SDGs Game. Retrieved from https://2030sdgsgame.com/
3 Centre for Systems Solutions (2018). About That Forest. Retrieved from https://aboutthatforest.socialsimulations.org/#contact
4 Centre for Systems Solutions (2018). The World's Future. Retrieved from https://worldsfuture.socialsimulations.org
5 Progress Namibia (2016). The Privilege Walk. Games for the SDGs. Retrieved from https://cms.my.na/assets/documents/p1c1cv42qm1va1v5pnpte09b9t4.pdf
6 Centre for Systems Solutions (CRS) and International Institute for Applied Systems Analysis (IIASA) (2018). Energy Transition Game. Retrieved from https://energytransition.socialsimulations.org/en
7 Perspectivity.org. (2021). The Perspectivity Climate Challenge. Retrieved from https://perspectivity.org/work/serious-gaming/
8 Cool Choices (2019). Cool Choices. Retrieved from https://coolchoices.com/our-game-platform/
9 Ściańska–Anna, J. G. K. W., & Jonczyk, L. Gamification in CSR Communication, *Marketing Identity* 1(1), 473–490.
10 Progress Namibia (2016). Debate on Poaching. Games for the SDGs. Retrieved from https://cms.my.na/assets/documents/p1c1cv42qm1va1v5pnpte09b9t4.pdf
11 Lejeune, A., & Nkambou, R. (2013). A Table Game to Elicit Green Capacities in Business Models. In ISPIM Conference Proceedings (p. 1). The International Society for Professional Innovation Management (ISPIM).
12 Gerlach, Robert. (2017). Methods for Sustainable Product- & Business Model Innovation – Lecture Notes. Game Retrieved from https://www.threebility.com/sustainable-business-model-game
13 Dewulf, K. (2010). Play it forward: a game-based tool for sustainable product and business model innovation in the fuzzy front end. In 6th EMSU conferences (ERSCP-2010). TUDelft.
14 games4sustainability.org (2021). Tradeoff! Retrieved from https://games4sustainability.org/gamepedia/tradeoff
15 SDGs Global Youth Innovators (2018). SDGs Action Card Game. Kanazawa Institute of Technology. Retrieved from https://www.kanazawa-it.ac.jp/sdgs/education/application/game-en.html
16 Centre for Systems Solutions (CRS) and Center for Sustainability Transformation (2018). Green & Great. Retrieved from https://greenandgreat.socialsimulations.org
17 Sterman J., Miller D. and Hsueh J. (2021). Clean Start. Retrieved from https://mitsloan.mit.edu/teaching-resources-library/cleanstart-simulating-a-clean-energy-startup
18 Centre for Systems Solutions (2018). Decisions for the Decade. Retrieved from https://games4sustainability.org/gamepedia/decisions-for-the-decade
19 Ściańska–Anna, J. G. K. W., & Jonczyk, L. Gamification in CSR Communication, *Marketing Identity* 1(1), 473–490.
20 Frumert C. & Bartning A. (2019). Pitch Your Green Idea. Retrieved from https://www.pitchyourgreenidea.de
21 Acaroglu, L. (2021). Design play cards. Retrieved from https://www.leylaacaroglu.com/portfolio/2016/12/16/design-play-cards
22 AtKisson, A. (1991). The innovation diffusion game: a tool for encouraging participation in positive cultural change in your office, your organization, or in the world at large. *Context*, 28, 58–62.

List of figures

https://doi.org/10.1515/9783110725582-029

Index

https://doi.org/10.1515/9783110725582-030

www.ingramcontent.com/pod-product-compliance
Lightning Source LLC
Chambersburg PA
CBHW082233240926
51846CB00014B/1410
9783110725544